Mod ern Legal Drafting
A Guide to Using Clearer Language

This clear structured and referenced book shows how and why ritional legal language has developed some of the peculiar characteristics that sometimes make legal documents inaccessible to the end users. It examines recent reforms in the UK, Australia and North America, and provides a critical examination of case law and the rules of interpretation. Practical elements are also covered. Detailed case studies illustrate how obtuse words and phrases can be reworked or removed. Particularly useful is the step-by-step guide to drafting in the modern style, using examples drawn from four types of legal documents: leases, company constitutions, wills and conveyances. Readers of this book will receive clear instructions on how to make their writing clearer and their legal documents more useful to clients and colleagues. This book will benefit all law students and professionals.

Peter Butt lectures in Law at the University of Sydney. He was a founding director of the Centre for Plain Legal Language and is the author of numerous books, including *Land Law* (3rd edition, 1996) and *The Standard Contract for Sale of Land in New South Wales* (2nd edition, 1998).

Richard Castle is an English solicitor, formerly an affiliated lecturer in the Department of Land Economy at the University of Cambridge. He is currently working in New Zealand. His previous books include *Barnsley's Land Options* (3rd edition, 1998) and *Rent Review Manual* (with David Clarke, 1996).

Modern Legal Drafting
A Guide to Using Clearer Language

Peter Butt
Solicitor, Australia

Richard Castle
Solicitor, England and Wales

CAMBRIDGE
UNIVERSITY PRESS

PUBLISHED BY THE PRESS SYNDICATE OF THE UNIVERSITY OF CAMBRIDGE
The Pitt Building, Trumpington Street, Cambridge, United Kingdom

CAMBRIDGE UNIVERSITY PRESS
The Edinburgh Building, Cambridge CB2 2RU, UK
40 West 20th Street, New York, NY 10011–4211, USA
10 Stamford Road, Oakleigh, VIC 3166, Australia
Ruiz de Alarcón 13, 28014 Madrid, Spain
Dock House, The Waterfront, Cape Town 8001, South Africa

http://www.cambridge.org

First published 2001

Printed in Australia by Ligare Pty Ltd

Typeface Plantin (Adobe) 10/12 pt.   *System* QuarkXPress® [BC]

A catalogue record for this book is available from the British Library

National Library of Australia Cataloguing in Publication data
Butt, P. J. (Peter J.).
Modern legal drafting: a guide to using clearer language.
Bibliography.
Includes index.
ISBN 0 521 80217 2.
ISBN 0 521 00186 2 (pbk.).
1. Legal composition. 2. Legal documents – Interpretation
and construction. 3. Law – Language. I. Castle, Richard.
II. Title.
808.06634

ISBN 0 521 80217 2 hardback
ISBN 0 521 00186 2 paperback

Summary of Contents

Contents

Cases

Showing page numbers in **bold** (footnotes in brackets).

Statutes and Subsidiary Legislation

Showing page numbers in **bold** (footnotes in brackets).

Panels and Tables

Panels

Tables

Acknowledgements

This book is the product of many years practice and research in the techniques of drafting legal documents in modern, standard English. We are grateful to many people for their contributions towards the ideas and experiences that have helped shape our views.

Richard Castle would particularly like to thank:
- the law librarian of the University of Exeter, and the librarians of the University of Plymouth and the College of St Mark and St John Plymouth for the use of their facilities
- the staff of Devon public libraries for their unfailing helpfulness
- colleagues on the drafting courses formerly run by the Centre for Commercial Law Studies, for their inspiration
- Professor John Adams of Queen Mary & Westfield College London for his advice and guidance on early work which led to this book
- his clients and colleagues in Plymouth who directly and indirectly provided a good deal of the material which appears here
- Wendy Castle for her support and untiring efforts in typing, retyping and retyping again many early drafts
- Sarah, Emma and Ally for their indulgence and motivation during the years of research and writing.

Peter Butt would particularly like to thank:
- the librarian and staff of the law schools in the Universities of Sydney and Bristol
- his students at the University of Sydney, who for a decade have provided inspiration and feedback in lecture courses on plain-language drafting techniques
- Marion Butt, for her efforts in typing the later drafts of the book.

Both of us would also like to thank a number of colleagues who reviewed drafts of the manuscript, and whose enthusiastic support for the project was a great encouragement. They include Robert Eagleson (Australia), Mark Adler (England) and David Elliott (Canada).

We gratefully acknowledge those who have given permission to reproduce copyright material used in the book: Her Majesty's Stationery Office (Panel 1, page 2; Panel 3, page 69); Australia and New Zealand Banking Group Limited (Panel 6, page 110); Wellington District Law Society's Collection, Special Printed Collections, Alexander Turnbull Library, New Zealand (Panel 8, page 123); and VicRoads (Panel 10, page 148, ©VicRoads 1991). Every effort has been made to trace and acknowledge copyright and we would be pleased to hear from those we have been unable to contact.

Finally, we emphasise that this book is very much a joint undertaking. Although we worked separately for a long time on opposite sides of the world, the final product is the result of our labours together for some six years. We take joint and several responsibility for it – or rather (see p. 173) we take responsibility for it separately and together.

PETER BUTT
RICHARD CASTLE

Introduction

Traditional legal language

The English language of today is still recognisably the language of Chaucer and Shakespeare, of Abraham Lincoln and Winston Churchill, of the Book of Common Prayer and the Authorised Version of the Bible. It is also the language of lawyers in many countries: the United Kingdom, the United States, Canada, Australia, New Zealand and India, to name but a few. In English, lawyers draft documents and compose letters; in English, lawyers formulate statutes and propagate regulations; in English, lawyers prepare pleadings and argue their cases.

Legal English, however, has traditionally been a special variety of English. Mysterious in form and expression, it is larded with law-Latin and Norman-French, heavily dependent on the past, and unashamedly archaic. Antiquated words flourish, such as *herein, therein, whereas* – words long lost to everyday language. A spurious sense of precision is conjured through liberal use of jargon and stilted formalism: *the said, aforesaid, the same*. Oddities abound: oath swearers do not believe something, they *verily* believe it; parties do not wish something, they are *desirous* of it; the clearest photocopy only *purports* to be a copy; and so on. All this – and much more – from a profession which regards itself as learned.

Some infelicities of expression, some overlooked nuances, some grammatical slips, can be forgiven. Lawyers are only human, and in the day-to-day practice of law they face an overwhelming weight of words. But what cannot be forgiven is the legal profession's systematic mangling of the English language, perpetrated in the name of tradition and precision. This abuse of language cannot be justified, legally or professionally. Nor, increasingly, do clients accept it, showing a mounting dissatisfaction with vague excuses such as 'That's the way we always put it' or 'That's how we say it in legal jargon'.

Speaking generally, today's legal English evolved over the 300-year period that spanned the setting up of the first printing press in England

1

(1476) and the American Declaration of Independence. Its terminology
and style remain largely frozen in the form they had reached by the early
years of the nineteenth century. Nothing much has changed since then,
despite sporadic efforts at reform. The lack of change is evident in Panel
1, taken from the charges register of an English land title: notice the
similarity of language in documents over 200 years apart.

In more recent times, typewriters, word processors and computers
have brought changes in the format, layout and length of legal
documents. The language, however, has remained largely unchanged.
How odd it must seem to non-lawyers that the law's antique language
lingers on, harking back to another age, so numbing and relentless that
even lawyers themselves sometimes fail to read it (or fail to understand it
if they do). How odd that legal gobbledegook lies dormant in office files,

---

Title Number : DN37753

Schedule of Restrictive Covenants

1. The following are details of the covenants contained in the Conveyance
    dated 25 January 1750 referred to in the Charges Register:-

    AND the said John Jeffery doth for himself his heirs and assigns and
    every of them further covenant promise and agree to and with the said
    Duke his heirs and assigns and every of them by these presents THAT he
    the said John Jeffery his heirs or assigns shall not nor will open or
    work any Quarry or quarries of stone or any mines or minerals in or upon
    the said premises or any part thereof (other than for building or
    repairing the said premises) without the Licence and consent of the said
    Duke his heirs or assigns for the purpose first had and obtained.

2. The following are details of the covenants contained in the Conveyance
    dated 5 August 1958 referred to in the Charges Register:-

    "The Purchasers to the intent that this covenant shall bind so far as may
    be the property hereby assured into whosesoever hands the same may come
    and to the intent likewise that this covenant may enure for the benefit
    of and be annexed to the land in the said Parish of Plymstock which
    immediately after the execution of this Deed may remain vested in the
    Vendor and the Company or either of them and to each and every part of
    such land taken separately HEREBY COVENANT jointly and severally with the
    Vendor and as a separate covenant with the Company that the Purchasers
    and their successors in title will at all times hereafter observe and
    perform the covenants and conditions on the part of the Purchasers
    contained and set forth in the Second Schedule hereunder written

    The Vendor and the Company reserve the right to release alter or vary any
    of the covenants to which any other part or parts of the Thornyville
    Estate is shall or may be subject and to alter or vary the lay-out of
    The Thornyville Estate or any part thereof and to sell any part or parts
    of the Thornyville Estate free from the said covenants or subject to such
    other covenants stipulations and conditions as the Vendor or the Company
    may think fit.

Panel 1 Charges register extract

precedent books and computers, ready to be recycled at a moment's notice in documents produced in the early twenty-first century.

Pressures for reform

All areas of human endeavour have their advocates for reform. But reformers, including legal reformers, are often disappointed.[1] Radical thinkers like Jeremy Bentham, Lord Brougham and Lord Denning, who urged reforms not only in the substance of the law but also in its language, in the end have had relatively little impact. Lawyers have a vested interest in preserving their mystique, and part of that mystique is wrapped up in traditional legal language. But today there are clear signs that the need for traditional legal language is being questioned.

This questioning has been fuelled largely by the consumer movement of the second half of the twentieth century. Non-lawyers now expect to be able to understand what they are asked to sign. Consumer groups urge customers to seek answers and explanations. Some lawyers see this as a threat, but others see it as a challenge. They recognise that a clearer, crisper style relieves them from the drudgery of acting as interpreter, of having to translate the antique into the contemporary. They also perceive the advertising advantage their documents provide in marketing their expertise. Even those lawyers whose prime concern is to avoid negligence claims can see that 'plainness' might prove an advantage over gobbledegook: for when a document is drawn in straightforward, up-to-date, no-nonsense English, clients are hard-pressed to assert afterwards that they did not understand it.

Yet the advocates of standard, modern English – or, to use the term now becoming widespread, plain English – should not be complacent. Among lawyers, proponents of plain English are in a minority. Many lawyers have difficulty in accepting anything other than traditional legal terminology; the ancient sonorous language of the law embodies all they stand for. But improvements are appearing, notably in commercial documents. Commercial lawyers appear more likely than their conveyancing colleagues to use standard, modern English. Perhaps this is because commercial work often involves putting new ideas and new methods into a legal setting; in contrast, conveyancing often harks back to the Middle Ages.

Change will come, but it will be slow. There will be no storming of the citadel, no victory parade, no triumphal march through the streets. Traditional legal language will be a long time dying. But die it will, under

---

1 See, for example, the hopelessly optimistic predictions following the 1845 English land law reforms, in 'Conveyancing Reform' (1845) 2 *Law Review*, p. 405.

the weight of the reality that change is inevitable. Wittgenstein once wrote of language, 'Everything that can be put into words can be put clearly.'[2] Legal language is no different.

What this book does

Our purpose in this book is to encourage legal drafters to write in modern, standard English by illustrating why it is preferable to traditional legal English. We start in Chapter 1 by considering the influences that affect today's legal drafter. We also examine the factors that help perpetuate traditional styles of legal drafting, factors such as the fear of negligence claims and the familiarity that comes from using a conventional style. Chapter 2 deals with the interpretation of legal documents, and explains why drafters in the modern style can be assured that their efforts will not fall foul of the so-called rules of interpretation. Chapter 3 traces the move towards modern English in legal drafting in various countries. In Chapter 4 we consider some of the benefits of drafting in plain language, showing how it can improve the image of lawyers and help avoid negligence claims. This leads us, in Chapter 5, to discuss what to avoid when drafting modern documents. Chapter 6 explains how to draft modern documents, covering not only obvious points such as language and punctuation but other important factors such as structure and layout. Lastly, Chapter 7 puts the principles to the test by analysing some traditional legal clauses and rewriting them in modern, standard English.

---

2 Ludwig Wittgenstein, *Tractatus Logico-Philosophicus*, trans. D. F. Pears and B. F. McGuinness (London: Routledge & Kegan Paul, 1961), p. 51.

1   What Influences the Legal Drafter

The traditional style of legal writing is the product of many influences. Some influences are constant, some are sporadic. They rarely exist in isolation; usually, many operate together. This chapter reviews the main influences on traditional legal drafting:

* familiarity and habit – the security that comes from adopting forms and words that have been used before and seen to be effective
* conservatism in the legal profession, allied to the common law tradition of precedent
* fear of negligence claims
* the means of production
* pressures to conform to professional norms
* the desire to avoid ambiguity
* the mixture of languages from which the law derives its vocabulary
* payment by length of document
* payment by time
* the litigious environment of legal practice.

Some of these influences are largely historical, with little direct effect today, such as the mixture of languages and payment by length of document. Others, however, remain relevant.

The stylistic hallmarks of traditional legal drafting are apparent in many types of documents. Some of the best (or worst) examples are leases, their dense prose and 'torrential' style intimidating even the hardiest reader.[1] But other documents exhibit a similar style: conveyances, wills, trust deeds, insurance policies, mortgages, and shipping documents, to name a few. The common thread pervading them all is

---

1 Law Com No 162, *Landlord and Tenant: Reform of the Law* (1987), paras 3.6, 3.7. Hoffmann J., in *Norwich Union Life Insurance Society v British Railways Board* [1987] 2 EGLR 137 at 138, found the flood of words in a lease so 'torrential' that he thought there might be 'some justification' in counsel's argument that he should depart from the normal principle of construction that requires effect to be given to every word in a clause.

tradition, going back hundreds of years. This tradition is so powerful that it has been impervious to reform through the centuries and continues to resist reform even today, when change might be thought an easy option. A tradition so persistent merits detailed scrutiny.

Familiarity and habit

Lawyers prefer to use documents that have been tested in operation. They prefer the familiar to the new. In a sense, this should not be surprising: all human beings share this trait. For lawyers, however, the trait creates particular problems, because eventually they come to write legal documents in a style that is peculiarly time-warped. It is traditional; it is inculcated in law schools; it is used by judges and legislators; it is how they always write. Knowing no other style, they never pause to question it. After all, what incentive is there to do so? All the pressures are the other way.

To illustrate, consider the following extract from a contemporary conveyance. The document comes from England, but it could have come from any country where English is the language of the law:

> AND excepting and reserving also in fee simple unto the Company their successors in title owners or owner for the time being of the parts not herein comprised of the said Building Estate the right to connect with any drain or drains made or to be made in through or under the said pieces or parcels of land thereby conveyed any drain or drains belonging to any adjoining or adjacent site or sites on the said Building Estate for the purpose of forming one or more general drain or drains or otherwise.

This drafting is the product of habit, not design. Written from scratch, it could have looked more like this:

> Reserving in fee simple the right to connect any drain in any part of the rest of the estate with any drain in the conveyed land.

Compared to the earlier version, this reduced version seems disarmingly simple. In fact, though, it assumes a high degree of expertise – so high that few lawyers would be bold enough to attempt it. Let us explore some of the technical knowledge required for the reduced version.

First, since new rights are created (whether to use existing drains or drains to be built), it is sufficient to use 'reserving' in place of 'excepting and reserving'. Most drafters, however, would instinctively play safe with the arcane distinctions between exceptions and reservations (see p. 24), and would retain the conventional 'excepting and reserving'.

Second, what of the phrase 'in fee simple'? This term has come down from medieval times. In many jurisdictions which have inherited the

English common law, landowners do not 'own' their land in any absolute sense. Rather, they 'hold' the land 'of [from] the Crown' under what is essentially a feudal concept. The Crown grants interests in land, to be held of the Crown. In the theory of the common law, the largest possible interest is the 'fee simple'. But despite the medieval theory, for practical purposes a person who holds the fee simple is the owner of the land, and no misunderstanding or ambiguity arises from calling that person the 'owner' of the land or the owner of the 'freehold'. So 'fee simple' can be discarded in favour of a more modern term. Indeed, this change has statutory blessing. For example, in England and Wales, s 1(2) of the *Law of Property Act* 1925 provides:

> The only interests or charges in or over land which are capable of subsisting or of being conveyed or created at law are –
> (a) an easement, right, or privilege in or over land for an interest equivalent to an estate in fee simple absolute in possession or a term of years absolute ...

In the light of this provision, it would be possible to say 'Reserving for the equivalent of a freehold the right to connect ...'. Indeed, it would be possible to go further and simply say: 'Reserving the right to connect ...'. Given its context in the conveyance, the parties must have intended this easement to be a perpetual right (as distinct from an easement intended to last for a specified number of years). This intention is implemented without the need for formalistic phrases, under s 60 of the English *Law of Property Act* 1925, which provides that a 'conveyance' of land passes the fee simple, read with s 205 of the same Act, which defines 'conveyance' to include every assurance of property 'or of an interest therein'. In practice, however, simplified usage of this kind is not seen. The technical 'in fee simple' is retained, on the illusory justification that it is legally essential. The mystification it causes to non-lawyers is considered irrelevant.

The point of this example is that drafting a reservation requires expertise. So, too, does drafting many other legal documents. Few lawyers risk changes in terminology, for it puts their expertise on the line. It is easier and safer to stick with the familiar.

Conservatism

The common law traditionally looks backwards, seeking authority from things past. A clear example is the principle of *stare decisis* (to stand by things decided): lawyers defer to past judicial decisions, moving from them only reluctantly.

However, reliance on past judicial decisions – 'precedents', as lawyers call them – can curb innovation. The pattern of the present is fixed by reference to the past, and there is a reluctance to alter the law in general to deal with a problem in particular. This reluctance is reflected in the well-known saying 'Hard cases make bad law'. When confronted by a manifest injustice, it is easy to lose sight of principle; there is a fear of setting a precedent for the future.

Of course, some lawyers do not allow themselves to be fettered by precedent. For them, rigid adherence to principle can inhibit justice. Among judges, perhaps the best-known example in modern times is Lord Denning. His 1979 book, *The Discipline of Law*, contains a chapter called 'The doctrine of precedent', which he concludes in his customary clear and forthright style:

> Let it not be thought from this discourse that I am against the doctrine of precedent. I am not. It is the foundation of our system of case law. This has evolved by broadening down from precedent to precedent. By standing by previous decisions, we have kept the common law on a good course. All that I am against is its too rigid application – a rigidity which insists that a bad precedent must necessarily be followed. I would treat it as you would a path through the woods. You must follow it certainly so as to reach your end. But you must not let the path become too overgrown. You must cut out the dead wood and trim off the side branches, else you will find yourself lost in thickets and brambles. My plea is simply to keep the path to justice clear of obstructions which would impede it.[2]

Lord Denning had earlier dealt with a similar theme, but with particular emphasis on lawyers' language. In his Romanes Lecture at Oxford in 1959, entitled *From Precedent to Precedent*, he said:

> You will have noticed how progressive the House of Lords has been when the lay peers have had their say, or at any rate, their vote on the decisions. They have insisted on the true principles and have not allowed the conservatism of lawyers to be carried too far. Even more so when we come to the meaning of words. Lawyers are here the most offending souls alive. They will so often stick to the letter and miss the substance. The reason is plain enough. Most of them spend their working lives drafting some kind of document or another – trying to see whether it covers this contingency or that. They dwell upon words until they become mere precisians in the use of them. They would rather be accurate than be clear. They would sooner be long than short. They seek to avoid two meanings, and end – on occasions – by having no meaning. And the worst of it all is that they claim to be the masters of the subject. The meaning of words, they say, is a matter of law for them and not a matter for the ordinary man.[3]

---

2 Lord Denning, *The Discipline of Law* (London: Butterworths, 1979), p. 314.
3 Quoted in ibid., p. 293.

These criticisms are hardly new. Getting on for 300 years ago Jonathan Swift had expressed similar views. In *Gulliver's Travels* (1726) his hero describes a society of men in England bred from youth to prove 'by words multiplied for the purpose' that black is white and white is black 'according as they are paid':

> It is a Maxim among these Lawyers, that whatever hath been done before, may legally be done again: And therefore they take special Care to record all the Decisions formerly made against common Justice and the general Reason of Mankind. These, under the name of Precedents, they produce as Authorities to justify the most iniquitous Opinions; and the Judges never fail of decreeing accordingly ...
>
> It is likewise to be observed, that this Society hath a peculiar Cant and Jargon of their own, that no other Mortal can understand, and wherein all their Laws are written, which they take special Care to multiply; whereby they have wholly confounded the very Essence of Truth and Falshood, of Right and Wrong; so that it will take Thirty Years to decide whether the Field, left me by my Ancestors for six Generations, belong to me, or to a Stranger three Hundred Miles off.[4]

So far, we have used the word 'precedents' to mean court decisions of the past. However, English and Commonwealth lawyers also use the term to describe model legal forms. These model forms, published specifically for use by the legal profession, are employed by lawyers in every facet of legal practice. They influence not only the language of legal documents but also their style and layout. They are found in precedent books, which are generally derived from earlier precedent books, which in turn were derived from yet earlier precedent books, and so on backwards to the origins of the first precedent books.

Books of model forms were first published in England in the sixteenth century.[5] Their number proliferated in succeeding centuries.[6] Also published were books of simplified legal principles, like *Every Man His Own Lawyer* and *The Justice of the Peace and Parish Officer*. Of these, David Mellinkoff of the University of California at Los Angeles, said:

---

4 *Gulliver's Travels* (Oxford: Basil Blackwell, 1959), pp. 249, 250. This is part of a general diatribe against lawyers.
5 The history of conveyancing precedent books is traced in *Martin's Practice of Conveyancing* (London: Maxwell & Son, 1844), vol. 2, pp. 24 ff.
6 Sir William Holdsworth, *A History of English Law* (London: Methuen and Sweet & Maxwell), vol. 12 (1938), p. 375. Examples from the 18th century are: Nicholas Covert, *The Scrivener's Guide*, 3rd edn (London: Elizabeth Nutt, 1716); *The Attorney's Compleat Pocket-Book*, 5th edn (London: J. Worrall, 1764); *The Attorney and Solicitor's Complete Assistant* (London: J. Worrall, 1767); Anthony Macmillan, *A Complete System of Conveyances of, and Securities upon, Lands* (Edinburgh: Elphingston Balfour, 1787).

Such books preserved in detail a continuity of archaic English, bad grammar, and deficient punctuation, in form available to every scrivener and dabbler in the law, with or without the slightest knowledge of what he was writing. They gave greater currency to the similar language of the more learned formbooks and of the few archaic forms enshrined for the literate by Blackstone. Where English letters blossomed with originality and sparkle in the eighteenth century, the law was encased in a hard shell of fixed pattern, its language determined by forms and the deadweight of precedent. The mass of misplaced precedent, attached to the forms by coincidence rather than art, dropped into the hands of a legal profession unprepared to cope with the bulk of its expanding business. The time had not yet come for any mass re-examination; there was too much movement in the law itself to look for more than the show of security. That appearance at least the forms gave, and lawyers embraced the illusion.[7]

Given their derivative nature, it is hardly surprising that even current precedent books are couched in a traditional style.

Mellinkoff has shown that many of the early drafters of precedents were uneducated laymen.[8] Others, though, were able barristers.[9] Of the latter, perhaps the most famous was Sir Orlando Bridgman, later Chief Justice of Common Pleas and styled 'the father of conveyancers'.[10] His forms of conveyance, first published in 1682 (though compiled earlier), continue to influence current practice, as witness the traditional 'covenants for title' still used in many countries.[11]

The tyranny of the precedent books is still with us. They continue to be published, hundreds of thousands of words pouring off the printing presses each year, swamping the legal profession with sentence upon sentence for pleadings, affidavits, declarations, wills, leases, conveyances, notices, bills of lading, mortgages, trust deeds, hire-purchase agreements, assignments, bonds, highway agreements, covenants – and any other documents that one lawyer imagines another might need. Two of the better-known collections in England are *Atkin's Court Forms* and *Butterworths' Encyclopaedia of Forms and Precedents*. Each runs to more than forty volumes. *Atkin* lines the shelves of most barristers' chambers; and most solicitors' firms of any size have the *Encyclopaedia*.

---

7 David Mellinkoff, *The Language of the Law* (Boston and Toronto: Little, Brown and Co., 1963), p. 199.

8 Ibid., p. 194.

9 Holdsworth, *History of English Law*, 3rd edn, vol. 3 (1923), p. 653; vol. 6 (1924), p. 446.

10 A title bestowed by Mr Serjeant Hill, in *Goodtitle v Funcan* (1781) Dougl 565 at 568; 99 ER 357 at 359.

11 They were compiled in 1649–60. M. J. Russell, 'Brevity v Verbosity' (1962) 26 Conv (NS) 59 reproduces some of Bridgman's material. For an example of current practice in Australia, see *Conveyancing Act* 1919 (NSW), s 78. In England and Wales, the language of these covenants has been updated: *Law of Property (Miscellaneous Provisions) Act* 1994.

To many practitioners, the contents of the precedent books are gospel. Some lawyers even cling to the belief that adopting precedents from books such as these will save them from claims in negligence. However, this reliance on precedent books is misplaced. Standard forms have their place, but legal documents should be drafted for the needs of the particular client, in the light of the circumstances of the particular transaction. Just as the needs of clients differ, so do the needs of their documents. Yet, as Robinson has written, 'the majority of members of the branches of the profession are addicted to the use of precedent books, office forms, and printed forms. The thinking seems to be that the needs of a client must be satisfied by some cure prescribed years ago.'[12]

Blind adherence to precedents is one cause of the complexity of modern legal documents. In *Penn v Gatenex Co.*, Lord Evershed MR condemned the unthinking use of precedent books. Commenting on a tenancy agreement for a flat, he said:

> the second clause contained no less than 18 separate covenants on the part of the tenants comprehending such matters as the keeping of rabbits and reptiles, the mowing of lawns and the weeding of gardens, which may have owed their presence more to precedents than the requirements of the actual contract being made.[13]

Sometimes, slavishly-copied precedents are not merely inappropriate to the particular transaction: they are dangerous or even wrong. 'Botched clauses'[14] find their way into the precedent books; and once there, they are perpetuated. For example, in *Dunn v Blackdown Properties Ltd*, the grant of an easement in a form found in several precedent books was held to be void because it infringed the rule against perpetuities.[15] Again, a number of cases dealing with the rule against perpetuities have pointed out the dangers of an uncritical adoption in modern wills or trusts of 'royal lives clauses' found in old precedent books.[16] Yet still the precedent books are relied on and treated – whether good or bad, appropriate or inept – as holy writ.

These two aspects of 'precedents' – reliance on past decisions and dependence on published forms – are compounded by a third: the

---

12 Stanley Robinson, 'Drafting – Its Substance and Teaching' (1973) 25 *Journal of Legal Education*, p. 514.
13 [1958] 2 QB 210 at 218.
14 *Re Gulbenkian's Settlements* [1970] AC 508 at 517. This case is discussed further in Chapter 2.
15 [1961] Ch 433, CA.
16 See especially *Re Villar* [1928] Ch 471, which Morris and Leach cite as 'an awful warning against the use of out-of-date editions of law books': J. H. C. Morris and W. Barton Leach, *The Rule Against Perpetuities* (London: Stevens & Sons, 1962), p. 61 fn 43. See also discussion in *Clay v Karlson* (No. 2) (1998) 19 WAR 287 at 293.

customary methods of learning in practice. Richard Preston, writing in the early 19th century, explained how lawyers taught themselves to draft documents:

> The misfortune of a person, who either as clerk to a solicitor, or as a student in a conveyancer's chambers, begins to study the practice of conveyancing, is, that he is taught by form, or precedent, rather than by principle. He is made to copy precedents, without knowing either their application, or those rules on which they are grounded. When he begins to prepare drafts, he is led to expect all his information from these forms; and his knowledge is, in the end, as limited as the means by which he has been instructed.
>
> One of the principal difficulties to be surmounted, by a person so educated, is to gain sufficient strength of mind, and resolution, to free himself from the shackles of precedent.[17]

Sadly, the same can be said today. Training in law firms, universities, and colleges of law reinforces the budding lawyer's natural desire to seek comfort in the precedents of yesteryear. As a result, lawyers are reluctant to set aside what has been used for years and presumed to work.

Fear of negligence claims

Fear of negligence claims governs the professional life of many lawyers. To some extent, this fear is justified. Courts regard lawyers as a special class, who should provide a high standard of care. This was apparent as long ago as 1914, when the House of Lords in *Nocton v Lord Ashburton* held a solicitor liable for breach of fiduciary duty for giving negligent advice to a client.[18] Decades later it was confirmed in *Ross v Caunters*, a decision which greatly enlarged the legal profession's potential liability.[19] Solicitors posted a will to a client (the testator) for him to sign. They told the client that his signature needed to be witnessed, but failed to warn him that the spouse of a beneficiary should not be a witness. Under English law, a gift to a beneficiary is void if the beneficiary or the beneficiary's spouse witnesses the will. Megarry V-C held that, by analogy with earlier authorities, the solicitors owed a duty of care not only to their client but also to the beneficiary.[20] So the beneficiary recovered from the solicitors what he should have received from the will. The principle of

---

17 Richard Preston, *A Treatise on Conveyancing*, 3rd edn, 3 vols (London: W. Clarke & Sons, 1819–1829), vol. 1, p. ix.
18 [1914] AC 932.
19 [1980] Ch. 297.
20 The authorities were *Donoghue v Stevenson* [1932] AC 562, HL; *Hedley Byrne v Heller* [1964] AC 465, HL; *Dorset Yacht Co. Ltd v Home Office* [1970] AC 1004, HL.

Ross v Caunters has since been confirmed by the House of Lords in England and the High Court in Australia.[21]

As other decisions show, lawyers may be open to claims for negligence even though they act in accordance with usual professional practices.[22] This may put lawyers in a liability class of their own. The law sometimes treats members of other professions more kindly. For example, doctors have been held not to be negligent where they have adopted normal professional procedures, and there is no higher duty on financial advisers.[23]

In short, lawyers are more at risk of negligence claims today than their predecessors ever were, and more at risk than members of other professions. And clients now have no qualms about suing their lawyers. Whatever may have been the position in the past, there is now no difficulty in getting one lawyer to act against another in a negligence claim.

Small wonder, then – as several Law Commissions have noted[24] – that many a lawyer's natural caution and conservatism reinforces fears that innovative legal drafting might prove dangerous and give rise to negligence claims. But these fears, if unchecked, can colour the whole approach to professional life. They can (and often do) lead to the use of ossified phrases and antiquated forms that have long lost their relevance to the people they are intended to affect. They can (and often do) lead to the indiscriminate accretion of page upon page of surplusage – as witness the scourge of unamended preliminary enquiries in English conveyancing

---

21 *White v Jones* [1995] 2 AC 207; *Hill v Van Erp* (1997) 188 CLR 159. However, there are limits to the duty a solicitor owes to non-clients: see, for example, *Clarke v Bruce Lance & Co.* [1988] 1 WLR 881; *Al-Kandari v J. R. Brown & Co.* [1988] QB 665 at 672 (Lord Donaldson MR); *Gran Gelato Ltd v Richcliff (Group) Ltd* [1992] Ch 560.

22 See *Edward Wong Finance Co Ltd v Johnson Stokes & Master* [1984] AC 1296, PC. See also *G. & K. Ladenbau (UK) Ltd v Crawley & de Reya* [1978] 1 WLR 266 (failure to search commons register). Even the barrister's traditional immunity from negligence for work done in court has disappeared in England (*Hall v Simons* [2000] 3 WLR 543, HL), though not yet in Australia and some other common law countries.

23 For doctors, examples are *Bolam v Friern Hospital Management Committee* [1957] 1 WLR 582; *Hills v Potter* [1983] 3 All ER 716; *Clark v Maclennan* [1983] 1 All ER 416; *Whitehouse v Jordan* [1981] 1 WLR 246, CA; *Sidaway v Bethlem Royal Hospital Governors* [1985] AC 871, HL; and note *Ashcroft v Mersey Health Authority* [1983] 2 All ER 245 at 247 (Kilner Brown J): 'it could be said that the more skilled a person is the more the care that is expected of him'. But compare *Rogers v Whitaker* (1992) 175 CLR 479, holding that ultimately the question of liability is decided by the court, not by the medical profession. For financial advisers, see *Stafford v Conti Commodity Services Ltd* [1981] 1 All ER 691 (commodity brokers). Banks, however, may also be liable even if they follow accepted practice: *Lloyds Bank Ltd v E. B. Savory & Co.* [1933] AC 201.

24 Law Com No. 162, *Landlord and Tenant: Reform of the Law* (1987), para 3.7; Law Reform Commission of Victoria, *Plain English and the Law* (Report No. 9, 1987), p. 49.

or requisitions on title in other jurisdictions.[25] And they can (and do) lead to documents of excruciating length, replete with clauses aimed at every possible contingency, whether immediate or remote, relevant or fanciful, with little regard for the circumstances of the transaction or the essence of the bargain between the parties.

The consequences of these fears are exacerbated when coupled with the legal profession's long-held notion that traditional words and phrases carry meanings that have been settled by judicial interpretation.[26] We will have something to say about this notion in a later chapter. Here it is enough to comment that a term that has been the subject of judicial interpretation may well be suspect, for if the term were clear it would not have been litigated in the first place.[27]

Means of production

Another influence on legal drafting is the way in which legal documents are physically produced. A number of the characteristics of legal style can be traced to this influence. Over the centuries the means of production has changed, but its influence on drafters remains.

Handwriting

Before the invention of printing, legal documents were necessarily hand-written. Various forms of stylised Latin script evolved, with abbreviations 'incomprehensible to any but the initiated'.[28] The best-known of these scripts was court hand, used in the records of the superior courts of law.

After William Caxton set up the first printing press in England in 1476, printed works soon proliferated. Not much printing, though, found its way into private legal documents. Until the typewriter took over in the twentieth century, legal documents were for the most part handwritten by clerks who were often poorly educated and poorly paid.[29] The clerk

---

25 See Richard Castle, 'Preliminary Enquiries: a Welcome Initiative' (1987) 84 *Law Society's Gazette*, p. 2257. The problem has been considerably lessened in England since the introduction of the Law Society's TransAction scheme. For criticisms of the undue width of standard requisitions, see *Re Ford and Hill* (1879) 10 Ch D 365 at 369; *Emmet on Title* (19th edn, 1986, looseleaf), para [5.077].

26 See William C. Prather, 'In Defense of the People's Use of Three Syllable Words' (1978) 39 *Alabama Lawyer*, p. 395.

27 However, to say, as some do, that a term that has been litigated must necessarily have something wrong with it, is to go too far: see Charles A. Beardsley, 'Beware of, Eschew and Avoid Pompous Prolixity and Platitudinous Epistles' (1941) 16 *California State Bar Journal*, p. 66.

28 Mellinkoff, *Language of the Law*, p. 86.

29 Geoffrey Best, *Mid-Victorian Britain, 1851–75* (London: Fontana, 1979), p. 109.

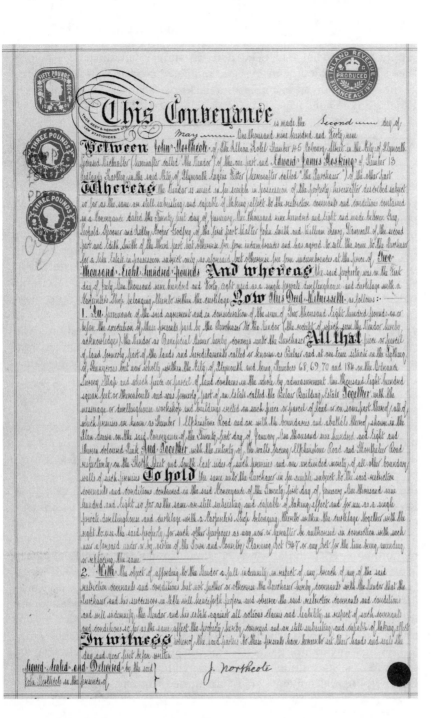

This Conveyance is made the Second day of May One thousand nine hundred and Forty nine **Between** John Northcote of the Albion Hotel Number 4-5 Coburg Street in the City of Plymouth Licensed Victualler (hereinafter called "the Vendor") of the one part and Edward James Hosking of Number 13 Gardenia Hartley in the said City of Plymouth Engine Fitter (hereinafter called "the Purchaser") of the other part **Whereas** the Vendor is seised in fee simple in possession of the property hereinafter described subject to or far as the same are still subsisting and capable of taking effect to the restrictive covenants and conditions contained in a Conveyance dated the Twenty first day of January One thousand nine hundred and Eight and made between Guy Leopold Spooner and Kitty Mooré Godfrey of the first part Walter John Smith and William Henry Dunnell of the second part and Edith Smith of the third part but otherwise free from incumbrances and has agreed to sell the same to the Purchaser for a like Estate in possession subject only as aforesaid but otherwise free from incumbrances at the price of **Two Thousand Eight hundred pounds And whereas** the said property was on the First day of July One thousand nine hundred and Forty eight used as a single private dwellinghouse and curtilage with a Carpenter's Shop belonging thereto within the curtilage **Now this Deed Witnesseth** as follows:—

1. In pursuance of the said agreement and in consideration of the sum of Two Thousand Eight hundred pounds on or before the execution of these presents paid by the Purchaser to the Vendor (the receipt of which sum the Vendor hereby acknowledges) the Vendor as Beneficial Owner hereby conveys unto the Purchaser **All that** piece or parcel of land formerly part of the lands and hereditaments called or known as Belair and at one time situate in the Tything of Pennycross but now wholly within the City of Plymouth and being Numbers 68, 69, 70 and 184 on the Ordnance Survey Map and which piece or parcel of land contains in the whole by admeasurement One thousand eight hundred square feet or thereabouts and was formerly part of an estate called the Belair Building Estate **Together** with the messuage or dwellinghouse workshop and buildings erected on such piece or parcel of land or on some part thereof and all of which premises are known as Number 1 Elphinstone Road and are with the boundaries and abuttals thereof shown in the Plan drawn on the said Conveyance of the Twenty first day of January One thousand nine hundred and Eight and thereon coloured pink **And Together** with the entirety of the walls facing Elphinstone Road and Montpelier Road respectively on the North West and South East sides of such premises and one undivided moiety of all other boundary walls of such premises **To hold** the same unto the Purchaser in fee simple subject to the said restrictive covenants and conditions contained in the said Conveyance of the Twenty first day of January One thousand nine hundred and Eight so far as the same are still subsisting and capable of taking effect and for use as a single private dwellinghouse and curtilage with a Carpenter's Shop belonging thereto within the curtilage Together with the right to use the said property for such other purposes as may now or hereafter be authorised in connection with such user as aforesaid under or by virtue of the Town and Country Planning Act 1947 or any Act for the time being amending or replacing the same ————

2. With the object of affording to the Vendor a full indemnity in respect of any breach of any of the said restrictive covenants and conditions but not further or otherwise the Purchaser hereby covenants with the Vendor that the Purchaser and his successors in title will henceforth perform and observe the said restrictive covenants and conditions and will indemnify the Vendor and his estate against all actions claims and liability in respect of such covenants and conditions so far as the same affect the property hereby conveyed and are still subsisting and capable of taking effect **In witness** whereof the said parties to these presents have hereunto set their hands and seals the day and year first before written ————

Signed Sealed and Delivered by the said John Northcote in the presence of,

J. northcote

Panel 2 Handwritten conveyance

simply copied what had been done in similar circumstances before. Preparing legal documents by hand remained common until as recently as the 1950s. For an example of a 1949 handwritten conveyance, see Panel 2 on previous page.

The typewriter

Typewriters were invented in the United States in 1867, and began to be commercially successful seven years later when Remington & Sons started to produce them. In legal practice, World War I provided an impetus to their use. Men were away fighting, and women were employed to operate these small machines. The manual typewriter with a moving platen remained the basic model until IBM introduced the 'golfball' in the 1960s. Electric typewriters then took over generally, until a decade or so later they in turn were replaced by the next generation: electronic typewriters with a memory function, proportional spacing, and justification of the right-hand margin.

The typewriter lessened the impact of the rising price of labour. As a result, the nineteenth-century reforms designed to curb verbosity in legal documents (pp. 27–30) had less effect than they might otherwise have had.

The computer and word processor

Now that the computer has supplanted the typewriter, word processing programs are frequently blamed for legal documents that are over-long, unnecessarily complicated and not tailored to the task in hand. But word processors do not think. The writer still must formulate the ideas, make the judgments and compose the text. As Christopher Turk and John Kirkman point out in their book *Effective Writing*, new technology changes the processes of writing, not its principles.[30]

Nevertheless, word processors are particularly apt to encourage monotonous repetition of words or whole chunks of text. This tendency is particularly evident in modern commercial leases, almost all of which are now produced on word processors. Drafters can make do with wordings they have used before, cutting and pasting unthinkingly, sidestepping the task of amending for slightly changed circumstances. As a result, leases become uniform, repetitive and prolix, lacking logical organisation.[31]

Obviously word processors have the potential for greatly improving the standard of legal drafting, making it easy to hone and clarify expression. But the potential remains largely unrealised. Instead, word processors

---

30 2nd edn (London and New York: E. & F. N. Spon, 1989), p. 120.
31 See ibid., p. 122.

'regurgitate complexity and verbiage'.[32] Lawyers 'put more store on the convenience of their word processor than clarity for the reader'.[33]

The dictating machine

Most lawyers use dictating machines. They are worthy tools for effectively using the time of both fee-earner and typist, but they can be over-employed. The mind can only accommodate so much, and what was dictated only moments before can be forgotten. Consistency disappears and inaccuracy appears.

Combining printed precedents with variables spoken into a machine can be difficult. The machine is picked up and used between appointments, after a telephone call, or whenever time permits; if something more pressing occurs, the machine is put down. The threads of what went before must then be collected when opportunity next arises.

Dictating machines are particularly unsuited to composing formal documents, except in the most experienced hands. The longer the document, the more difficult the task. Since the invention of the tape cassette in the 1950s and particularly the introduction of the Philips mini-cassette in 1966, dictation to secretaries via shorthand has declined almost to extinction. A secretary could read back what went before, and was often asked to. Although it is possible to replay a tape, any attempt to find more than the immediately preceding piece is likely to be frustrating. Certainly it is not possible to keep checking back for consistency and accuracy as it is with a document, whether handwritten or typed.

Perhaps dictating machines will become less important as more lawyers acquire computer keyboard skills. (Even keyboard skills may become redundant as voice-recognition technology improves – but that is likely to be some way ahead.) In the meantime, the lapses of a tired fee-earner dictating into a machine are all too often revealed, usually in correspondence but sometimes in formal documents too.

Professional pressures

The pressures of professional legal practice are numerous. Three in particular call for attention here: lack of time; demands of clients; and the perceived need to conform to the conventions of other lawyers. All three can influence drafting styles.

---

32 *Smith v Australia and New Zealand Banking Group Ltd* (1996) NSW Conv R 55–774 at 55,936 (Kirby P.).
33 *Saloma Pty Ltd v Big Country Developments Pty Ltd*, Young J, Supreme Court of New South Wales, 15 December 1997, p. 1.

Lack of time is the easiest to identify. Successful lawyers are busy people – indeed, success and lack of time are logical concomitants. Needless to say, lack of time can seriously impede clear drafting. To write succinctly takes time. In 1656 Pascal apologised to the Jesuit fathers for making his letter so long, because he did not have time to make it shorter.[34]

Equally pressing are the demands of clients: the lawyer naturally wants to give clients what they want – after all, clients pay the fees. Yet this can adversely affect the drafting of documents. Faced with a client's demand to include a provision (or a set of provisions), the lawyer may feel disinclined to explain that the point is already covered, or that it could be better dealt with another way, or that it need not be dealt with at all. One commentator has put it this way:

> The client asks you to include, as standard, a covenant not to put rubbish bins in the common parts [of the building]. The easy way out is to stick in the extra clause, probably at the end of the other covenants to save renumbering; but why not point to the existing covenant against nuisance, the right for the landlord to make regulations, and the fact that the tenant has no right to put out dustbins in the first place. If the client is not persuaded, the covenant should be put in its rightful place among the others dealing with similar matters.[35]

Also pressing is the tendency to conform to professional conventions. This arises partly from the way that legal drafting is learned. Earlier, we showed how legal training encourages the unthinking use of precedents. On the whole, in England and many Commonwealth countries legal drafting is not taught at universities or in the law schools. Students are not exposed to the techniques of clear, precise drafting. For the most part, drafting is learned on the job, picked up piecemeal in chambers by the pupil barrister or in the office by the solicitor's trainee. Little guidance is given. Small wonder, then, that learners begin nervously, by reference to models in the precedent books or in office forms. Wanting to become respected members of the group, they naturally conform to the language conventions of that group.[36] Inevitably, old forms, old styles, old words and old phrases are perpetuated. The result is traditional legal language, preserving professional mystique but precluding lay comprehension.

Straining to avoid ambiguity

Ambiguity is the chief curse of legal writing. Both lawyers and non-lawyers regard avoidance of ambiguity as the legal writer's goal; and to

---

34 *Provincial Letters* XVI (4 December 1656).
35 Nick Lear (1987) 84 *Law Society's Gazette*, p. 1630.
36 Law Reform Commission of Victoria, *Plain English and the Law*, para 31.

give them their due, most lawyers strive to achieve the goal. Of course, this goal is to be applauded, at least where 'ambiguity' is understood in its dictionary sense of the admission of more than one meaning; of being understood in more than one way; or of referring to more than one thing at the same time. The distinguished American writer on legal drafting, Reed Dickerson, called ambiguity 'perhaps the most serious disease of language'.[37] The law reports are littered with cases dealing with ambiguity of one kind or another. Perhaps this is not surprising, for even the shortest and simplest words can be difficult to analyse and use with precision.

Nonetheless, it is important to keep the goal of ambiguity-free drafting in perspective. Language can be wrenched out of context. Perverse interpretations are almost always possible. Not every word or sentence is ambiguous; nor is every word or sentence a lawyer writes subject to 'every conceivable misinterpretation'.[38] The lawyer's fear of ambiguity is one of the principal reasons why the language of legal documents has reached its present parlous state.[39] So much so that whether the documents communicate meaning to those who are bound by them has become of secondary importance.

The mixture of languages

Legal English reflects the mixture of languages which has produced the English language generally. The principal sources of the modern legal lexicon are French and Latin.[40] But they are not the only sources. Another is Scandinavian: by AD 900 invaders from Scandinavia had installed themselves in the eastern part of Britain called the Danelaw. The Scandinavian influence gives us the word *law* itself.[41]

As to the French influence: the Norman invaders of 1066 spoke a dialect form of French, known as Norman French. As a result of the conquest, French became the official language of England, though most people still spoke English. For nearly 300 years, French was the language of legal proceedings, with the consequence that many words in current legal use have their roots firmly in this period.[42] They include

---

37 *The Fundamentals of Legal Drafting*, 2nd edn (Boston and Toronto: Little, Brown and Co., 1986), p. 32.
38 Sir Ernest Gowers, *The Complete Plain Words* (London: Pelican, 1962), p. 19.
39 David Crystal and Derek Davy, *Investigating English Style* (London: Longman, 1969), p. 193.
40 Law Reform Commission of Victoria, *Plain English and the Law*, p. 14.
41 Robert Burchfield, *The English Language* (Oxford and New York: Oxford University Press, 1995 reissue), pp. 12, 175: Albert C. Baugh and Thomas Cable, *A History of the English Language*, 4th edn (London: Routledge, 1993), p. 97.
42 Burchfield, *English Language*, p. 14; Baugh and Cable, *History of the English Language*, p. 145.

property, estate, tenement, chattel, appurtenance, lease, encumbrance, seisin, tenant and *executor.*

French continued in use in England from the Norman Conquest until the fourteenth century. It came to be known as Anglo-French. Like all languages, it drew on other linguistic influences, in this case not only Norman French but also Central French (the dialect of Paris). Central French preferred an initial *ch*, so the Norman *catel* corresponds to the Central *chatel*. The first gives us *cattle*; the second gives us the word familiar to lawyers, *chattel*.[43] And like all languages, it evolved over time, giving rise to various forms of law French.[44]

During this period, Latin remained the language of record – that is, the language of formal records and statutes.[45] But because only the learned were fluent in Latin, it never became the language of oral pleading or discussion. Of course, Latin had long been an influence on the English language, though not as a result of the Roman occupation (which had left no impact on the language, apart from a few corrupted place-names).[46] Latin initially made its mark when it was brought by the first Christian missionaries in AD 597.[47] As Christianity came to be adopted in most parts of the land, Latin words were taken into the language and adapted to English formations.[48]

Thus for some centuries following the Norman invasion, England was tri-lingual: English remained the spoken language of the great majority of the population, but virtually all writing was in French or Latin. English had no place in legal matters. The first known appearance of an English word in a legal document was in a report (in Latin) of a case brought by Henry III (1216–72), where the clerk called the king's action *nameless* (pointless).[49]

On the battle between Latin, French, and English in legal documents, Pollock and Maitland write:

---

43 Burchfield, *English Language*, p. 16; Baugh and Cable, *History of the English Language*, p. 171.
44 Mellinkoff, *Language of the Law*, ch. IX. Sir Frederick Pollock, in *A First Book of Jurisprudence*, 6th edn (London: Macmillan, 1929), p. 299, gives fascinating examples of the degeneration of law French. The examples are of living Anglo-Norman, as spoken in 1292 (taken from YB 20 Ed I, pp. 192–3); decaying Anglo-Norman, as spoken in 1520 (taken from YB 12 Hen VIII, p. 3); and degenerate law French, reported in the 17th century (taken from Dyer's *Reports* 188b, in the notes added to the 1688 edition).
45 Sir Frederick Pollock and F. W. Maitland, *The History of English Law Before the Time of Edward I*, 2nd edn (2 vols, Cambridge: Cambridge University Press 1968), vol. 1, pp. 82, 86.
46 Robert McCrum and others, *The Story of English*, rev. edn (London: Faber & Faber, 1992), p. 52.
47 Ibid., p. 64.
48 Burchfield, *English Language*, p. 11.
49 McCrum, *Story of English*, pp. 73, 76.

Legal instruments in French come to us but very rarely, if at all, from the twelfth century; they become commoner in the thirteenth and yet commoner in the fourteenth, but on the whole Latin holds its own in this region until it slowly yields to English, and the instruments that are written in French seldom belong to what we may call the most formal classes; they are wills rather than deeds, agreements rather than charters of feoffment, writs under the privy seal, not writs under the great seal.[50]

The beginning of the demise of French in the law can be traced to 1356, when the mayor and aldermen of London ordered proceedings in the sheriff's court of London and Middlesex to be in English.[51] In 1362 the *Statute of Pleading* enacted (in French) that all proceedings should be in English, though they should be enrolled in Latin.[52] Pollock and Maitland remark that this came too late:

> It could not break the Westminster lawyers of their settled habit of thinking about law and writing about law in French, and when slowly French gave way before English even as the language of law reports and legal text-books, the English to which it yielded was an English in which every cardinal word was of French origin.[53]

As the printed word became more commonplace, some writers made a deliberate effort to adopt words derived from Latin, with the aim of making their text appear more learned. This happened also in the law. Some of the legal words taken from Latin in this way are *adjacent, frustrate, inferior, legal, quiet,* and *subscribe.*[54] Some writers also affected Latin word order. This led to an ornate style, consciously adopted to impress rather than inform. Even today, Latin grammar is responsible for some of the ornateness and the unusual word order of legal documents. It also lies behind the all-pervasive *shall* constructions, discussed further in Chapters 5 and 6.[55]

Different documents came to adopt English at different times. Wills began to be written in English about 1400. The petitions of the Commons were enrolled in French until 1423, after which they were often in English. Statutes were in Latin until about 1300, in French until 1485, in English alongside French for a year or two, and in English alone from 1489.[56] The abbreviated French used by lawyers was a serviceable and

---

50 Pollock and Maitland, *History of English Law*, vol. 1, p. 85.
51 Baugh and Cable, *History of the English Language*, p. 145.
52 36 Ed III c 15.
53 Pollock and Maitland, *History of English Law*, vol. 1, p. 85.
54 Baugh and Cable, *History of the English Language*, p. 180.
55 For the complexities of Latin construction, see H. C. Nutting, *The Latin Conditional Sentence* (Berkeley: University of California Press, 1925).
56 Baugh and Cable, *History of the English Language*, p. 150.

accurate shorthand,[57] and written pleadings in law French (despite the statute of 1362 and a similar one in 1650)[58] became more and more technical. But as the seventeenth century progressed, there arose new branches of law governed by principles not so easily expressed in French. These included new branches of commercial law. Also, many developments in land law were introduced by courts of equity, whose language had always been English.[59]

English law's linguistic progression – through French, Latin and English – is sometimes cited to explain the legal tradition of using two or three words where one will do. Lawyers, it is said, saw some benefit (if not strict need) in drawing from the law's diverse language stocks, particularly in periods of transition from one language to the next. In this way words from one language stock came to be used in conjunction with words from another language stock. There is some evidence to support this assertion: as we show below, certain common word pairings that have survived in modern legal usage are indeed drawn from different languages. But the argument does not hold true for all common pairings: many are drawn from the same language. The 'language stocks' argument is not an adequate explanation for all usages. More likely, whether drawn from the same or from different language stocks, word pairings merely exemplify the lawyer's natural proclivity towards verbosity. The following examples illustrate the point.

'Null and void'

'Null' comes from the Latin *nullus*, or from the Old French *nul*. 'Void' comes from the Old French *voide*. In legal documents, the two words are synonymous. Occasionally the phrase 'absolutely null and void' is seen, or even 'absolutely null and void and of no further force or effect whatsoever'. ('Absolutely' in this context means simply 'without condition or limitation'; usually it can be discarded, though sometimes it is useful to lend emphasis.)[60] So common is the doublet that for most lawyers 'null' or 'void' used singly seems odd. The pairing has virtually become one word. Strictly, though, 'void' alone would do.[61]

---

57 Holdsworth, *History of English Law*, 2nd edn (1937), vol. 6, p. 572.
58 C. H. Firth and R. S. Rait, *Acts and Ordinances of the Interregnum*, 1642–1660, vol. ii (Abingdon: Professional Books, 1978), p. 455. A statute similar to the 1650 statute was enacted in 1731: 4 Geo II, c 26.
59 Holdsworth, *History of English Law*, 2nd edn (1937), vol. 6, p. 572.
60 See *Re Delamere's Settlement Trusts* [1984] 1 All ER 584, CA.
61 An argument might be made for retaining the doublet in bijural countries such as Canada. See L. Mailhot and J. D. Carnwath, *Decisions, Decisions ...* (Quebec: Les Editions Yvon Blais Inc., 1998), p. 100, quoting Susan C. Markman, Senior Counsel, Department of Justice, Canada, at the Canadian Bar Annual Meeting, August 1997: 'The plain language advocates tell us there is no reason to use the lawyers' standby 'null and void' but the drafter mindful of the sensibilities of the two English-speaking audiences will want 'null' for civil lawyers and 'void' for common lawyers.'

'Observe and perform'

This pairing is frequently seen in promises relating to land, as in: 'to observe and perform all the covenants and stipulations set out in the charges register and to indemnify the Lessor against all actions in respect of any non-observance or non-performance'.[62]

'Observe' comes from the Latin *observare*: to watch, attend to, guard. 'Perform' comes from the Anglo-Norman *perfourmer*. It might be thought that the doublet could be justified on the ground that 'observe' is merely passive, while 'perform' involves some action, so that (for example) 'observe and perform' reflects the distinction between restrictive and positive covenants so well known in English and Commonwealth law.[63] But the courts have decided otherwise: in the context of legal obligations, there is no difference between 'observe' and 'perform'.[64]

'Fixtures and fittings'

This doublet is common in the context of land transactions. 'Fixture' derives from the late Latin *fixura*, and is the description applied to something that has become so attached to land that the law regards it as forming part of the land.[65] The origin of 'fitting' (with its adjective 'fit': suited, answering the purpose, appropriate) is unknown.

When used in conjunction with 'fixtures', 'fittings' merely serves to confuse.[66] Usually, the two terms are used as synonyms: that is, fittings are fixtures.[67] To some users of the word, however, 'fittings' are chattels – that is, not fixtures at all.[68] To other users, 'fittings' describes items that have been attached (and so are fixtures) but that remain essentially removable, such as fitted carpets, kitchen racks, and bathroom cabinets. If we turn to the case law, we see that judges generally distinguish, not between fixtures and 'fittings', but between fixtures and 'chattels'.[69]

---

62 A shortened version from Theodore B. F. Ruoff and C. West, *Land Registration Forms*, 3rd edn (London: Sweet & Maxwell, 1983), p. 133.

63 As to this distinction, see Peter Butt, *Land Law*, 3rd edn (Sydney: LBC Information Services, 1996), ch. 17.

64 See *Grey v Friar* (1854) 4 HLC 565; *Croft v Lumley* (1858) 4 HLC 672; *Bass Holdings Ltd v Morton Music Ltd* [1988] Ch 493, CA; *Ayling v Wade* [1961] 2 QB 228 at 235, CA.

65 See Butt, *Land Law*, pp. 22–32.

66 See J. E. Adams, 'Fixtures and Fittings – Time for Some Clear Thinking' (1986) 136 *New Law Journal* (UK), p. 652; Richard Castle, 'Estate Agents' Particulars – Incorporation in the Contract' (1987) 84 *Law Society's Gazette*, p. 326.

67 See Marcus Binney, 'Preying on the Churches', *The Times*, 3 December 1988, p. 10.

68 See Adams J. E. (1986) 136 *New Law Journal*, p. 652; D. N. Clarke and J. E. Adams, *Rent Reviews and Variable Rents*, 3rd edn (London: Longman, 1990), p. 328.

69 See *Elitestone Ltd v Morris* [1997] 1 WLR 687. Perhaps 'fixtures and fittings' is paralleled by 'goods and chattels'. 'Goods' (Old English *god*) and 'chattels' (Old French *chatel*) are treated as near-synonyms, although strictly speaking 'chattels' embraces 'goods'. See Robert E. Eagleson, 'Legislative Lexicography', in E. G. Stanley and T. F. Hoad, *Words for Robert Burchfield's Sixty-Fifth Birthday* (London: D. S. Brewer, 1988), p. 83.

'Right and liberty'

This familiar pairing often heads a list of appurtenant rights, as in: 'full right and liberty for the Tenant to pass and repass with or without vehicles over and upon the roads shown and tinted brown on the said plan'.[70] 'Right' comes from the Old English *riht*. 'Liberty' comes from the Latin *libertas*, through the Provençal *libertat*. The words are synonymous.

'Excepting and reserving'

'Exception' comes from the late Latin *exceptio*: exception, restriction, limitation. 'Reservation' comes from the late Latin *reservatio*, itself derived from the verb *reservare*: to keep back, lay up, reserve, to keep for some purpose. The pairing commonly heralds a qualification to the transfer of a property. Usually it is intoned as if the words were synonyms. The law draws a clear difference between them, however. An 'exception' is a subtraction from something already in existence, while a 'reservation' is a creation of something new out of the thing granted.[71] For example, a right of drainage through an existing pipe is an exception, while a new right of way over the property sold is a reservation. Indiscriminate pairing of the words sometimes demonstrates the drafter's ignorance of the essential difference between them.

'Use and enjoyment'

The roots of both these words lie in Latin: *usus*; and *gaudere*, to rejoice. In a legal context, however, 'enjoyment' means simply the use of something; it bears no connotation of pleasure, happiness or recreation.[72] So the words are synonyms. Similarly, 'hold and enjoy' are legal synonyms, though 'hold' comes from the Old English *haldan* (and the Old Frisian *halda*, Old Saxon *haldan*, Old High German *haltan*, and Old Norse *halda*).

---

70 A shortened version from Ruoff and West, *Land Registration Forms*, p. 151.
71 *Emmet on Title*, 19th edn, ed. J. T. Farrand (London: Longman, 1986), para 15.027; Butt, *The Standard Contract for the Sale of Land in New South Wales*, 2nd edn (Sydney: LBC Information Services, 1998), para [10.78]. Leading judicial discussions of the distinction include: *Cooper v Stuart* (1889) 14 App Cas 286 at 289–90 (PC); *Attorney-General (New South Wales) v Dickson* [1904] AC 273 at 277 (PC).
72 In *Kenny v Preen* [1963] 1 QB 499, Pearson LJ said that 'enjoy' in this context is a translation from the Latin 'fruor', denoting the exercise and use of a right in the sense of having the full benefit of it, rather than deriving pleasure from it.

'Free and uninterrupted'

This phrase is commonly found in the grant of easements, as where the grantee is given 'the free and uninterrupted right of passage and running of gas electricity water soil and other utility services through the grantor's land'.[73]

'Free' is from the Old English *freo*. 'Uninterrupted' is a combination of the Old English *un* (a prefix expressing negation), the Latin *inter* (between, among), and the past participle of the Latin *rumpere* (to break). The two words are not synonyms in everyday English. When joined in a legal context, however, they are used as synonyms. If the services run freely through the pipes, they are uninterrupted; so one word could be discarded. But why use the words at all? 'The right to run services through the pipes and cables' would grant in clear terms what was intended.

'Easements rights and privileges'

The root of 'easement' is the Old French *aisement*. 'Right' is Old English, as we have seen. 'Privilege' is from the Latin *privilegium*, itself a compilation of *privus* (private) and *leg, lex* (law). An easement is a particular kind of privilege, and a privilege is a particular kind of right. In many instances the widest word – 'right' – would do for all three.

'Agreed and declared'

'Agreed' has its roots in the Latin *ad gratus* (pleasing, welcome) and 'declared' in the Latin *de clarus* (clear). The words are sometimes said to be synonymous and are almost certainly used with that intention.[74] Strictly, however, they are capable of performing different functions. An 'agreement' is an arrangement between people; it arranges, or rearranges, the relationship between them. A 'declaration' is a formal statement about an existing state of affairs; it is not in itself an agreement, though it may amount to a warranty or create an estoppel.

'Freed and discharged'

As we have seen, 'freed' comes from the Old English *freo*. 'Discharge' comes from the Old French *descharger*. The word 'charge' in law has

---

73 From Ruoff and West, *Land Registration Forms*, p. 151.
74 For example, Stanley Robinson, *Drafting* (Sydney: Butterworths, 1979), p. 13.

several meanings,[75] but '*dis*charge' always carries the sense of unloading, unburdening or freeing. So 'freed' and 'discharged' are synonyms.

'Full and sufficient'

This is a common pairing, and appears in the usual form of indemnity: a person gives a 'full and sufficient indemnity' to someone.[76] 'Full' is directly from the Old English. 'Sufficient' comes from the Latin *sub*, plus *facere* (to do). In a legal context, the two words are used as synonyms, but in fact they do not have the same sense. A 'full' indemnity must be 'sufficient' indemnity, but a sufficient indemnity need not be a full indemnity. Here too, we may ask whether the words are needed at all. An 'indemnity' must be a 'full' indemnity or it is not an indemnity at all. The drafter uses the words 'full and sufficient' out of a sense of caution, to safeguard against all eventualities. They could be left out altogether; nothing would be lost, and clarity and directness might well be gained.

Payment by length

From the earliest times, officials of the English common law courts were paid by fees, the staffing of all the central courts being self-supporting. Many court officials bought their office, and naturally were keen for their investment to show a return.[77] One way was to charge fees for preparing and filing documents.[78] Litigants were required to pay for office copies, regardless of whether they wanted them and sometimes regardless of whether the documents were ever prepared.

Originally, fees were based on the overall length of documents. Various devices were invoked to make documents longer: wide margins, greater line-spacing, and, of course, more words. Sir Matthew Hale (1609–76), Chief Justice of the King's Bench, in his influential book *A History of the Common Law in England*,[79] gave his reasons for the development of lengthy pleadings ('as our vast Presses of Parchment for any one Plea do abundantly witness'). One reason was: 'These Please being mostly drawn by Clerks, who are paid for Entries and Copies therof, the larger the Pleadings are, the more Profits come to them, and the dearer the Clerk's Place is, the dearer he makes the Client pay.'

---

75 For example: a criminal accusation; a judge's instruction to the jury; expenses; an encumbrance on land to secure payment of a debt.
76 For an example, see Ruoff and West, *Land Registration Forms*, p. 160.
77 Holdsworth, *History of English Law* (3rd edn, 1927), vol. 1, pp. 255, 257.
78 Mellinkoff, *Language of the Law*, p. 188.
79 First published posthumously in 1713. The quotations are from the 1971 edition by C. M. Gray, University of Chicago Press, pp. 111, 112.

Like court officials, lawyers too came to be paid by length. Longer pleadings meant more income. Occasionally the judges themselves were frustrated by the prolixity. In one famous case in 1596, a pleader was fined £10 and sent to Fleet Street prison for drafting pleadings which ran to 120 pages.[80] The judge thought that sixteen pages would have sufficed. To add ignominy to penalty, the judge ordered that a hole be cut in the offending document, that the pleader's head be poked through the hole, and that the pleader be paraded around the courts of Westminster 'bareheaded and barefaced', with the document hanging 'written side outward'. More recently, pleadings exceeding 2600 pages were lodged in a South Australian case; they were later reduced to about 360 pages and then reinflated to 500 pages. The judge expressed his distaste in epithets such as 'contradictory', 'embarrassing and oppressive', 'meaningless', and 'so convoluted that [the pleadings are] well nigh impossible ... to comprehend'.[81]

Prolixity also became endemic in private legal documents, such as contracts and deeds. An easy way for a lawyer to increase the length of a document was by adding 'recitals'. Typically heralded by 'whereas', recitals introduced the operative part of the document by stating at considerable length the background to the transaction. While occasionally performing the useful function of putting the transaction into context – a function they can still serve today, as we see in Chapter 6 – more often than not they were superfluous, adding legal feel without legal purpose. They were merely an easy way of increasing the size of the document and hence the fee.[82]

Attempts to curb the excesses failed. Early in the nineteenth century, in a submission to the Real Property Commissioners, one writer suggested that deeds could be reduced to less than a quarter of their customary length, and pointed to payment by length as the main obstacle to reform.[83] In 1845, Joshua Williams wrote in his *Principles of the Law of Real Property*:

> The payment to a solicitor for drawing a deed is fixed at 1s. for every seventy-two words, denominated a *folio*; and the fees of counsel, though paid in guineas, average about the same. The consequences of this false economy on

---

80 *Mylward v Weldon* (1596) Tothill 102; 21 ER 136. A fuller report appears in Spence's *Equitable Jurisdiction* (1846), pp. 376–7.

81 *South Australia v Peat Marwick Mitchell & Co.* (Supreme Court of South Australia, Olsson J, 15 May 1997). Aspects of the case are reported at (1997) 24 ACSR 231.

82 Mellinkoff, *Language of the Law*, p. 190.

83 Alexander Hordern in a letter to Edward J. Littleton MP, reported in *Real Property Commissioners First Report* (1829): House of Commons Sessional Papers (HCSP) 1829, vol. 10, p. 446; see also p. 586 (T. J. Hogg Esq.). See also *Report from the Select Committee on Land Titles and Transfer* (1879): HCSP 1878–79, vol. 11, at p. 7.

the part of the public has been that certain well known and long established lengthy forms, full of synonyms and expletives, are current among lawyers as *common forms*, and by the aid of these, ideas are diluted to the proper remunerating strength; not that a lawyer actually inserts nonsense simply for the sake of increasing his fee; but words, sometimes unnecessary in any case, sometimes only in the particular case in which he is engaged, are suffered to remain, sanctioned by the authority of time and usage. The proper amount of verbiage to a common form is well established and understood, and whilst any attempt to exceed it is looked on as disgraceful, it is never likely to be materially diminished till a change is made in the scale of payment.[84]

In 1844, the journal of the reforming Law Amendment Society, *Law Review*, published an article promoting standard forms which would have effectively thwarted the practice of payment by length.[85] The president of the society was the radical Lord Brougham. The next year, Brougham introduced into parliament the *Conveyancing Act* 1845 and the *Leases Act* 1845, both of which provided short forms of standard covenants. The Acts also provided that the length of a deed was to be irrelevant on taxation of costs. Section 3 of the *Leases Act* (which was not repealed until 1989)[86] read:

> That in taxing any Bill for preparing and executing any Deed under this Act it shall be lawful for the Taxing Officer and he is hereby required, in estimating the proper Sum to be charged for such Transaction, to consider, not the Length of such Deed, but only the Skill and Labour employed, and Responsibility incurred, in the Preparation thereof.

Shortly afterwards, in an article entitled 'The Conveyancing Acts of 1845', the *Law Review* expressed its optimistic opinion that the lawyer's client

> will soon express himself in favour of the new Acts. The law will always be stronger than the lawyer. There is no class of persons who will excite so little sympathy as a body of lawyers resisting a change attempted to be made in favour of the public, and possibly affecting the profits of the profession. Books will be written (we already perceive symptoms of them) to prove that it is unsafe and unwise to rely on the new plans; they will, nevertheless, be acted on. Learned conveyancers under the bar, and still more learned conveyancers at the bar, will argue, sneer, contemn, denounce, rail, ridicule – it will all be in vain.[87]

---

84 Joshua Williams, *Principles of the Law of Real Property* (London: S. Sweet, 1845), p. 147.
85 'Recent Alterations in Conveyancing Forms' (1844) 1 *Law Review*, p. 158. See also another anonymous article, 'Conveyancing, its Early History and Present State' (1845) 1 *Law Review*, p. 382.
86 *Statute Law (Repeals) Act* 1989.
87 (1845) 3 *Law Review*, p. 177.

The optimism proved misplaced. The legal profession, prompted chiefly by a fear that fees would fall, refused to use the short forms supplied by the 1845 Acts.[88] In a first response to the passing of the Acts, the *Legal Observer* was hostile on this account.[89] Brougham made several attempts to overcome the anxiety about fees.[90] Others made similar attempts. In a paper to the Juridical Society in 1862, Joshua Williams expressed himself in his usual forthright way:

> But to tell a man that the more he aims at conciseness, the worse he shall be paid; that the more copies and abstracts he gets done by the law-stationer, the more prosperous he shall be; that it matters not what is in a letter, so long as he writes it; is surely not the way to encourage a genuine industry. And it is curious to see how much the minds of some clerks and others, who have not enjoyed the benefits of a liberal education, are warped by this state of things. I have before now met with some, who seemed to think that their sole duty to their principals consisted, first in expanding every idea into the largest possible number of words, and secondly in making as many deeds as possible out of every transaction.[91]

In 1878–79 a parliamentary select committee investigating registration of deeds and titles looked also at payment by length.[92] By this time it was generally accepted that legal documents had become far too convoluted. Several witnesses urged that a scale based on the value of the transaction would help make documents shorter.[93] Nehemiah Learoyd was frank with the select committee when asked why Brougham's Acts had fallen on stony ground:

> hitherto we have been paid according to the length of the instrument, and there has been no mode of payment which the law has recognised which allows for the responsibilities of our work; so that if I draw a deed which is 60 folios in length, a folio being 72 words, I am paid for it and it probably compensates me for my labour; but if I can find a mode of putting it into a dozen lines, I am entitled to only a few shillings as the remuneration for the transaction, though my responsibilities may be as many thousands of pounds.[94]

---

88 M. J. Russell, 'Brevity v Verbosity' (1962) 26 Conv (NS) 45 at 54.
89 (1845) 30 *Legal Observer*, p. 369, anonymous article 'Conveyancing Reform and Professional Remuneration'.
90 See Russell, 'Brevity v Verbosity', p. 54.
91 *On the True Remedies for the Evils which Affect the Transfer of Land* (London: S. Sweet, 1862), p. 13.
92 *Report from the Select Committee on Land Titles and Transfer* (1878, 1879): HCSP 1878, vol. 15, p. 467; 1878–79, vol. 11, p. 1.
93 Ibid. (1879): HCSP 1878–79, vol. 11, pp. 7, 8.
94 Ibid. (1878): HCSP 1878, vol. 15, p. 559.

The select committee recommended abolishing payment by length and substituting scales of charges based on value ('ad valorem').[95] Its recommendation was accepted, and for the next ninety years scale fees held sway. The 1883 Remuneration Order[96] introducing them was made under the *Solicitors' Remuneration Act* 1881, which received royal assent on the same day as the *Conveyancing Act* 1881. That Act contained effective and widespread provisions designed to shorten deeds. It was a major step forward. The worst excesses of noun upon noun, verb upon verb, and qualification upon qualification, were never to be seen again.

However, far from abandoning the idea of payment by length, the 1883 Remuneration Order preserved it by allowing solicitors to elect to charge 'according to the present system as altered by Schedule II hereto'.[97] Many of the fees in that schedule were set according to the number of words (expressed as 'folios'), a direct financial inducement to undue length. This option of payment by length persisted in England until the Solicitors' Remuneration Order of 1953[98] decreed for the first time that one of seven factors in deciding a fair and reasonable payment should be 'the number and importance of the documents prepared or perused, without regard to length'.

Payment by time

Payment by time spent on a task is a standard way of assessing legal fees in many countries. For example, in England, solicitors' fees for 'non-contentious business' (that is, work not in connection with litigation) are governed by the Solicitors' (Non-Contentious Business) Remuneration Order 1994. This Order lists a number of factors in assessing fees:

> A solicitor's costs shall be such sum as may be fair and reasonable to both solicitor and entitled person having regard to all the circumstances of the case and in particular to:-
> (a) the complexity of the matter or the difficulty or novelty of the questions raised;
> (b) the skill, labour, specialised knowledge and responsibility involved;
> (c) the time spent on the business;
> (d) the number and importance of the documents prepared or perused, without regard to length; ...

---

95 Ibid. (1879): HCSP 1878–79, vol. 11, p. 13.
96 *Solicitors' Remuneration Order* 1883 (SR & O Rev 1948, xxi, p. 205).
97 Ibid., para 6. The *Solicitors' Remuneration Order* 1953 (SI 1953, No. 117) substituted 'in accordance with' for 'according to the present system as altered by', and substituted a new Schedule II.
98 SI 1953, No. 117, para 6.

Para (c) speaks of 'time spent'. Similar wording appeared in the former Order, the Solicitors' Remuneration Order 1972 (which in turn drew on terminology in the Solicitors' Remuneration Order 1953). Thus, where time spent is relevant, the longer the time, the higher the fee – a strong inducement to expand the time taken on a task. Of course, there is no direct and automatic relationship between the time spent and the size of the bill; but equally, there is no incentive to work quickly or to prepare short documents. Indeed, ever since the 1972 Order the Law Society of England and Wales has been at pains to emphasise that solicitors should keep records of the time taken for a task.[99] The result has been an obsession with time-recording and hourly charging rates, particularly in larger law firms. Of the factors listed in the Remuneration Order, time spent has become dominant. And so payment by time – cousin to payment by length – continues to bedevil the practice of law.[100]

The litigious environment

In this chapter we have sought to highlight some of the reasons why legal drafters are reluctant to depart from the traditional style of legal writing. Before leaving the topic we should mention one more: the litigious environment in which lawyers work. This environment plays a large role in perpetuating a settled style. Lawyers draft documents against an adversarial background. There is always the risk that documents will come under judicial scrutiny. Even in the process of drafting, the lawyer cannot ignore the potential effect of the words on a judge.

Judges have evolved a complex set of principles to help clarify ambiguity and resolve uncertainty in legal documents. For some lawyers, these principles of interpretation encourage a defensive style: drafters attempt to anticipate them and thus avoid their application. The result is drafting that is reactive, not proactive – drafting that harks back to precedent and tradition, with little or no concern for clarity, brevity, or ease of comprehension.

As we show in the next chapter, however, the principles of interpretation need not stand in the way of a crisp, modern style.

---

99 See the Law Society's booklet, *The Expense of Time* (first published in 1972; several editions since).

100 For an incisive discussion of some of the issues, see L. Fisher, 'The Crude Yardstick of the Billable Hour' (1996) 70 *Australian Law Journal*, p. 160.

This chapter examines the ways in which legal documents are interpreted. After reviewing some judicial comments on the parlous state of traditional legal drafting, we discuss the complex series of principles – sometimes overlapping, sometimes conflicting – which courts have evolved to help clarify meaning in legal documents. In the process, we consider whether those who draft legal documents can or ought to draft so as to avoid the application of these principles. We then consider the all-important role of context in interpreting legal documents – for, as will be seen, context often resolves problems of interpretation.

We conclude the chapter by pointing out the dangers of a too-strict reliance on precedent when interpreting legal documents. A paramount principle emerges from the case law: decisions on the meaning of particular words or phrases in one document provide little or no guidance to their meaning in another.[1] Each document is unique. To interpret it, one single question should be asked: what did these parties mean by these words in this context?

What judges have said about traditional legal drafting

Judges have not been reluctant to criticise poorly drafted documents. Epithets have included 'botched', 'half-baked', 'cobbled-together', 'doubtful', 'tortuous', 'archaic', 'incomprehensible legal gobbledegook', and 'singularly inelegant'.[2] We will look at some cases of recent decades where judges have criticised the language, form or content of traditionally drafted legal documents.

---

1 See, for example, *Sefton v Tophams Ltd* [1967] AC 50 at 84 (Lord Wilberforce); *Re Donald* [1947] 1 All ER 764 at 766 (Lord Greene MR); *Housden v Marshall* [1959] 1 WLR 1 at 5 (Harman J); *Aspden v Seddon* (1874) 10 Ch App 394 at 397 (Jessel MR).
2 'Doubtful': *Overseas Union Insurance Ltd v AA Mutual International Insurance Co. Ltd* [1988] 2 Lloyd's Rep 63 at 69 (Evans J). The citations for other epithets are given below.

The botched clause[3]

A 1929 settlement gave power to pay income to:

> any person or persons in whose house or apartments or in whose company or under whose care and control or by or with whom the said [Mr] Gulbenkian may from time to time be employed or residing.

As Lord Reid pointed out in the House of Lords, this clause did not make sense as it stood.[4] One of the permutations was 'by whom [Mr] Gulbenkian is residing'. Lord Reid was surprised to learn that such a 'botched clause' had somehow found its way into a standard book of legal precedents. Nevertheless, he said that clients ought not to be penalised for their lawyer's slovenly drafting; and that since no rational person would insert such a provision, it might be necessary to relax the stricter interpretation standards of an earlier era, to see whether a reasonably clear intention lay behind the words.

The half-baked clause[5]

A developer contracted with landowners to develop the landowners' site in return for a 99-year lease of the site. Clause 4 of the agreement provided:

> if for any reason due to the wilful default of the tenant [that is, the developer] the development shall remain uncompleted on 29th September 1983 the lease shall forthwith be granted and completed.

By 1984 the development had not even started. So, in October 1984, the landowners treated the agreement as repudiated. The developer countered with the argument (among others) that, even if it was in wilful default, it was entitled to the lease under clause 4. Not surprisingly, the Court of Appeal rejected the developer's argument. In the court's view, clause 4 was part of a commercial agreement and the parties must have intended to make a sensible commercial arrangement (discussed further on p. 50). Hence, the Court implied a condition precluding the developer from enforcing the agreement if it was in wilful default. Both sides conceded that clause 4 was inept. Dillon LJ thought it 'half-baked'.[6]

---

3 *Re Gulbenkian's Settlement* [1970] AC 508 at 517 (Lord Reid).
4 At 507.
5 *Alghussein Establishment v Eton College* [1988] 1 WLR 587, HL.
6 A comment which Lord Jauncey of Tullichettle on appeal thought not to be 'overstated': [1988] 1 WLR 587 at 594.

The cobbled-together insurance policy[7]

The mortgagee of a ship took out an insurance policy to protect itself against loss if the ship was damaged. The policy consisted of two parts. One was a standard printed form ('the SG form'), which, although 'dignified'[8] by inclusion as a schedule to an Act of 1906, had been described as long ago as 1791 as 'absurd and incoherent'.[9] The other part of the policy was a set of eight typed conditions known as 'Mortgagee's Interest Clause 1'. These conditions were a translation from Swedish, since they had originated in Sweden and had later been adopted in English marine insurance policies. The court was urged to give certain words in these conditions their plain and ordinary meaning. Lloyd LJ said that he did not know whether those words had a plain and ordinary meaning in Swedish, but he was certain they had no plain and ordinary meaning in English. The task of construing the contract as a whole against the commercial background was 'not made easy' when a medieval English form was combined with a translation from modern Swedish. Lloyd LJ said that the courts had been protesting for years about the drafting of marine insurance contracts, and he hoped that the SG form would never again be used in combination with 'Mortgagee's Interest Clause 1' without at least some explanation on how they were to be read together. Purchas LJ hoped that in future marine insurance policies would be properly drawn and designed for the specific purpose involved, rather than 'cobbled together' by joining inconsistent sets of contractual terms taken from policies which were alien both to the market and to the purposes for which they were produced.

The disastrous letter[10]

A firm of solicitors wrote a letter of advice to their client Socpen, who were the landlords of offices in London. The offices were leased to a tenant. The lease contained a 'break' clause, allowing either the landlord or the tenant to cancel the lease in 1980. The letter concerned the effect of the break clause, and was addressed to the landlord's secretary, who was not a lawyer, and who was inexperienced in property management. At issue in the High Court was the meaning of the letter.

The *Times* described the letter as 'obscure'.[11] But on closer examination, the letter was not so much muddled as wrong. The lease gave either

---

7 *The Alexion Hope* [1988] 1 Lloyd's Rep 311 at 320, CA (Purchas LJ).
8 To adopt the description of Purchas LJ, ibid. at 320.
9 See *Brough v Whitmore* (1791) 4 Term Rep 206 at 210; 100 ER 976 at 978.
10 *Socpen Trustees Limited v Wood Nash & Winters*, Jupp J, Queen's Bench Division, 6 October 1983. The case is unreported.
11 'Obscure Legal Advice Cost Firm £90,000', *Times*, 7 October 1983, p. 5.

party the right to terminate the lease in 1980, whereas the letter indicated that only the tenant had that right. Though hardly a model of clarity, the letter was not hopelessly obscure; worse examples can be found. Nevertheless, the judge said that part of the letter was phrased in 'very obscure English' and that it had 'anaesthetized [the secretary] into an oblivion' over the effect of the break clause. In the judge's view, the result of the letter from the landlord's point of view was 'disastrous'. The solicitors were negligent in failing to advise the landlord that it could have used the break clause to bring the lease to an end. As a result of that negligence, the landlord had lost the right to relet the offices at a higher rent. The judge ordered the solicitors to pay the shortfall, amounting to £95,000.

The notices that defied understanding[12]

Under United States legislation, elderly people could claim reimbursement from medical insurers for certain medical expenses. The insurer could reduce the claim on certain specified grounds. The claimant could then seek a review of the insurer's decision; and after the review, the insurer was required to send a notice telling the beneficiary of the basis of its decision. The beneficiary then had a right to appeal against the review. As a practical matter, in order to decide whether to appeal, the beneficiary had to be able to assess two points: whether the insurer had properly classified the medical services that had been provided; and whether the insurer had properly computed the reasonable charge for that service. The case arose because the insurer sent (to hundreds of thousands of claimants) a form of notice which, the court ruled, was unintelligible to the average beneficiary. According to the evidence, about 48 per cent of elderly people in New York had an eighth-grade education or less; yet to understand the notice required a sixteenth-grade education. The notices

> defy understanding by the general populace. They are filled with confusing cross-references to 'control numbers' and are composed of paragraphs that seem strung together randomly. Explanations are couched in technical jargon. The words and phrases 'approved charges', 'customary charges', 'prevailing charges', 'locality', 'economic index' and 'physicians' old and new profile', which are the substance of the [notice], are specialized Medicare vocabulary. To a layman unfamiliar with Medicare regulations, this language has no real meaning ...
>
> The language used is bureaucratic gobbledegook, jargon, double talk, a form of officialese, federalese and insurancese, and doublespeak. It does not qualify as English.[13]

---

12 *David v Heckler* 591 F Supp 1033 (1984).
13 Ibid., pp. 1037, 1043.

The court held that the notices were so complex that the beneficiaries had been denied due process.

The tortuous rent review [14]

Surveyors negotiated a formula for rent reviews in a proposed lease, and set out that formula verbally in correspondence. Solicitors then drew up an agreement to grant the lease. In accordance with standard practice, they attached to the agreement a draft form of the proposed lease, containing the solicitors' attempt to embody the surveyors' formula. The language of this attempt Hoffmann J characterised as 'tortuous'. In fact, not only was it tortuous: it was wrong, for the solicitors' formula differed from the surveyors' formula. However, the solicitors' language was so complex that no-one noticed the difference. When the formal lease was granted some time later, it incorporated the surveyors' formula; strictly, it should have incorporated the formula in the draft lease (the solicitors' formula). Only on the first rent review did anyone notice that the two formulas differed. Simpler language should have avoided the discrepancy. Hoffmann J suggested that the mistake would not have occurred if the formula had been expressed algebraically instead of verbally. The case showed, he said, 'that a very modest degree of numeracy can save a great deal of money'. [15]

The archaic bond [16]

Main contractors of a leisure complex required subcontractors to provide a performance bond for 10 per cent of the value of the subcontract. This could have been achieved by a relatively simple document, but the document which the parties signed was lengthy and complex, drafted in traditional style. Its complexity was compounded by an eccentric order of provisions. The first part acknowledged that the subcontractors and the surety were bound to the main contractors in the specified sum. Then followed a testimonium stating that the parties had sealed the document. This was followed by recitals, which in turn were followed by the condition upon which the bond was given, namely, that the obligation would be 'null and void' if the subcontractors complied with their contract or if the surety paid damages for breach up to the specified sum. In the Court of Appeal, Beldham LJ (echoing comments of Saville LJ) described the wording of the bond as 'archaic, difficult to interpret and

---

14 *London Regional Transport v Wimpey Group Services Ltd* [1986] 2 EGLR 41 (Hoffmann J).
15 Ibid. at 900.
16 *Trafalgar House Construction (Regions) Ltd v General Surety & Guarantee Co. Ltd* [1996] AC 199 at 208, HL (Lord Jauncey of Tullichettle).

ill-suited to its obvious commercial purpose'.[17] When the case reached the House of Lords, Lord Jauncey of Tullichettle said he found 'great difficulty in understanding the desire of commercial men to embody so simple an obligation in a document which is quite unnecessarily lengthy, which obfuscates its true purpose and which is likely to give rise to unnecessary argument and litigation as to its meaning'.[18] In our opinion, though, commercial people do not generally desire to express themselves in unnecessarily complex ways. Complexity intrudes because lawyers draft the documents – even if the clients later adopt the documents as standard forms. Lord Atkin once said that old-fashioned language is not the fault of lawyers;[19] but that view does not stand close scrutiny.

The gobbledegook guarantee[20]

Two bank customers signed a bank's standard form of guarantee. The customers thought they were signing a guarantee limited to $10,000, but in fact the guarantee was for an unlimited amount. The judge described the clause which dealt with the extent of the guarantee as 'a single sentence of 57 lines in length couched in incomprehensible legal gobble-degook'.[21] It was so complex that the judge thought that neither the customers, nor the two bank officials who had been present when the customers signed, had any real understanding of the nature and effect of the clause.[22] (Nor, it seems, did the bank's counsel who argued the case in court.)[23] The customers had not read the document before signing it, but 'they would have been little wiser had they attempted the exercise'.[24] The judge, Higgins J, held that the customers were bound only to the extent of $10,000.

The singularly inelegant document[25]

A rifle association signed a document by which it acknowledged that it occupied government land in Sydney for use as a rifle range. When the

---

17 (1994) 10 Const LR 240.
18 [1996] AC 199 at 209.
19 *Trade Indemnity Co. Ltd v Workington Harbour and Dock Board* [1937] AC 1 at 17.
20 *Houlahan v Australian and New Zealand Banking Group Ltd* (1992) 110 FLR 259.
21 Ibid. at 263. The law report omits the full text of the clause, but it contained 1193 words. On average, each clause in the document contained 330 words.
22 Ibid. at 262–3. To similar effect are the comments of Young J in the New South Wales Supreme Court, that a chattel lease transaction 'was written in such legalese that not even the New South Wales office manager of the [lessor] realised what it meant': *Goldsbrough v Ford Credit Australia Ltd* [1989] ASC 58,583 at 58,590.
23 (1992) 110 FLR 259 at 263.
24 Ibid.
25 *NSW Rifle Association v Commonwealth of Australia*, unreported, New South Wales Court of Appeal, 15 August 1997, Powell JA.

government tried to terminate the occupation, the rifle association sought an order that the document gave it the right to remain for as long as it wished to use the land as a rifle range. The New South Wales Court of Appeal held that the rifle association had no right to remain. Two of the three members of the court held that the document was not contractual in nature. Powell JA described the document as 'singularly inelegant', reminiscent of the efforts of the 'blundering attorney's clerk' and revealing 'sloppy draftsmanship and confusion of thought'.[26] The Australian High Court later refused leave to appeal from this decision, on the ground that the documents were 'so inelegantly drawn, and their intention to operate contractually [was] so problematic' that the case was not a suitable vehicle for reconsidering the law regarding intention to enter into contractual relations.[27]

The principles of legal interpretation

From judicial condemnation of poor drafting, we now turn to consider the principles which courts have evolved to help interpret documents that come before them. In truth, these 'principles' are merely guidelines – presumptions which may be weak or strong depending on circumstances. Sometimes they are called 'rules' – 'rules of construction' – but in fact they are all rebuttable.

These principles of interpretation are well-known to lawyers, and form part of their linguistic consciousness. So it might be thought that the principles have a direct effect on the way legal documents are written. In reality, however, lawyers probably pay little heed to the principles of interpretation when they draft documents. Nor should they. Documents should be drafted with sufficient clarity to render unnecessary any recourse to rules of construction on points of language.[28] The late Reed

---

26 The same judge some years earlier had castigated a partnership agreement as 'hardly a shining example of the draftsman's art — indeed, it is not going too far to describe it as exuding the glutinous aroma of pastepot and scissors': *Van der Waal v Goodenough* [1983] 1 NSWLR 81 at 87–8. The judge has returned to this simile on other occasions: *New South Wales Rifle Association v Commonwealth* (unreported, NSWCA, 15 August 1997); *New South Wales Rugby League Ltd v Australian Rugby Football League Ltd* (1999) 30 ASCR 354 at 371. The reference to the 'blundering attorney's clerk' appears to be a reference to Bacon VC's use of that phrase in *Re Redfern* (1877) 6 Ch D 133 at 138, repeated by Joyce J in *Re Dayrell* [1904] 2 Ch 496 at 499.

27 (1998) 72 ALJR 713 at 714.

28 Piesse, *Elements of Drafting*, 9th edn, ed. J. K. Aitken (Sydney: Law Book Company, 1995), p. v. See also Robert C. Dick, *Legal Drafting*, 3rd edn (Toronto: Carswell, 1995), p. 17: 'A drafter should not use the rules of interpretation as crutches but should be capable of drafting without having to rely on or resolve difficulties in meaning through the use of the rules.' For a different view, see Charles Bennett, *Drafting Residential Leases*, 2nd edn (London: Longman, 1990), p. 8.

Dickerson, a leading United States exponent of legal drafting, accurately described the reality:

> For the draftsman, many rules of interpretation are simply irrelevant. These are the rules by which courts resolve inconsistencies and contradictions or supply omissions that cannot be dealt with by applying the ordinary principles of meaning. They are irrelevant because the draftsman who tries to write a healthy instrument does not and should not pay attention to the principles that the court will apply if he fails. He simply does his best, leaving it to the courts to accomplish what he did not. The draftsman who adverts to what the courts will do in such cases is likely to relax his efforts, thus passing the drafting buck to the courts and forcing them to deal with an inferior instrument.[29]

Internal and external factors

The interpretation of legal documents has two aspects: internal and external. The internal aspect looks only at the language of the document; in contrast, the external aspect looks beyond the document for evidence of its meaning and legal effect.

The internal aspect is the dominant one. The internal canons of interpretation apply unless they are displaced, and a party who seeks to displace them bears the burden of proof.[30] Yet a moment's thought will bring home the obvious point that a document can never be complete in itself. A number of external factors are potentially relevant. They include: the background against which the document was prepared; the factual matrix from which it sprang;[31] the circumstances and the relationship of the parties; the terms which (though physically absent from the document) will be implied if necessary; the general law; and the purpose which the document or a part of it was designed to achieve. All these have a powerful but unspoken effect on a document's operation, and neither the parties nor the courts ignore them.[32]

Particularly relevant are the circumstances in which the courts will imply terms into contracts. These deserve our attention before we turn to the 'principles' of interpretation themselves.

---

29 Reed Dickerson, *Fundamentals of Legal Drafting*, 2nd edn (Boston: Little, Brown & Co., 1986), p. 47.

30 See *Odgers' Construction of Deeds and Statutes*, 5th edn, ed. G. Dworkin (London: Sweet & Maxwell, 1967) p. 28; Sir Roland Burrows, *Interpretation of Documents*, 2nd edn (London: 1946), p. 94.

31 The term 'factual matrix', now common, appears to have been first used in *Reardon Smith Line Ltd v Yngvar Hansen-Tangen ('The Diana Prosperity')* [1976] 1 WLR 989 at 997 (Lord Wilberforce), HL.

32 Compare *Schuler AG v Wickman Machine Tool Sales Ltd* [1974] AC 235, in which the House of Lords held that in general the parties' subsequent actions are not relevant in construing the document.

Implication of terms

Courts imply terms into contracts on a number of grounds. Some are required by statute; others are required by the common law. In either case, the implication affects the interpretation of the contract, since the result is to add to the contract a provision which is not evident merely from reading the document itself.

To deal first with implication by statute: an example is the implication of merchantable quality under sale of goods legislation.[33] Another is the implication of habitable quality under residential tenancy legislation.[34] The implied terms give a contract a content over and above its printed terms.

As to implication at common law: courts imply terms into contracts on grounds of custom or usage, whether in the trade generally or merely between the particular parties.[35] They also imply terms on the basis of business efficacy.[36] Sometimes an inference from the written language of the agreement is so obvious that it needs no stating; thus, *Gardner v Coutts & Co.* held that the grant of a right of first refusal to A precluded the grantor not only from selling the property without first offering it to A, but also from making a gift of it without first offering it to A.[37] Occasionally courts imply terms that are really rules of law: an example is the principle that a professional person must act with reasonable care and skill. Similarly, courts impose constructive trusts to satisfy the demands of justice and good conscience, without necessary reference to any express or presumed intention of the parties.[38] Other doctrines, too, are invoked to alter the relationship between the parties, regardless of the express words the parties may have used to describe their relationship; examples are estoppel, rescission, restitution and rectification. Indeed, judges sometimes disregard even the clear words of a document in order to reach a desired result.[39]

---

33 For a detailed discussion, see Roy Goode, *Commercial Law*, 2nd edn (London: Penguin Books, 1995), ch. 11.

34 For examples in England and Wales, see *Landlord and Tenant Act* 1985, ss 8, 11. For examples in Australia, see *Residential Tenancies Act* 1987 (NSW), ss 25, 26.

35 See, for example, *Peter Darlington Partners Ltd v Gosho Co. Ltd* [1964] 1 Lloyd's Rep 149: the rule that the supplier must supply the quantity and quality agreed was displaced by evidence of trade usage permitting a limited shortfall in the purity of seed against an appropriate reduction in the price.

36 *The Moorcock* (1889) 14 PD 54, CA: in a contract for the use of a jetty by a ship there was to be implied a term that the jetty owner would pay for any damage that the ship might suffer by settling on the river bed.

37 [1967] 3 All ER 1064 (Cross J).

38 See *Carl Zeiss Stiftung v Herbert Smith & Co. (No. 2)* [1969] 2 Ch 276 at 301 (Edmund Davies LJ); *Baumgartner v Baumgartner* (1987) 164 CLR 137; *Bahr v Nicolay* (No. 2) (1988) 164 CLR 604.

39 For example, *Bishop v Bonham* [1988] 1 WLR 742, where the Court of Appeal held that a mortgagee's court-imposed duty to obtain a proper price on sale overrode the mortgagee's express power to sell 'as [the mortgagee] may think fit' and with exemption from 'liability for any loss howsoever arising'.

One area where the courts have intervened readily, in apparent disregard of the terms of the document, is landlord and tenant. Two examples come easily to mind. One is the principle, well-established in England, that there can be no contracting out of the Rent Acts.[40] The other, well-established in many countries, is the principle that the parties may be found to have entered into a 'lease' despite deliberately casting their agreement in the form of a 'licence'. An example is *Street v Mountford*.[41] There, a written agreement had been carefully crafted in the form of a licence, so as to avoid all semblance of a lease. Headed 'licence agreement', it scrupulously avoided words like 'landlord', 'tenant', or 'rent' – words which might suggest a lease. Further, above the grantee's signature appeared these printed words: 'I understand and accept that a licence in the above form does not and is not intended to give me a tenancy ...'. Despite all this, the House of Lords held that the agreement created a tenancy. The deliberate language and form of 'licence' was not conclusive of the legal relationship the parties had created. Similar decisions have been reached in other cases, both in England and elsewhere.[42]

Document must be read as a whole

Turning now to the internal principles of construction: the first to be considered holds that the document (or series of documents, if the transaction is to be carried out by a series) should be construed as a whole. As Viscount Symonds said in *Attorney General v Prince Ernest Augustus of Hanover*, 'no one should profess to understand any part of a statute or of any other document before he has read the whole of it. Until he has done so, he is not entitled to say that it or any part of it is clear and unambiguous.'[43]

This principle is well-known to lawyers. Yet they frequently disregard it by inserting copious cross-references, which the principle renders superfluous. Cross-referencing is sometimes helpful. But when overdone it can make a document more difficult to read, by forcing the reader to

---

40 See *Barton v Fincham* [1921] 2 KB 291, CA; *Appleton v Aspin* [1988] 1 WLR 410, CA.

41 [1985] AC 809. This decision quickly produced a substantial literature: see, for example, Street, 'Coach and Horse Trip Cancelled? Rent Act Avoidance after Street v Mountford' [1985] Conv 328; Bridge, 'Street v Mountford – No Hiding Place?' [1986] Conv 344; Clarke, 'Street v Mountford: The Question of Intent – A View from Down Under' [1986] Conv 39; Wallace, 'The Legacy of Street v Mountford' (1990) 41 *Northern Ireland Law Quarterly*, p. 143.

42 *AG Securities v Vaughan* [1990] 1 AC 417; *Bruton v London & Quadrant Housing Trust* [2000] 1 AC 406. Australian examples are *Radaich v Smith* (1959) 101 CLR 209 (predating *Street v Mountford*); *Lewis v Bell* (1985) 1 NSWLR 731 (NSW CA); *KJRR Pty Ltd v Commissioner of State Revenue* (1999) 99 ATC 4335 (Vic CA).

43 [1957] AC 436 at 463, HL.

jump backwards and forwards, interrupting the flow of ideas. Also, of course, it adds to the length of the document.

Eiusdem generis

Of all the rules of construction, this is probably the best-known to the competent drafter. It can be expressed in this way: where a list of two or more items belonging to the same 'genus' (that is, group or class) is followed by general words, the general words are construed as confined to the same class. To illustrate: in *Williams v Williams*[44] the Court of Appeal was asked whether bundles of unsorted cheques and paying-in slips were included within the description 'ledgers, day books, cash books, account books and other records used in the ordinary business of the bank'. Specifically, were unsorted cheques and paying-in slips covered by the words 'other records'? The court held they were not, because 'other records' were to be construed *eiusdem generis*, 'of the same genus', with the earlier terms in the list.

This rule (like the next two to be discussed) applies also in the construction of statutes, from which many illustrations can be drawn.[45] A clear example is *Hy Whittle Ltd v Stalybridge Corporation*,[46] where Buckley J held that bread and confectionery did not come within the description 'meat, fish, poultry, vegetables, fruit, and other provisions'. The list 'meat, fish, poultry, vegetables, fruit' pointed, he said, to a class of natural products – that is, products that had not been subjected to a manufacturing process. The phrase 'other provisions' was to read as confined to the same class. Bread and confectionery were manufactured items, the 'product of a baker's activities, converting natural flour into a finished article'.[47] Accordingly, they did not fall within the catch-all phrase 'other provisions'.

To take another example: a government proclamation authorised the making of a customs regulation banning the import of 'arms, ammunition, gunpowder, or any other goods'. It was held that the proclamation did not authorise a regulation banning the import of pyrogallic acid (used for film-developing), because the phrase 'any other goods' was to be construed as encompassing only goods of the class of arms, ammunition and gunpowder.[48]

---

44 [1988] QB 161, CA.
45 Alec Samuels, 'The *Eiusdem Generis* Rule in Statutory Interpretation' [1984] *Statute Law Review*, p. 180.
46 (1967) 65 LGR (UK) 344.
47 Ibid. at 354.
48 *Attorney-General v Brown* [1920] 1 KB 773.

Again, in an Australian case, a defendant was charged with breaching a regulation drafted in the following terms: 'No person shall by speaking, shouting, singing, playing upon, operating or sounding any musical or noisy instrument or doing anything whatsoever attract together a number of persons in any street or so as to obstruct traffic.'[49] The defendant had attracted a crowd (and thus obstructed pedestrian traffic) by standing on the steps of a theatre in a city street, dressed in a gorilla suit, gesticulating but without making any noise. He was acquited of the charge, because the phrase 'doing anything whatsoever' was to be read down by reference to the class inherent in the preceding list of specific activities – namely, activities that generated noise. The defendant's gesticulations being mute, he fell outside the genus of noisemakers.

The *eiusdem generis* rule can apply only where the specific words belong to a 'class'.[50] If they lack an identifiable class, the general words must usually be taken at face value and given the width of meaning they normally bear.[51] For example, an English case concerned the question whether the obligation to pay hiring charges for a ship ceased after the ship ran aground. The charterparty stated that hiring charges would cease 'in the event of loss of time from deficiency of men or owners' stores, breakdown of machinery, or damage to hull or other accident'. The court held that the words and phrases preceding 'or other accident' formed no particular genus or class – they expressed 'no common or denominating feature'.[52]

The *eiusdem generis* rule sometimes seems to defeat the drafter's intentions. In *S. S. Knutsford Ltd v Tillmanns & Co.* a bill of lading exonerated the ship's master 'should the entry and discharge at a port be deemed by the master unsafe in consequence of war [or] disturbance or any other cause.' The court held that 'any other cause' must be construed as within the class of events characterised by 'war [or] disturbance'. Icing-up of the sea was not in that class. Hence, the clause did not exonerate a master who judged a port unsafe because of the existence of ice.[53]

Like other 'rules' of construction, the *eiusdem generis* rule is intended as a guide to discerning the parties' true intentions. It is not to be applied slavishly, divorced from this purpose. This is clear from the following comments of Devlin J in *Chandris v Isbrandtsen-Moller Co. Inc.*:

---

49 *Hughes v Winter* [1955] SASR 238.
50 *R v Regos* (1947) 74 CLR 613 at 622–4 (Latham CJ).
51 *Mudie & Co. v Strick* (1909) 100 LT 701; *Ruapehu Alpine Lifts Ltd v State Insurance Ltd* (1998) 10 ANZ Insurance Cases 61–404. We add the qualification 'usually', because the context in which the general words are used and the subject matter of the contract may show that the parties intended to use them in a narrow sense (as in *Stag Line Ltd v Foscolo, Mango & Co. Ltd* [1932] AC 328: 'bunkering or other purposes').
52 *S. S. Magnhild v McIntyre Brothers and Co.* [1920] 3 KB 321 at 332.
53 [1908] AC 406, HL.

A rule of construction cannot be more than a guide to enable the court to arrive at the true meaning of the parties. The ejusdem generis rule means that there is implied into the language which the parties have used words of restriction which are not there. It cannot be right to approach a document with the presumption that there should be such an implication. To apply the rule automatically in that way would be to make it the master and not the servant of the purpose for which it was designed – namely, to ascertain the meaning of the parties from the words they have used.[54]

That said, the *eiusdem generis* rule has become something of a 'juristic fetish',[55] giving legal drafters genuine cause for concern. Drafters sometimes attempt to thwart the rule by casting the 'class' as widely as possible, hoping to make the general words embrace more. This is done by drafting lengthy lists, as in the following example taken from a repairing covenant in a lease:

> supplying, providing, purchasing, hiring, maintaining, renewing, replacing, repairing, servicing, overhauling and keeping in good and serviceable order and condition all appurtenances, fixtures, bins, receptacles, tools, appliances, materials, equipment *and other things* which the Landlord may deem desirable or necessary for the maintenance, appearance, upkeep or cleanliness of the Estate or any part of it.

The result is wordy, over-long clauses, impeding comprehension. Indeed, the result is doubly unfortunate, because this kind of defensive drafting may still fail to achieve its purpose: as long as a 'class' is apparent, the *eiusdem generis* rule remains applicable.

Some judges have expressed reservations about the rule, and have applied a modified form of it: prima facie, general words are to be given their general meaning, and are not to be restricted by the *eiusdem generis* rule 'unless you can find that in the particular case the true construction of the instrument requires you to conclude that they are intended to be used in a sense limited to things eiusdem generis with those which have been specifically mentioned before'.[56] But given the wide acceptance of the rule in its traditional form, only a brave drafter would rely on this limited view of its operation to justify giving an expansive meaning to general words that follow a list of specific items belonging to a class.

---

54 [1951] 1 KB 240 at 244.
55 *S. S. Magnhild v McIntyre Brothers and Co.* [1920] 3 KB 321 at 326.
56 *Anderson v Anderson* [1895] 1 QB 749 at 753; endorsed by the Australian High Court in *Attorney-General for New South Wales v Metcalfe* (1904) 1 CLR 421 at 427. See also *Mandalidis v Artline Contractors Pty Ltd* (1999) 47 NSWLR 568 at 585–6, arguing that the *eiusdem generis* rule has limited application in the construction of statutes of a reformatory nature.

Expressio unius

Another rule of construction states that express reference to one matter indicates that others are excluded. It is embodied in the maxim *expressio unius est exclusio alterius* – the expression of one thing is the exclusion of the other. Where parties have included express obligations in a contract, a court is wary about extending those obligations by resort to implication: the presumption is, that having expressed *some*, the parties have expressed *all* of the conditions by which they intend to be bound under the document.[57]

The *expressio unius* rule becomes particularly relevant where a document lists specific matters but omits others that might be thought to be relevant. The rule presumes that the omission was deliberate. This has a certain logic to it. For instance, where a contract lists a number of events entitling a party to set the contract aside, it seems reasonable to assume that the list is intended to be complete and that no other event will entitle the party to set it aside.

Examples of judicial application of the *expressio unius* rule are relatively rare. The clearest instances are cases involving the interpretation of statutes. To illustrate: an Australian statute gave film-makers certain benefits if their name appeared on films. The statute distinguished between film-makers who were corporations and those who were natural persons, and stated that 'in the case of a person other than a body corporate, that name [must be] his true name or a name by which he was commonly known.' It was held that by expressly allowing film-makers other than bodies corporate to use *either* their true name *or* the name by which they were commonly known, the statute allowed bodies corporate to enjoy the benefits only if they used their true name. Burchett J described the case as a 'classic instance' for applying the *expressio unius* rule:

> Parliament has expressly provided that a name other than the true name will do for the one case, provided the person is commonly known by it, while in the same sentence specifying 'the name of a person' for the other case. I can see no escape from the conclusion that a corporation which intends to avail itself of [the section] must use its very name.[58]

Again, a Canadian statute empowered the Director of Investigation and Research to intervene in proceedings before 'any federal board, commission or tribunal'. Did this empower the director to intervene in proceedings before provincial tribunals? The Supreme Court of Canada held that it did not, on the basis of the *expressio unius* rule. Having listed

---

57 *Broome's Legal Maxims*, 10th edn (1939), p. 443.
58 *Film Investment Corporation of New Zealand v Golden Editions Pty Ltd* (1994) 28 IPR 1 at 18.

the bodies before whom the director could intervene, the statute contained a 'clear implication' that intervention before other bodies was not permitted.[59]

In the context of statutory interpretation, the *expressio unius* rule has been described as a valuable servant but a dangerous master.[60] By this is meant that a too-rigorous application of the rule to statutes may be inappropriate where the '*exclusio*' results from the drafter's inadvertence, particularly as the inadvertence is likely to be a product of the pressures under which parliamentary drafters labour.[61] The same may perhaps be said about the rule's application to private legal drafters. However, only the most foolhardy of drafters would rely on judicial lenity to excuse inadvertent omissions.

Legal drafters enjoy enumerating, but long lists can be counterproductive. The *expressio unius* rule creates the danger that things not expressed in the list may be held to be deliberately omitted. By being too particular, the drafter will probably be held to have made the list exhaustive.

Noscitur a sociis

This rule can be expressed as follows: the meaning of a word or phrase can be controlled by the words or phrases associated with it. The Latin tag from which it is drawn can be translated: 'it is known by its neighbours'. Stanley Robinson treats the rule as part of the general principle that documents are to be read as a whole.[62] Most commentators, though, regard the rule as having a life of its own.[63] In reality, this rule – like the others – is simply part of a general store upon which courts draw to give meaning to a document in the face of the parties' differing interpretations.

To illustrate the operation of the rule: an insurance policy taken out by a fruit and vegetable importer was expressed to cover 'physical loss or damage or deterioration' arising out of strikes. A dock strike delayed

---

59 *Director of Investigation and Research v Newfoundland Telephone Company* [1987] 2 SCR 466 at 483–4. The case is discussed by John Mark Keyes, '*Expressio Unius*: The Expression that Proves the Rule' (1989) 10 *Statute Law Review*, p. 1.

60 *Colquhoun v Brooks* (1888) 21 QBD 52 at 65.

61 *Ryland Brothers (Australia) Ltd v Morgan* (1926) 27 SR (NSW) 161 at 168–9; *Bruce v Cole* (1998) 45 NSWLR 163 at 173 (Spigelman CJ), citing a number of Australian High Court warnings. For an example, see *Dean v Wiesengrund* [1955] 2 QB 120 (CA). Also, it may be inappropriate to apply the rule where its operation would restrict the operation of legislation which is clearly designed to reform the existing law, for legislation of that kind ought to be construed in a way that allows its purpose to be achieved: *Mandalidis v Artline Contractors Pty Ltd* (1999) 47 NSWLR 568 at 585–6.

62 *Drafting* (London: Butterworths, 1973), p. 84.

63 See, for example, Dickerson, *Fundamentals of Legal Drafting*, p. 48.

the arrival of the insured's produce at market. During the period of delay, market prices fell, with the result that the produce fetched lower prices than it would have done had the strike not occurred. Was the loss in market price covered by the words 'physical loss or damage or deterioration'? Pearson J held that it was not, applying the *noscitur a sociis* rule. Each of the three listed misfortunes involved physical damage to the produce – physical loss, physical damage, physical deterioration. The words did not extend to mere loss of market value.[64]

Just as the 'genus', or class, must be ascertained before applying the *eiusdem generis* rule, so the 'societas' to which the *socii* belong must be ascertained before applying the *noscitur a sociis* rule.[65] This can be a difficult exercise, on which different minds can reach different conclusions.[66] Nevertheless, the rule is apt to trap unwary drafters.

Contra proferentem

Under the *contra proferentem* rule, if ambiguity in a clause or document cannot be resolved in any other way, the clause or document is construed against the interests of the person who put it forward.[67] To illustrate: if a provision concerning the extent of cover under an insurance policy is ambiguous, one possible construction favouring the insurer and another favouring the insured, a court will adopt the construction favouring the insured.[68] Similarly, an ambiguous provision in a lease imposing obligations on the tenant is construed in favour of the tenant;[69] in a contract for the sale of land, it is construed in favour of the purchaser;[70] in a guarantee, it is construed in favour of the guarantor;[71] in a grant, it is construed in favour of the grantee;[72] and an ambiguous provision

---

64 *Lewis Emanuel & Son Ltd v Hepburn* [1960] 1 Lloyd's Rep 304.
65 *Letang v Cooper* [1965] 1 QB 232 at 247 (Diplock LJ); *Andrews v Strugnell* [1977] Qd R 284 at 286.
66 As in the Australian case of *R v Calabria*, which considered whether a person who dries out Indian hemp is caught by a provision which penalises a person who 'produces, prepares or manufactures' Indian hemp. According to the South Australian Full Supreme Court, on the basis of the *noscitur a sociis* rule, 'no' – see (1982) 31 SASR 423; but according to the Australian High Court on appeal, 'yes' – see (1983) 151 CLR 670.
67 Stated fully, the rule is *verba chartarum fortius accipiuntur contra proferentem*: the words of an instrument are taken most strongly against the party employing them.
68 *Rowlett, Leakey & Co. v Scottish Provident Institution* [1927] 1 Ch 55 at 69 (Warrington LJ); *Ruapehu Alpine Lifts Ltd v State Insurance Ltd* (1998) 10 ANZ Insurance Cases 61–404 at 74,442; *HEST Australia Ltd v McInerney* (1998) 71 SASR 526 at 534–5.
69 As in *John Lee & Son (Grantham) Ltd v Railway Executive* [1949] 2 All ER 581 (CA); *Gruhn v Balgray Investments Ltd* (1963) 107 *Solicitors Journal*, p. 112 (CA).
70 As in *Savill Brothers Ltd v Bethell* [1902] 2 Ch 523 at 537–8.
71 *Eastern Counties Building Society v Russell* [1947] 1 All ER 500 at 503; affirmed [1947] 2 All ER 734 at 736 (CA).
72 *Halsbury's Laws of England* (4th edn), Deeds, para 1472. But it is otherwise if the grantor is the Crown; there, the ambiguity is construed in favour of the Crown: *Viscountess Rhondda's Claim* [1922] 2 AC 339 at 335; *Minister for Natural Resources v Brantag Pty Ltd* (1997) 8 BPR 15,815 at 15,821–2 (NSWCA).

concerning the extent of the borrower's liability under a loan agreement is construed in favour of the borrower.[73]

The *contra proferentem* rule is applied only if the ambiguity cannot be resolved by any other legitimate means.[74] In that sense, it is a rule of last resort. Nevertheless, perhaps more than any of the other principles of interpretation, the rule accounts for the verbosity in many legal documents, particularly leases. It may also be the reason why exemption clauses (in contracts of all kinds) are cast in the widest possible terms.[75] Lawyers try to avoid the application of the principle (whose Latin tag adds an undue aura of learning)[76] by ensuring that the document confers on their client every conceivable variant of right. In this way a rule of last resort becomes a first principle of drafting.

The two golden rules of interpretation and drafting

Two 'rules' of legal interpretation we may term 'golden' rules. In contrast to the rules considered so far, which may encourage a drafting style that is defensive, prolix and over-cautious, these two rules (if properly understood) should promote a style that is clear, direct and concise.

Golden rule 1: The 'ordinary sense' of words

Words are to be given their ordinary sense. The meaning of an ordinary English word is not a question of law but of fact, to be found by taking all the circumstances of the case into consideration.[77] Lord Macmillan explained this so-called 'golden rule' of interpretation:

> The grammatical and ordinary sense of the words is to be adhered to unless that would lead to some absurdity or some repugnance or inconsistency with the rest of the instrument, in which case the grammatical and ordinary sense of the words may be modified so as to avoid that absurdity and inconsistency, but no further.[78]

---

73 As in *Budget Stationery Supplies Pty Ltd v National Australia Bank Ltd* (1996) 7 BPR 14,891.

74 *St Edmundsbury and Ipswich Diocesan Board of Finance v Clark (No. 2)* [1975] 1 WLR 468 at 477 (extent of use permitted under reservation of right of way); *Darlington Futures Ltd v Delco Australia Pty Ltd* (1986) 161 CLR 500 at 510 (limitation of liability clause in commercial contract).

75 Robinson, *Drafting*, p. 84 (fn). See the extended discussion in *Odgers' Construction of Deeds and Statutes*, pp. 98–105.

76 See *Ballard v North British Railway Co.* (1923) SC (HL) 43 at 46 (Lord Shaw of Dunfermline): 'If that phrase [*contra proferentem*] had not been in Latin, nobody would have called it a principle'.

77 *Cozens v Brutus* [1973] AC 854 at 861 (Lord Reid).

78 *Law and Language* (Birmingham: Holdsworth Club, University of Birmingham, 1931), p. 18.

This principle also embraces technical words: they are to be given their technical meaning, with the same qualification about absurdity, repugnance or uncertainty.

Golden rule 2: Consistent terminology

This rule may be stated: 'Never change your language unless you wish to change your meaning, and always change your language if you wish to change your meaning.'[79] It could also be expressed along these lines: 'Different words are taken to refer to different things, and same words to same things.' Like all rules of interpretation, it is only applied if the circumstances warrant.[80]

A striking illustration of the difficulties that can arise from a change in terminology is *Dickerson v St Aubyn*.[81] A landlord granted a lease of a flat for a term of seven years, with a right for the tenant to bring the lease to an end after five years. The tenant covenanted 'To paint in the last quarter of the *said term* with [a specified number of coats of paint]'. The tenant also covenanted to yield up the flat in repair 'at the end or sooner determination of *the tenancy*' and to allow inspection by prospective tenants 'during the last month of *the tenancy*'. The landlord covenanted to repair the outside walls and roofs and pipes 'at all times during the *said term*'. Was the tenant obliged to paint if the tenant brought the lease to an end after five years? The Court of Appeal had no trouble in finding that the answer was 'no'. By its language, the lease drew a distinction between 'the term' and 'the tenancy'. In the context of the lease, 'the term' meant the original period of seven years for which the lease was granted. Du Parcq LJ explained:

> Now, the period of time which has been referred to is seven years, and 'the last quarter of the said term' therefore means the last quarter of the seven years, and the tenant, if he has read this lease, knows that when he gets to that quarter he must paint, and having read that, he sees that, if he gives notice to terminate after five years he will never get to that quarter at all, and the obligation to paint will no more arise than the obligation to go on cleaning windows every two months after he has determined the lease. Counsel for the [landlord] rather suggested that this construction was based on a narrow view, and rather complained that it all turned on one word. It very often happens that very important decisions turn on one word, and it is as well that draftsmen should remember that.[82]

79 Piesse, *Elements of Drafting*, p. 18.
80 See *Watson v Haggitt* [1928] AC 127, PC.
81 [1944] 1 All ER 370, CA.
82 [1944] 1 All ER 370 at 371.

Commercial or purposive interpretation

If the internal rules fail to resolve difficulties in meaning, courts now invoke external factors, viewing the document from the outside. In particular, a court will interpret the document with reference to its commercial purpose and the factual background from which it springs.[83] In taking this approach, the court endeavours to give effect to the whole of the document, but rejects repugnant words if necessary.[84] This is sometimes called the 'purposive' construction, but it is better termed the 'commercial' interpretation.[85] Its classic exposition is found in *The Antaios*, where Lord Diplock said that if detailed and syntactical analysis of words in a commercial contract lead to a conclusion that flouts 'business commonsense', then the analysis must be made to yield to business commonsense.[86] Or, as Hoffmann J said in *MFI Properties Ltd v BICC Group Pension Trust Ltd*: 'if the language is capable of more than one meaning, I think the court is entitled to select the meaning which accords with the apparent commercial purpose of the clause rather than one which appears commercially irrational.'[87]

Of course, if taken to extremes, an analysis based on 'business commonsense' can be as nebulous as one based on concepts such as 'reasonableness'. To that extent, the 'commercial' interpretation can give rise to disputes, especially where a party to the document deliberately seeks to extricate itself from contractual obligations. But such a party rarely invokes the 'commercial purpose' principle as a means of attack. More often the principle is invoked by way of defence against a party who alleges that the document should be interpreted literally.

To those who would urge against the purposive or commercial approach to interpreting documents, two answers can be given. First, the approach is now entrenched.[88] Judges are unlikely to return to a literal approach. This reflects a movement in the law generally, away from conformity to a strict code and towards judgment on the merits.

---

83 See *Reardon Smith Line Ltd v Yngvar Hansen-Taugen* [1976] 1 WLR 989, HL; *Hyundai Shipbuilding and Heavy Industries Co. Ltd v Pournaras* [1978] 2 Lloyd's Rep 502, CA.

84 See *Forbes v Git* [1922] 1 AC 256, PC; *Cooke v Anderson* [1945] 1 WWR 657; *Adamastos Shipping Co. Ltd v Anglo-Saxon Petroleum Co. Ltd* [1959] AC 133, HL.

85 See *Mannai Investment Co. Ltd v Eagle Star Life Assurance Co. Ltd* [1997] AC 749 at 770 (Lord Steyn).

86 [1985] AC 191 at 201, HL.

87 [1986] 1 All ER 974 at 976. See also *Datastream International Ltd v Oakeep Ltd* [1986] 1 WLR 404 (Warner J); *Pearl Assurance PLC v Shaw* [1985] 1 EGLR 92 (Vinelott J); *British Gas Corporation v Universities Superannuation Scheme Ltd* [1986] 1 WLR 398 (Browne-Wilkinson V-C); *Basingstoke and Deane Borough Council v Host Group Ltd* [1988] 1 All ER 824, CA (Nicholls LJ).

88 See, for example, *Spiro v Glencrown Properties Ltd* [1991] Ch 537 (Hoffmann J); *Mannai Investment Co. Ltd v Eagle Star Life Assurance Co. Ltd* [1997] AC 749, HL.

The movement is particularly evident in the 'notice' cases that have followed the decision in *Mannai*, where technical deficiencies in the form of some notices are ignored if, in the context of the transaction, a reasonable person in the recipient's position could not have been in doubt about the purpose and meaning of the notice.[89]

Second, the parties can always forestall argument about the underlying purpose of a document by stating the purpose expressly in the document – in a preliminary clause, or in a declaration at the end, or elsewhere. Indeed, there is much to commend an express purpose statement in every clause or document of any complexity. For example, a statement in a rent review clause that its purpose is to provide an upwards-only rent review every three years may help clarify an inevitably complicated provision, catering as it must for matters such as interest, payment of arrears, and arbitration.

Some might also urge that the commercial or purposive approach prolongs litigation, by allowing the parties to garner extrinsic evidence that otherwise might be inadmissible. But judges can be relied on to ensure that trials are not unduly prolonged, and that extrinsic evidence is admitted only where strictly relevant (but see p. 54).

Importance of context

Thinking lawyers are prone to an obsession with ambiguity. However, while all ambiguities in legal documents are unfortunate, some are worse than others. Some can be clarified by a moment's reflection, and others by applying one or more of the principles discussed earlier in this chapter. In many cases, too, ambiguity is resolved by reference to the context in which the ambiguous word or phrase appears.[90]

To illustrate the importance of context, consider a gift by will in these terms:

I give to Albert all my black and white horses.

What does the testator mean by the words 'black and white horses'? Does he mean all his horses that are wholly black and all his horses that are

---

89 *Mannai Investment Co. Ltd v Eagle Star Life Assurance Co. Ltd* [1997] AC 749; *York v Casey* (Eng CA, unreported, 16 February 1998); *Ketchum International Plc v Group Public Relations Holdings Pty Ltd* (Eng CA, unreported, 17 October 1997); *Atari Corporation (UK) Ltd v Electronic Boutique Stores (UK) Ltd* [1998] QB 539; *Central Pacific (Campus) Pty Ltd v Staged Developments Australia Pty Ltd* (1998) V ConvR 54–575 (Vic CA); *Bava Holdings Pty Ltd v Pando Holdings Pty Ltd* (1998) NSW ConvR 55–862.

90 For an early example, see the Statute 25 Ed 3, which prohibited ecclesiastics from purchasing 'provisions' in Rome. The context indicated that by 'provisions' was meant not food but papal nominations to benefices.

wholly white? Or does he mean all his horses that are both black and white (piebald)? Reference to the context may help solve the uncertainty. If, at the date of his death,[91] the testator owned only piebalds, the potentially ambiguous words are clear: no wholly black horses or wholly white horses could have been included in the gift. Even if, at the date of his death, the testator owned white horses, black horses, and piebalds, Albert must surely be entitled to either all the wholly black horses and all the wholly white ones, or all the piebalds. In this latter situation, context would not resolve the ambiguity; but litigation over the ambiguity is not inevitable, for Albert and the other beneficiaries under the will might be able to agree on a division – particularly as the words, read in isolation, do not appear to give Albert all the testator's horses.

Consider another example, this time from a lease:

> The lessee may graze not more than twenty cows or sheep on the land.

This wording may be impossible to clarify merely by looking at the document. Is twenty the maximum number of animals? How many sheep are permitted? Can sheep and cows be mixed? However, reference to the circumstances known to the landlord and tenant at the date of the lease (for example, that the tenant then owned a total of twenty cows and sheep, or that the carrying capacity of the land was twenty cows or sheep) may clarify the uncertainty. Of course, in this example (as in the previous one) the fault may lie in vague instructions from the client – although a careful drafter would resolve the ambiguity before perpetuating it.

As linguists are at pains to emphasise, almost any word, phrase or sentence taken out of context can have two or more meanings.[92] Context often gives meaning to words and phrases that are capable of being read in more than one way; examples are 'juvenile magistrate', 'criminal solicitor', 'serious fraud office'. In reality, ambiguities like these generally pass unnoticed, because the reader unconsciously interprets the phrase within its context.

In summary, context and purpose are all-important when interpreting legal documents.[93] The commercial approach to interpretation leans heavily on both.[94]

---

91 A will generally 'speaks' from the testator's death, not the date on which the will was signed.
92 See, for example, Max Black, *The Labyrinth of Language* (London: Penguin Books, 1968), p. 167; John Lyons, *Semantics*, vol. ii (Cambridge, Cambridge University Press, 1977), p. 397; Geoffrey Leech, *Semantics* (London: Penguin Books, 1974), p. 77; G. P. Baker and P. M. S. Hacker, *Language, Sense and Nonsense* (Oxford: Basil Blackwell 1984), p. 310; John Lyons, *Language, Meaning and Context* (London: Fontana, 1981), pp. 14, 28.
93 See, for example, *Okolo v Secretary of State for the Environment* [1997] 2 All ER 911 at 914 (Sedley J); *Scottish Power plc v Britoil (Exploration) Ltd, The Times*, 2 December 1997, CA.
94 See *Mannai Investment Co. Ltd v Eagle Star Life Assurance Co. Ltd* [1997] AC 749 at 767 (Lord Steyn).

Modern restatement

The House of Lords has recently restated the principles governing the interpretation of contractual documents, in *Investors Compensation Scheme Ltd v West Bromwich Building Society*.[95] The case turned on a phrase in a claim form: 'Any claim (whether sounding in rescission for undue influence or otherwise) that you have ...'. This drafting the House of Lords thought slovenly. The facts are noteworthy because the convoluted claim form was supplemented by a short explanatory note, itself a model of clarity.[96] Had the note been used alone, the litigation might well have been avoided.

In giving his judgment, Lord Hoffmann referred to the 'fundamental change' that had overtaken the construction of contracts. Generally, contractual documents were to be construed in accordance with 'common sense principles by which any serious utterance would be interpreted in ordinary life'. Almost all the old 'intellectual baggage' of legal interpretation had been discarded. He summarised the modern principles of interpretation:

(1) Interpretation is the ascertainment of the meaning which the document would convey to a reasonable person having all the background knowledge which would reasonably have been available to the parties in the situation in which they were at the time of the contract.

(2) The background was famously referred to by Lord Wilberforce as the 'matrix of fact', but this phrase is, if anything, an understated description of what the background may include. Subject to the requirement that it should have been reasonably available to the parties and to the exception to be mentioned next, it includes absolutely anything which would have affected the way in which the language of the document would have been understood by a reasonable man.

(3) The law excludes from the admissible background the previous negotiations of the parties and their declarations of subjective intent. They are admissible only in an action for rectification. The law makes this distinction for reasons of practical policy and, in this respect only, legal interpretation differs from the way we would interpret utterances in ordinary life. The boundaries of this exception are in some respects unclear.

(4) The meaning which a document (or any other utterance) would convey to a reasonable man is not the same thing as the meaning of its words. The meaning of words is a matter of dictionaries and grammars; the meaning of the document is what the parties using those words against the relevant background would reasonably have been understood to mean.

---

95 [1998] 1 WLR 896 at 912. Applied in *Barclays Bank Plc v Weeks Legg & Dean* [1999] QB 309 at 331 (Pill LJ); *Acorn Consolidated Pty Ltd v Hawkslade Investments Pty Ltd* (1999) 21 WAR 425 at 434–6 (Owen J); and explained in *Bromarin AB v IMD Investments Ltd* [1999] STC 301 at 310 (Chadwick LJ).

96 [1998] 1 WLR 896 at 910 (Lord Hoffmann).

The background may not merely enable the reasonable man to choose between the possible meanings of words which are ambiguous but even (as occasionally happens in ordinary life) to conclude that the parties must, for whatever reason, have used the wrong words or syntax.

(5) The 'rule' that words should be given their 'natural and ordinary meaning' reflects the commonsense proposition that we do not easily accept that people have made linguistic mistakes, particularly in formal documents. On the other hand, if one would nevertheless conclude from the background that something must have gone wrong with the language, the law does not require judges to attribute to the parties an intention which they plainly could not have had.

Lord Hoffmann's second principle has been criticised on the basis that to include 'absolutely anything' as part of the admissible background is likely to increase both uncertainty and the costs of litigation.[97] In *Scottish Power plc v Britoil (Exploration) Ltd* Staughton LJ made a plea for restricting background material to what the parties had in mind and what was going on around them at the time they were making the contract.[98] But even with that caution in mind, the five principles can be applied to the interpretation of all private legal documents. We illustrate with three examples drawn from the areas of wills, patent applications, and standard forms.

Wills

Lord Hoffmann's principles reflect the so-called 'armchair principle', which has long been applied in interpreting wills.[99] This principle allows the admission of extrinsic evidence to explain the meaning of words and expressions in a will.[100] The court may receive 'evidence of the testator's habits of speech and of her or his family, property, friends and acquaintances in order that the court may read the will from the position of the person making it (as if sitting in the testator's armchair)'.[101] For example, in a South Australian case a testator devised property 'To Miss Doris Walters 121 William Street Norwood (Meals on Wheels)'. In fact, no Doris Walters lived at this address. The testator had, however, known a Miss Doris Taylor, who had lived at that address and had been associated with Meals on Wheels. Viewing the will from the testator's

---

97 Simon Price, 'Commercial Contract Interpretation through the Looking Glass' (1998) 142 *Solicitors Journal*, p. 176.

98 *The Times*, 2 December 1997.

99 See *Boyes v Cook* (1880) 14 Ch D 53 at 56 (James LJ).

100 F. V. Hawkins and E. C. Ryder, *The Construction of Wills*, 3rd edn (London: Sweet & Maxwell, 1965), pp. 12–21.

101 I. J. Hardingham, M. A. Neave and H. A. J. Ford, *Wills and Intestacy in Australia and New Zealand*, 2nd edn (Sydney: Law Book Co., 1989), pp. 284–5.

metaphorical armchair, the court held that the testator must have intended to benefit Miss Taylor, and construed the will accordingly.[102] Again, in an English case a will contained a gift to 'my son Forster Charter'. The testator had two sons, William Forster Charter and Charles Charter; he had no son Forster Charter. Even so, the court admitted evidence that the testator habitually called Charles by the name of Forster, and so the gift went to Charles.[103] There are many other cases to similar effect.[104]

In some jurisdictions, the 'armchair principle' has now yielded to statute. An example is s 21 of the *Administration of Justice Act* 1982 (England and Wales), under which extrinsic evidence (including evidence of the testator's intention) is admissible to construe parts of a will that are meaningless or ambiguous.[105]

Patent applications

Patent applications must be precise, in order to mark the exact confines of the invention. This encourages pedantry, jargon and repetition, in the hope of avoiding ambiguity.[106] Lord Hoffmann's five principles are particularly relevant in this highly specialised area.

Patents are sometimes attacked for alleged 'insufficiency'. This involves investigating whether the description of the patent is sufficient to enable those to whom the specification is addressed to understand how the subject-matter of the patent is to be made or worked.[107] The specification must speak for itself, but must be interpreted against the background of the invention and what the inventor was trying to achieve. For example, in *Henriksen v Tallon Ltd*, Henriksen's patent claim read:

> A fountain pen of the ball tip type, comprising a tubular ink reservoir provided at one end with a ball tip and at the opposite end with an air inlet, in which there is disposed between the column of ink in the reservoir and the air inlet a liquid or viscous or paste-like mass which does not mix with the ink and forms a plug which moves with the surface of the ink column and *prevents* air from contacting the surface of the ink [emphasis added].[108]

The Henriksen invention was a particular kind of ballpoint pen, in which a moveable plug kept the air from the ink in the tube. Tallon made a similar pen with a similar plug, but argued that they did not infringe

102 *Re Alleyn* [1965] SASR 22.
103 *Charter v Charter* (1874) LR 7 HL 364.
104 Some are cited by Lord Hoffmann in *Mannai Investment Co. Ltd v Eagle Star Life Assurance Co. Ltd* [1997] AC 749 at 776–8.
105 For an Australian counterpart, see s 36 of the *Wills Act* 1997 (Victoria).
106 See *Leonard's Application* [1966] Fleet Street Patent Law Reports 132 at 133 (Lloyd-Jacob J).
107 See *No-fume Ltd v Frank Pitchford & Co. Ltd* (1934) 52 RPC 28 at 34 (Luxmoore J).
108 [1965] RPC 434.

Henriksen's patent because their plug reduced the amount of air getting into the ink to 40 per cent, and so did not prevent air from contacting the surface of the ink. The House of Lords interpreted 'prevents' as meaning 'prevents for all practical purposes'. Because the Tallon pen was saleable and would last for a number of years, the court held that the claim was infringed; as a result, the Tallon pen was scotched. Lord Reid pointed out that even the most careful drafter sometimes uses phrases capable of more than one construction, and that it would be applying the wrong standard to hold that the claim was ambiguous merely because it was difficult to construe.[109]

This case is a clear example of the rule applied in patent cases, that a court will make allowances for the language used, in an endeavour to ascertain what the drafter must have intended. All of Lord Hoffmann's principles operated in the case. The court interpreted the claim by finding the meaning which the claim would reasonably convey against the actual background of technical knowledge. What Henriksen might really have intended (subjectively) was irrelevant; but the judges did not attribute to Henriksen any impossible intention, and wrong or incomplete words and syntax were not fatal.

Standard forms

Where parties embody their contract in a tried and tested standard form, the courts presume that the parties have chosen to govern their relationship on the basis of the law and practice which has evolved in the use of that form.[110] That law and practice – and particularly any judicial decisions on the meaning of words or phrases in the form – are part of the background material which the courts consider when interpreting the meaning of the contract.

To illustrate, in *The Annefield* the English Court of Appeal was asked to interpret a standard form charterparty. The form had been the subject of judicial interpretation in 1936, where the court paid regard to a practice which had existed since 1914. The Court of Appeal therefore adopted the same interpretation given in the 1936 case. Lord Denning MR said:

> Once a court has put a construction on commercial documents in a standard form, commercial men act upon it. It should be followed in all subsequent

---

109 [1965] RPC 434 at 443.
110 See, for example, *Dunlop & Sons v Balfour Williams & Co.* [1892] 1 QB 507 at 518, CA (Lord Esher MR); *The Nema* [1982] AC 724 at 737, HA (Lord Diplock); *Legal & General Insurance Australia Ltd v Eather* (1986) 6 NSWLR 390 at 394 (Kirby P).

cases. If the business community is not satisfied with the decision, they should alter the form.[111]

This approach is consistent with Lord Hoffmann's principles. The parties are presumed to know how the courts have interpreted earlier versions of the form and to intend their contract to be interpreted in that light. All this is part of the 'matrix of fact' against which the document has been drafted.

Dangers in using precedent as an aid to interpretation

Given the importance of purpose and context in construing documents, there are dangers in relying too much on precedent as an aid to interpretation. Sir George Jessel MR pointed to these dangers in *Aspden v Seddon*.[112] The duty of a judge, he said, is to ascertain the meaning of the particular document before the court, and reference to past decisions 'merely for the purpose of ascertaining the construction of a document' is to risk 'confusion and error'. A decision on construction in one case is a guide, but no more than a guide, to construction in a later case. An inflexible, step-by-step, precedent-based process can lead to absurdity:

> There is, first, document A, and a Judge formed an opinion as to its construction. Then came document B, and some other Judge has said that it differs very little from document A – not sufficiently to alter the construction – therefore he construes it in the same way. Then comes document C, and the Judge there compares it with document B, and says it differs very little, and therefore he shall construe it in the same way. And so the construction has gone on until we find a document which is in totally different terms from the first, and which no human being would think of construing in the same manner, but which has by this process come to be construed in the same manner.[113]

Courts do not regard themselves as controlled by the meaning given to words in earlier cases. This is because no two cases are ever exactly the same. Judicial examination of a word's meaning in an earlier case is useful only to the extent that it provides an analogy to prompt the approach to be taken in a later case.[114]

---

111 [1971] P 168.
112 (1874) 10 Ch App 394 at 397.
113 Ibid. at 398.
114 *Galcif Pty Ltd v Dudley's Corner Pty Ltd* (1995) 6 BPR 14,134 at 14,137 (Kirby P).

3 The Move towards Modern English in Legal Drafting

The modern style of legal drafting owes much to the plain English movement in law. This chapter considers the history of that movement in several countries, concentrating on the period from the 1960s to the present.

We begin with a reminder that calls to simplify legal language are hardly new. Some early examples were mentioned in Chapter 1. A number of leading nineteenth century reformers were scathing in their attacks on lawyers' language. One was Jeremy Bentham, who was particularly vitriolic in attacking the argument that 'precision' or 'certainty' demanded a repetitious style:

> For this redundancy – for the accumulation of excrementitious matter in all its various shapes, in all its various forms ... for all the pestilential effects that cannot but be produced by this so enormous load of literary garbage, the plea commonly pleaded [is] ... that it is necessary to *precision* – or to use the word which on similar occasions they themselves are in the habit of using, *certainty*.[1]

Later in the nineteenth century, the English barrister George Coode published his influential book, *On Legislative Expression*. In it, he rejected the convoluted style of traditional legal drafting: 'Nothing more is required than that instead of an accidental and incongruous style, the common popular structure of plain English be resorted to.'[2]

Many of Bentham's and Coode's suggestions were adopted by Lord Macaulay in his *Indian Penal Code*,[3] described by a modern legislative

---

1 *Nomography or the Art of Inditing Laws*, published in *Works* (Edinburgh: William Tait, 1838–43), vol. 3, p. 208. Bentham's views are surveyed in *Access to the Law: The Structure and Format of Legislation* (Melbourne: Law Reform Commission of Victoria, 1990), Appendix 4.
2 Reprinted in E. Driedger, *The Composition of Legislation* (Ottawa: Department of Justice, 1976), p. 376.
3 Macaulay's influence on statutory drafting is traced by Mark Duckworth, 'The Body of the Laws as a Popular Book', unpublished conference paper, delivered at Law and History Conference, Canberra, July 1995.

drafter as 'to this day a shining example of legal wisdom and clarity'.[4] In his introduction to the code, Macaulay wrote:

> There are two things which a legislator should always have in view while he is framing laws; the one that they should be, as far as possible, precise: the other that they should be easily understood. ... That a law, and especially a penal law, should be drawn in words which convey no meaning to the people who are to obey it is an evil.[5]

Yet the work of these and other reformers failed to have any lasting effect. Most legal drafting of the nineteenth and twentieth centuries was couched in the traditional style. As Arthur Symonds – not so well known as Bentham or Coode, but an experienced legislative drafter with perceptive views on legal writing – lamented of legislation:

> our legislators often dream wisely, and talk after the fashion of their dreams; but from ignorance and want of skill in the workmanship of details, which they leave to the routine performance of mere artisans, they seldom succeed in giving to the people a law intelligible either to themselves or the persons for whose especial guidance the law was designed. The beauty of a piece of mechanism is shewn in the completeness of all its parts, and their combined action towards one grand general result. There is nothing excessive – nothing wanting. Each part has its special use, and is indispensable. Apply these principles to English laws, what are they? The clumsiest pieces of workmanship which the unskilled labour of man ever made.[6]

Calls for reform resurfaced from time to time during the first half of the twentieth century, but went largely unheeded. Then in the 1960s and 1970s, the demands of the consumer movement gave new urgency to the campaign for change.

The United Kingdom

In the United Kingdom, the modern plain English movement in law can be traced to a number of specific developments. First, for the practising lawyer, came two books of precedents by Anthony Parker. Unlike previous precedent books, which perpetuated a style frozen in time, these books were radically modern in approach. Then, about twenty years after the first Parker book, two organisations came to focus on the obstacles to understanding inherent in traditional styles of legal drafting. They

---

4 Sir William Dale, 'A London Particular' [1985] *Statute Law Review*, pp. 13–14.
5 *Works of Lord Macaulay*, ed. Lady Trevelyan; London (Longmans, Green & Co., 1879), vol. 7, p. 423.
6 Arthur Symonds, *The Mechanics of Law-Making* (London: Edward Churton, 1835), p. iv.

were the Plain English Campaign and the National Consumer Council, both originally formed to help the general public in their dealings with officialdom and commerce. About the same time, a newly formed organisation of lawyers, aptly named Clarity, added its voice to the growing demands for change in traditional styles of legal drafting. These organisations were later joined by another, the Plain Language Commission. Since then, the United Kingdom government has played a role in helping eradicate legalese from government departments and official forms, and in sponsoring moves towards plainer language in legislation.

The Parker books

In 1964 Butterworths published a slim volume of conveyancing precedents edited by solicitor Anthony Parker: *Modern Conveyancing Precedents.* It was unlike any precedent book which had gone before. It used ordinary English, shunned tautology, and avoided excessive caution ('the said City of London'). Parker was a vivid writer, with an apt turn of phrase. He wrote in the preface:

> Many lawyers today feel that draftsmen of traditional conveyancing documents use English as a bludgeon, and that they attempt by casting about repeated blows to beat the subject into submission; these lawyers would like to use a less primitive weapon, yet they have no precedents to help them. It is hoped that this book, which uses modern language, may assist. Others may resent the break with tradition, and to them I would say that the change is not due to any lack of respect for legal history; engineers may admire Stephenson's 'Rocket' as a lesson in the foundations of mechanics, but they would not put into service a replica.

Parker explained the main aims of his forms in this way:

1. To produce the full legal effect intended.
2. To make documents more comprehensible to clients, and thus to assist in relations between solicitors and the public.
3. To avoid the abuse of the English language found in traditional precedents.
4. To avoid the confusion of thought and expression found in some traditional precedents.
5. To make documents shorter, and so save time and money for the legal profession.[7]

He achieved those aims. An illustration was his standard adaptable mortgage. The clauses were expressed in clear, concise English, discarding many unnecessary legal complexities. Gone was the legal date for

---

7 Anthony Parker, *Modern Conveyancing Precedents* (London: Butterworths, 1964), p. 4.

redemption under which the borrower promised to repay the whole loan on a fixed day six months after the date of the mortgage: that was pure fiction, a device merely to bring the lender's remedies into potential use, neither party expecting or wanting the money to be repaid so soon. Gone too was the fiction that for some purposes the parties were in a landlord–tenant relationship. Parker's precedent gave the lie to Lord Macnaghten's aphorism that 'no-one by the light of nature ever understood an English mortgage of real estate'.[8]

Four years after the conveyancing precedents, *Parker's Modern Wills Precedents* appeared.[9] Its expressed aims were similar to those of the earlier work. In the preface, Parker urged the use of 'minor' rather than 'infant'; the rejection of 'enjoy' in the sense 'to have the advantage of' (as in, 'to enjoy the drains and sewers'); and the adoption of the straightforward 'give' instead of 'give, devise and bequeath'. With the benefit of hindsight, these exhortations seem tame; when they were published, however, they heralded significant changes in drafting styles.

The Parker books were ahead of their time. Parker asserted (in his Editor's Notes to *Modern Conveyancing Precedents*) that he was steering a middle course. But the legal profession thought his precedents too radical. They did not catch on, and most non-registered conveyancing documents and wills seen today are still in the traditional form.

Plain English Campaign

In 1976 Martin Cutts and Chrissie Maher helped to establish an advice centre in Salford, Greater Manchester, England. This was the Salford Form Market, where for three years they worked to simplify supplementary benefit forms and leaflets. In 1979 Cutts and Maher took the bold decision to launch a broader, national initiative: the Plain English Campaign.[10] Since then, the Plain English Campaign has expanded enormously. It attracts considerable media attention, especially with its annual plain English awards, which ridicule the worst examples of traditional legal writing.

---

8 *Samuel v Jarrah Corporation Ltd* [1904] AC 323 at 326, HL. Compare the lament of an Australian judge (Fox J) on the fate of a person signing a traditionally-worded mortgage: 'It is surely a sad commentary on the operation of our legal system that a borrower should be expected to execute a document which only a person of extraordinary application and persistence would read, [and] which, if read, is virtually incomprehensible and which, in any event, has a legal effect not disclosed by its language.': *Richards v The Commercial Bank of Australia* (1971) 18 FLR 95 at 99–100.

9 An Australian edition also appeared: F. C. Hutley, *Australian Wills Precedents* (Sydney: Butterworths, 1970).

10 Martin Cutts and Chrissie Maher, *The Plain English Story* (Stockport: Plain English Campaign, 1986). The Plain English Campaign's website is at <www.plainenglish.co.uk>.

Though neither Cutts nor Maher were lawyers, they were not afraid to tackle traditional legal writing head-on. They redrafted a large range of legal documents, private and public. Insurance policies in particular proved amenable to the Campaign's crusade for rewriting in plain style.

The Campaign's organisers were not content merely to replace legal jargon with everyday words. To them (as indeed for all proponents of clear writing), plain English involved considering not only language but also content and layout.[11] These three elements are well illustrated in one of the Campaign's early publications, *Writing Plain English*.[12] Among other things, the booklet recommended that writers of official prose should:

- decide what is the essential information, and stick to it
- choose words learnt early in life
- select a clear, legible typeface
- construct sentences simply, with one or two clauses in a sentence
- create a total effect which is pleasing.

In the sphere of legal writing, the Plain English Campaign has helped to clarify texts such as regulations, articles of association, consumer contracts, police procedures and shareholder information. A notable success was its work on the British Aerospace aircraft lease, which the Campaign rewrote in conjunction with Clifford Chance and Allen & Overy – two of the world's leading law firms. They reduced the lease to one-third of its original length. One of the first transactions to use the new lease involved six Airbus A320 aircraft, a deal worth US$180 million. The lease helped reduce the time taken for the transaction from the normal six months to six and a half weeks.

In recent years, the Campaign has expanded internationally, opening a branch in the United States. It has also conducted workshops in countries where training in plain English drafting is not otherwise readily available.[13]

Arguably, the Campaign's most lasting achievement has been to change the attitude of everyday consumers. As a result of the Campaign's pioneering work, consumers who find themselves unable to understand a document are now confident to ask: 'What does this mean, in plain

---

11 See, for example, Robert Eagleson, *Plain English in Official Writing* (Canberra: Department of Sport, Recreation and Tourism, 1985), p. 4.

12 Martin Cutts and Chrissie Maher, *Writing Plain English* (Stockport: Plain English Campaign, 1984).

13 These countries include South Africa. The Campaign's projects in that country included preparing and testing a plain language version of the *Human Rights Commission Act* 1995 (SA). For the results of the Commission's work, see Philip Knight, *Clearly Better Drafting – A Report to the Plain English Campaign* (1996).

English?' A generation ago they would have been more timid, ascribing the document's incomprehensibility not to poor drafting but to their own lack of ability.

Plain Language Commission

Martin Cutts left the Plain English Campaign in 1989 and formed the Plain Language Commission in 1994.[14] The Commission is best-known for its accreditation mark, the Clear English Standard. This appears on some 4000 documents, each vetted for clarity of language and presentation. The Commission emphasises its involvement not only in writing, but also in editing, training and typography. It provides training in legal drafting for some of the leading law firms in England and Wales. And like the Plain English Campaign, the Commission runs a regular competition to reward the best and worst examples of official prose, the latter with the Golden Rhubarb Trophy.

In 1993, Martin Cutts responded to a challenge from the first parliamentary counsel in the United Kingdom to redraft a statute in plain English without significant loss of meaning. The result was a discussion paper, *Unspeakable Acts?*, in which Cutts rewrote the *Timeshare Act* 1992.[15] The parliamentary drafter responsible for the original Bill mounted a robust defence,[16] and Cutts revised his redraft. When the two texts are compared – as they are comprehensively in Cutts's later paper, *Lucid Law*[17] – there can be little doubt that the Cutts version is far easier to understand and apply, demonstrating the truth of Driedger's assertion that mysterious incantations and special rules of grammar and composition are as unnecessary in statutes as they are in private legal documents.[18]

In a follow-up to *Lucid Law*, the Plain Language Commission redrafted portions of the United Kingdom tax law, working with a team of tax and accountancy experts. Both projects were highly influential in persuading the United Kingdom government to rewrite its tax law, a project discussed below.

---

14 The Commission's website is at <www.plainlanguage.demon.co.uk>.
15 Martin Cutts, *Unspeakable Acts?* (Stockport: Words at Work, 1993).
16 Euan Sutherland, 'Clearer Drafting and the Timeshare Act 1992: A Response from Parliamentary Counsel to Mr Cutts' (1993) 14 *Statute Law Review*, p. 3.
17 Martin Cutts, *Lucid Law* (Stockport: Plain Language Commission, 1994); compare Bennion, 'Don't Put the Law into Public Hands' (subtitled: 'Leave legal wording alone, says Francis Bennion'), *The Times*, 24 January 1995, trenchantly criticising the Cutts version. Cutts has also written *The Plain English Guide* (Oxford: Oxford University Press, 1995).
18 See Elmer Driedger, *A Manual of Instructions for Legislative and Legal Writing* (Ottawa: Minister of Supply and Services Canada, 1982), vol. 1, p. 2.

National Consumer Council

In 1975 the United Kingdom government established the National Consumer Council to identify and represent the interests of consumers. The Council is a non-statutory body, financed by the government but otherwise independent of it, with fourteen members nominated by the president of the Board of Trade.

The National Consumer Council has worked with the Plain English Campaign to promote plain English. The year 1980 saw the publication of *Gobbledegook*, a critical review of official forms and leaflets by broadcaster Tom Vernon on behalf of the Council. *Small Print* (1983), with its emphasis on layout as well as content and language, took the form of a report to the Council by the Plain English Campaign. *Plain Words for Consumers: The Case for a Plain Language Law* followed in 1984.

Also in 1984, the Council published its booklet *Plain English for Lawyers*. The first section included the following passage:

> Sadly, lawyers have an almost universal reputation for mystifying their work. Their prose baffles their clients and alienates the public. They go on using a particular phrase, sentence, paragraph or entire agreement because it is familiar. It offers an effortless solution. And as Lord Denning said, when presenting the 1982 Plain English Awards, 'Lawyers try to cover every contingency, but in so doing they get lost in obscurity'. The wordy, repetitive phrases of legal documents in 1984 still conjure up a musty Dickensian image and make them unintelligible to most non-lawyers – the very people who are the ultimate users of many of these documents. Consumer contracts, in particular, are incomprehensible to the consumers who sign them.
>
> But legal writing does not have to be like this. Enlightened lawyers have recognised that good professional writing does not read as though it has been written by a lawyer. There is nothing clever about sounding clever. The result is usually pompous and obscure.

The booklet included a number of guidelines:

* use a logical order
* use familiar forms of address
* leave out surplus words
* use familiar, concrete words
* use short sentences
* use verbs to describe activities and processes; keep verbs in the active voice
* use punctuation sensibly
* arrange your words with care
* avoid language quirks.[19]

Like many plain language publications, the booklet emphasised the importance of writing from the viewpoint of the reader. It concluded that

---

19 National Consumer Council, *Plain English for Lawyers* (London, 1984), p. 9.

its 'guidelines' were not inflexible rules, to be followed slavishly. But there was one golden rule: 'to write with the interests and abilities of your reader constantly in mind'.[20] This, of course, prompts the question: who is the reader? The Council's assumption, unexpressed, was that the reader of a legal document is the user of the document. This is where plain language drafters depart from drafters who use the more traditional style. The traditional school of legal drafting assumes that the reader is a lawyer – either the lawyer for the other party to the transaction, or the judge who would rule on the document if it were challenged in court.

The Council has since published other booklets directed to the legal profession, exhorting a simpler, more direct style of legal drafting.[21]

Clarity

Clarity is an international organisation of lawyers devoted to improving legal drafting.[22] It has strong memberships in the United Kingdom, Australia, Canada and the United States of America, and it is also represented in many non-English-speaking countries.

Clarity's beginnings can be traced to a letter of 12 January 1983 to the English *Law Society's Gazette* from a surveyor, D. J. Swinburne, who lamented that modern-day leases still seemed to be drafted 'in the language of the early 19th century'. The writer told how he[23] had been engaged in difficult negotiations for a lease, which resulted in terms which he could present as heads of agreement on a single A4 page. His client had turned to him 'in utter bewilderment' when the solicitor later produced the draft lease. The concise terms of the heads of agreement had been 'almost completely lost within the antique legal padding' of the lease. The lease referred to the land as extending to 'three acres, two roods and nineteen perches', while the Ordnance Survey plan showed the land as extending to 3.619 acres (1.466 hectares). The 'quite ordinary house' on the land was referred to throughout the lease as 'the messuage or dwellinghouse'. In the repair clause, the tenant was asked to paint 'with three coats at least of good oil paint', and was also to 'stain, varnish, distemper, stop, whiten and colour'. The writer ended by seeking 'some assurance from your profession that before we arrive in the 21st century your profession will have abandoned the meaningless, Victorian verbiage in legal documents and produce something relevant to this century at least'.

---

20 Ibid., p. 26.
21 For example, *Making Good Solicitors: The Place of Communication Skills in Their Training* (1989); Plain Language, Plain Law (1990).
22 Clarity's website is at <www.adler.demon.co.uk>.
23 We are assuming that the writer was male, though nothing in the letter indicates either way.

The plea did not fall on deaf ears. The *Gazette* of 2 March 1983 published an answer from John Walton, a local government solicitor, who urged lawyers to do something about it. He proposed a movement to simplify legal English from within the profession – an 'organised group of solicitors, barristers and legal executives whose aims would be to write in good, clear English and to persuade others to do the same'. There could be an exchange of precedents to give guidance in producing documents that were both 'certain in meaning and intelligible to ordinary people'. The name of the organisation, he suggested, could be 'Clarity'.

The response was encouraging enough for Walton to announce some three months later in the *Gazette* the birth of Clarity.[24] The organisation's aim was to encourage the legal profession to use good, clear English. This would be achieved by

- avoiding archaic, obscure and over-elaborate language in legal work;
- drafting legal documents in language both certain in meaning and easily understandable;
- exchanging ideas and precedents, not to be followed slavishly, but to give guidance in producing good legal English; and
- exerting a firm but responsible influence on the style of legal English, with the hope of achieving a change in fashion.

Membership was to be open to anyone in a position to influence the use of legal English. It was not to be confined to lawyers. A newsletter for the exchange of ideas would be produced, as well as a register of precedents.

The first newsletter appeared in August 1983. By the time of the first annual meeting on 8 September 1984, membership stood at 257. Since then it has risen steadily to more than 1000 worldwide. The newsletter has now been supplemented by a weighty journal, also called *Clarity*. The organisation's former chairperson, Mark Adler, has written a book and several articles on legal drafting.[25] Clarity has as its patrons two judges – one from England, the other from Australia – each with a reputation for clear writing.[26]

Tribunals and organisations have sought Clarity's views on simplifying legal language. The National Consumer Council consulted Clarity before finalising its *Plain Words for Consumers and Plain English for Lawyers*. The Farrand Committee on the simplification of conveyancing

---

24 John Walton, 'The Case for "Clarity": Improvement of Legal English' (1983) 80 *Law Society's Gazette*, p. 1484.

25 Mark Adler, *Clarity for Lawyers* (London: Law Society, 1990); 'Bamboozling the Public' [1991] *New Law Journal*, p. 1032; 'British Lawyers' Attitudes to Plain English' (1993) 28 *Clarity*, p. 29.

26 The patrons are Sir Christopher Staughton (formerly a Lord Justice of Appeal in England and Wales), and Justice Michael Kirby (of the Australian High Court).

invited Clarity's views. Clarity also commented on the first draft of the 1990 Standard Conditions of Sale (England). The property information form in the English Law Society's TransAction package reflects Clarity's suggested draft. In these and other ways, Clarity has helped change the legal profession's attitude to drafting.

The United Kingdom Government

The United Kingdom government in recent years has done a great deal for the cause of plain English. The government's input can be traced to the 1940s, when the Treasury invited Sir Ernest Gowers to write his works *Plain Words* (1948) and *ABC of Plain Words* (1951) as a contribution to governmental efforts to improve official English. These two books later led to *The Complete Plain Words*.

A more recent impetus came from Sir Derek Rayner's report to the prime minister in January 1982, called *Review of Administrative Forms*. A white paper, *Administrative Forms in Government*, soon followed. These revealed that over 2000 million government forms and leaflets were used by the public each year, at a cost of about £200 million; they also revealed enormous inefficiencies in their use, due in no small part to their complexity. The white paper proposed immediate action: a systematic review of existing forms; a critical look at proposed new forms; staff to design, control and review forms; the development and extension of training; and an annual report to each permanent secretary. In particular, the white paper required departments to ensure that forms became progessively more intelligible, with language 'plain and simple, avoiding jargon'.[27]

Progress reports to the prime minister were made in February 1983 and September 1987. Meanwhile, in 1984 the government had issued a ten-page guidance booklet to the Management and Personnel Office, entitled *The word is … Plain English*. This booklet, designed by the Plain English Campaign, carried the following message from minister Lord Gowrie:

> The message is simple. Using plain English is the best way to write. The audience will pay more attention to what you have to say if you can capture their interest and if they don't have to waste time unravelling the language.
>
> The first step is also simple. Put yourself in the position of your readers. Then you will see why your letters, minutes or reports will be more acceptable and more convincing if they are written in plain English.

Based on the booklet, a pamphlet called *Making It Plain* appeared in 1988. Addressed to the civil service as a whole, the pamphlet bore on its

---

27 *Administrative Forms in Government*, Cmnd 8504 (London: HMSO, 1982), p. 3.

cover the authority of a forceful prime minister, Margaret Thatcher. The extract in Panel 3 conveys something of the Thatcher style.

Achievements since the Rayner review of 1982 have been formidable. Government forms have become easier to understand and simpler to complete. Departments have won awards from the Plain English Campaign. According to one source, by 1988

- 125,000 forms had been reviewed
- 27,000 forms had been scrapped
- 41,000 forms had been redesigned
- £14,000,000 had been saved.[28]

The message that forms and documents could be couched in clear, simple language seems to have been heard by government departments and is getting home to government lawyers. As long ago as 1988, Inland Revenue published a booklet, *Is it Legal?*, which aimed to encourage designers to prepare forms that the public could understand and complete easily. As the booklet recognised, most of the department's actions were governed by legislation, much of it complex. In designing forms, the department had to act within its powers; and describing difficult concepts in plain English was demanding work. But there was 'no reason why forms written in modern, easily understood English should not be just as valid as their sometimes less comprehensible predecessors'.[29]

As well as simplifying government forms, the United Kingdom government has supported moves to a plainer style of legislative drafting. These moves can be traced to the Renton Committee, established in 1973. The committee's terms of reference began: 'With a view to achieving greater simplicity and clarity in statute law ...'. Its 1975 report highlighted the complexities in the traditional style of legislative drafting and recommended changes.[30]

While the report generated a deal of comment,[31] parliamentary drafters largely ignored its chief recommendations. Substantial change took several more decades,[32] and then came in an unexpected guise: reform of taxation

---

28 Bernard Saunders, 'Paperwork: A Time for Action', *Management Services*, March 1988, pp. 19, 20. See also J. M. Foers, *Forms Design: An International Perspective* (London: Inland Revenue, 1987), p. 39.
29 Inland Revenue, *Is it Legal?* (London: HMSO, 1988), p. 3.
30 *The Preparation of Legislation*, Cmnd 6053 (London: HMSO, 1975).
31 See Lord Hailsham of St Marylebone, 'Addressing the Statute Law' [1985] *Statute Law Review*, p. 4; Sir William Dale, 'A London Particular' [1985] *Statute Law Review* 11; Lord Simon of Glaisdale, 'The Renton Report – Ten Years On [1985] *Statute Law Review*, p. 133; Richard Thomas, 'Plain English and the Law' [1985] *Statute Law Review*, p. 139; Justice Nazareth, 'Legislative Drafting: Could our Statutes be made Simpler?' [1987] *Statute Law Review*, p. 81; Sir Patrick Mayhew, 'Can Legislation Ever be Simple, Clear and Certain?' (1990) 11 *Statute Law Review*, p. 1.
32 Writing in 1990, Lord Renton claimed that 39 of the report's 81 recommendations had been adopted: 'Current Drafting Practice and Problems in the United Kingdom' (1990) 11 *Statute Law Review*, p. 12.

Can I say exactly what I mean in plain English?

Of course you can. More to the point, will your reader understand exactly what you mean if you don't use plain English?

The reason for most of your writing is to transmit information or ideas from *your* mind clearly, convincingly and politely to your *reader's* mind. Of course, you may have to use technical terms. But then it is even *more* important to use plain English to explain your ideas.

There's no need to sacrifice accuracy for clarity. Follow Einstein – "I like to make things as simple as possible, but not simpler".

But don't plain words mean more words?

Sometimes, but not often. The real aim is to make your writing quicker to read and easier to understand.

Generally you will find that plain English is shorter. One local authority put its instructions for drawing up contracts into plain English. The old instructions had 3,679 words. The new ones said the same in 1,850 words. What's more, loopholes which had been obscured by jargon in the old instructions were exposed – and closed.

And isn't plain English ugly?

No! The example of tortured officialese on page 1 is hardly beautiful! It's exhausting. You have to unravel the language to find the meaning.

Let thy speech be short, comprehending much in few words

– Ecclesiasticus 32:8

Panel 3 Making it plain

laws. The aim was to simplify the tax laws by using plain English, adopting a more logical structure and numbering system, and ensuring greater consistency of definitions.[33] In an exposure draft, the drafting committee said of its drafting style:

> We use colloquial English wherever we can, adopting shorter sentences written using the active, rather than the passive, voice. We replace archaic expressions with more modern ones, taking care not to change the law inadvertently by rewriting words or expressions that have a well understood meaning. We try to harmonise definitions across the Acts where possible, and then make it easier for the reader to find defined terms. We group similar rules together in one place, and make greater use of signposts to guide the reader to other relevant provisions. And we continue to explore other techniques for making legislation more accessible – method statements, formulae and, where appropriate, tables.[34]

The timetable has proved over-ambitious, and the difficulties and delays in the consultation process have seemed irksome.[35] Yet this enormous task, paralleled in Australia and New Zealand, is under way. One well-known tax lawyer, originally sceptical, was reported as being surprised at how significant an improvement could be made 'just by rewriting'.[36]

More recently, the government has supported sweeping changes to the court system in England and Wales. These changes (called the Woolf reforms, after the Lord Chief Justice whose recommendations they implement) include simplifying the language of pleadings and other documents used in court. Lord Woolf had been appointed to review the procedures for civil justice in England and Wales. His work reached fruition in April 1999, when new rules, practice directions and forms came into force. Pre-action protocols were also published. The changes wrought a revolution in civil procedure. Familiar terms such as *plaintiff, ex parte* and *discovery* were discarded, to be replaced by *claimant, applications without notice* and *disclosure*. The Civil Procedure Rules themselves are user-friendly and direct, and the new forms seem clear and well-designed. The rules start with the overriding objective: 'These Rules are a new procedural code with the overriding objective of enabling the court to deal with cases justly.'[37] Proceedings are begun by a claim form rather than by a writ or originating application.[38] Among other

---

33 See [1997] *Solicitors Journal*, p. 920.
34 Exposure Draft 9 (February 2000), vol. 1, para 2.14.
35 See (1998) 95/22 *Law Society's Gazette*, p. 6.
36 See (1999) 96/15 *Law Society's Gazette*, p. 8.
37 Civil Procedure Rules 1998 (SI 1999 No. 3132), r 1.1(1). This bold beginning echoes the admirably drafted s 1 of the *Arbitration Act* 1996 (England and Wales), which sets out succinctly the principles of arbitration. For praise of the *Arbitration Act*, see A. Samuels, 'How to Do It Properly: The Arbitration Act 1996' (1997) 18 *Statute Law Review*, p. 58.
38 Rule 7.2(1).

things, particulars of claim must include a concise statement of the facts on which the claimant relies.[39] Given the new case management powers which the rules bestow on the courts[40] and the time and money invested in educating judges at all levels, it seems likely that the Woolf reforms will prove something of a catalyst for change, at least for litigators.

Australia

The plain English movement in Australia began in the 1970s. Its acknowledged leader since those days has been Dr Robert Eagleson, formerly Professor of English at the University of Sydney. In an article in 1985, Dr Eagleson pointed out that writing plainly was not something invented in the twentieth century. Of the 'reinstatement' of plain English in Australia, he said:

> The first tangible sign of revival came in 1974 when Sentry Life Insurance Co and Nationwide Mutual Insurance Co released their plain language car and house insurance policies. Only two years later in 1976 and four years before a similar development in the UK, the National Roads and Motorists' Association (NRMA) in New South Wales produced the first of its Plain English insurance policies. The next year the Real Estate Institute produced its residential and commercial leases in Plain English.[41]

In 1983, Dr Guy Powles told an Australian Senate enquiry into national language policy of the grave need for a major study of legal English in Australia. The purpose was to find out how much was gobbledegook, mere professional jargon, or pompous officialese; how much was designed to obscure meaning or to deceive; what were the language requirements of an effective and fair legal system; and what policies and actions were needed to meet these requirements.[42] The 1984 Senate report which followed recommended setting up a national task force to look into ways to reform legal language.[43] The recommendation was never implemented.

A decisive step was taken on 7 May 1985, when the Hon J. H. Kennan, Attorney-General of Victoria, made a ministerial statement to the state Legislative Council 'on the matter of plain English'. After expressing the Victorian government's commitment to clear legislative

---

39 Rule 16.4(1)(a).
40 Rules, part 3.
41 Robert Eagleson, 'The Plain English Debate in Australia', Festschrift in honour of Arthur Delbridge, 48 (1985), *Beiträge zur Phonetik und Linguistik*, p. 143.
42 Reported in Victorian Parliament, *Plain English Legislation* (Melbourne, 1985) extract from parliamentary debates, ministerial statement by J. H. Kennan, 7 May 1985, p. 3.
43 Senate Standing Committee on Education, *A National Language Policy* (1984), para 3.17. The report is discussed in 'Legalese and Courtspeak' (1985) 59 *Australian Law Journal*, p. 189–91.

drafting, he set out what he referred to as a 'new format' for drafting bills. This he modestly called 'Kennanization'.[44] He said:

> In a sense, however, the steps which have been taken so far represent only the tip of the iceberg ... What needs to happen now is to have a process whereby Parliamentary Counsel draft Bills, and legislation officers draft subordinate legislation, from the outset in plain English. This requires a radical departure from tradition and a break with the thinking of the past. It requires imagination, a spirit of adventure and a boldness not normally associated with the practice of law or with the drafting of legislation or subordinate legislation. I am confident, however, that under the leadership of the Chief Parliamentary Counsel we have cause for optimism in Victoria.[45]

Following this statement, Kennan referred the question of plain English in legislation and other government communications to the Law Reform Commission of Victoria. In August 1986, the commission issued a discussion paper, *Legislation, Legal Rights and Plain English*. In a general review of the topic, it made the following valuable points:

- Quality of information is more important than quantity. Attempts to cover all possible contingencies can be counterproductive.
- A plain English document strives to be eminently readable, in the sense of ease of absorption.
- Plain language is concerned with communication and efficiency. It aims to produce documents which the intended audience can easily read and readily understand.
- Any division between content and language is artificial.
- Writers should bear in mind the way that readers approach their task, especially the way that readers react to abstract material.
- The major source of incomprehensibility is not technical words but convoluted structures, incoherent organisation, and a perspective which ignores the real audience.

The discussion paper led in June 1987 to the most comprehensive and scholarly treatment of the topic ever published: *Plain English and the Law* (Report No 9 of the Law Reform Commission of Victoria).[46] It ran to four volumes. The first volume was the report itself; the second was a drafting manual; the third (and largest) was a redraft of the company takeovers code;[47] and the fourth contained redrafts of other forms and

---

44 For judicial castigation of 'Kennanisation', see *Halwood Corporation Ltd v Roads Corporation* [1998] 2 VR 439 at 446 (Tadgell JA).

45 *Plain English Legislation*, p. 7.

46 The Irish Law Reform Commission has recently undertaken a similar study: *Consultation Paper on Statutory Drafting and Interpretation: Plain Language and the Law* (1999).

47 See the article by the commission's chairperson, D. St L. Kelly, 'The Takeovers Code: A Failure in Communication' (1987) 5 *Company and Securities Law Journal*, p. 219.

supplementary material. Volume 3 (the takeovers code) had two aims: to show that legislation, even on the most complex subject, could be written in plain English; and to show that the traditional style of legislative drafting could be substantially improved without loss of precision.

After analysing drafting defects in legislation enacted by the Victorian Parliament in 1985 and 1986, the commission made a powerful plea for what it called the 'plain English approach to communication':

> 'Plain English' involves the use of plain, straightforward language which avoids these defects and conveys its meaning as clearly and simply as possible, without unnecessary pretension or embellishment. It is to be contrasted with convoluted, repetitive and prolix language. The adoption of a plain English style demands simply that a document be written in a style which readily conveys its message to its audience. However, plain English is not concerned simply with the forms of language. Because its theme is communication, it calls for improvements in the organisation of the material and the method by which it is presented. It requires that material is presented in a sequence which the audience would expect and which helps the audience absorb the information. It also requires that a document's design be as attractive as possible in order to assist readers to find their way through it.[48]

As with the extract from the UK National Consumer Council quoted earlier in this chapter, the unstated assumption is that the audience is the client or lay person who uses the document, not a lawyer or a judge.

Another significant step occurred in 1990, when the Law Foundation Centre for Plain Legal Language was established at Sydney University's Faculty of Law. The centre's stated aim was 'to promote the study and use of plain language in public and private legal documents (including legislation and official forms)'.[49] The centre produced some substantial plain English legal documents, and conducted training programs in legal drafting for judges, practising lawyers and law students. Three of its activities merit special mention. The first was its monthly 'words and phrases' column in the New South Wales *Law Society Journal*. Each month, the centre chose a 'traditional' legal word or phrase, researched the interpretation it had received in the courts, and then suggested a plain English equivalent that would capture the legal nuances of the original.[50]

---

48 Law Reform Commission of Victoria, *Report No. 9: Plain English and the Law* (Melbourne, 1987), vol. 1, p. 45.

49 For an introduction to the centre's activities, see 'Eliminating Legalese: New Body to Clear the Fog from Legal Documents' (1992) 30 *New South Wales Law Society Journal*, p. 77.

50 Words and phrases researched in this way included: *aid and abet; deemed; escrow; estate or interest; fit and proper; force majeure; give, devise and bequeath; goods and chattels; heirs, executors, administrators, successors and assigns; joint and several; last will and testament; notwithstanding; null and void; per stirpes; pro bono; provided that; rest, residue and remainder; right, title and interest; said; signed, sealed and delivered; time of the essence; whereas; without prejudice.* The centre's collected articles are published as *Law Words* (Sydney: Centre for Plain Legal Language, 1995).

The second was its work on the design of legislation, a joint project with the New South Wales Parliamentary Counsel's Office. This project dealt with matters such as typography, use of headings, running heads, white space, page size, text layout, numbering systems, and text justification, in an effort to produce a format that was attractive and readable.[51] Most of the recommendations have been adopted in New South Wales statutes. The third was the centre's research on the economic benefits of plain English documents – the subject of much anecdotal material but limited empirical evidence. The resulting publication makes a strong case that plain English documents are far more efficient than their traditional counterparts.[52]

In 1990s, Australian parliamentary drafters began to adopt a plain language style. This is a marked departure from the former style of legislative drafting – a style which mirrored, perhaps even surpassed, the complexities of traditional drafting in other English-speaking countries.[53] Indeed, the move to simplicity has been so marked that legislative drafters now use techniques far in advance of those commonly used in the private legal profession.[54] At Commonwealth level, the change in style began hesitantly,[55] but it is now entrenched, as it is in some states – notably New South Wales and Queensland.[56] Illustrations of the new

---

51 The centre's results were published in a discussion paper, *Review and Design of NSW Legislation* (Sydney: NSW Parliamentary Counsel's Office, 1994).

52 For the results of the research, see *The Gains from Clarity* (Sydney: Centre for Microeconomic Policy Analysis, Centre for Plain Legal Language, and Law Foundation of NSW, 1996).

53 Research by the Law Reform Commission of Victoria indicated the number of years of formal education required to comprehend some traditionally drawn Australian statutes: for example, income tax legislation (27 years: *Australian Financial Review*, 27 September 1991, p. 19); dividing fences legislation (29 years: Richard Wright, Executive Director of the Commission, 'I'm not from here, I just live here', unpublished paper, 7 September 1990, pp. 2–3); credit legislation (22 years: ibid., pp. 3–6); and in vitro fertilisation legislation (32 years: ibid., pp. 6–7). Similar results have been found in New Zealand: L. Tan and G. Tower, 'The Readability of Tax Laws: An Empirical Study in New Zealand' (1992) 9 *Australian Tax Forum* 355. To give parliamentary drafters their due, the overly complex style was partly a response to the excessively literalist approach of the Australian High Court in the 1960s and 1970s, particularly in cases involving income tax legislation. See the imponderable tax provisions which bewildered even Australia's highest court in *Hepples v Commissioner of Taxation* (1992) 173 CLR 492.

54 Examples are the *Native Title Amendment Act* 1998 (Cth) and *A New Tax System (Goods and Services Tax) Act* 1999 (Cth), both of which deal with matters of great complexity in a style that is simple and direct.

55 See I. Turnbull, 'Legislative Drafting: Use of Plain English' [1987] *Australian Current Law*, p. 36,047; and compare Turnbull, 'Clear Legislative Drafting: New Approaches in Australia' (1991) 11 *Statute Law Review*, p. 161; Turnbull, 'Legislative Drafting in Plain Language and Statements of General Principle' (1997) 18 *Statute Law Review*, p. 21; D. Murphy, 'Plain Language in a Legislative Drafting Office' (1995) 33 *Clarity*, p. 3; D. Berry, 'Legislative Drafting: Could our Statutes be Simpler?' [1987] *Statute Law Review*, p. 92.

56 A ground-breaking example is the *Local Government Act* 1993 (NSW), described by Justice Kirby of the Australian High Court as a 'paragon in our midst' (book review of *Decisions, Decisions* (by Justices Mailhot and Carnwath, (1999) 73 *Australian Law Journal*, p. 292), and by the minister introducing the Bill into parliament as 'in a format which breaks new ground in Australia and which will be understood by all who need to see it' (G. Peacocke, NSW

drafting techniques can be seen in two Commonwealth projects to simplify legislative language in the complex areas of corporations law and taxation. Both projects have produced substantial working papers and discussion papers, setting out their drafting techniques and inviting public comment.[57] Both have now resulted in legislation that is simple and direct, a far cry from the conventional style of their predecessors. Both have also spawned a welter of published comment, some favourable and some critical.[58] The taxation law project inspired similar projects in the United Kingdom, as we have seen, and in New Zealand.[59]

The Law Societies of some of the Australian states have established plain language committees, along the lines of similar Bar Association committees in the United States of America (discussed below). The New South Wales committee – now sadly defunct – helped to engender change in the local profession's drafting habits.[60] Its chairperson has written a successful text on the use of plain language in law.[61] The New South Wales Law Society has produced a plain language style manual,[62] along with a number of plain English documents now in common use; they include a contract for the sale of land, a commercial lease, and an agreement for the sale of business. The society was also successful in persuading the New South Wales legislature to enact simplified forms of easement. Panel 4 shows one result, now enshrined in the *Conveyancing Act* 1919 (NSW).[63]

Legislative Assembly, *Parliamentary Debates*, 11 March 1993, p. 724). A number of the Act's drafting innovations appear to have been inspired by the draft Alberta *Municipal Government Act*, mentioned below. A Queensland example is the *Land Title Act* 1994 (Qld), exemplifying the drafter's ability to reduce even the most complex property concepts to plain English. For the views of the Act's drafter, see J. Leahy, 'The Advantages of Plain Legal Language', unpublished conference paper, 29th Australian Legal Convention, Brisbane, 26 September 1995.

57 For examples, see *Second Corporate Law Simplification Bill: Exposure Draft, Volume 1, Provisions* (Canberra: Australian Government Publishing Service, 1995); *Tax Law Improvement Project: Exposure Draft No. 9* (Canberra: Australian Government Publishing Service, 1997).

58 See, for example, 'Tarting up the Tax Law' (various authors), (1995) 30 *Taxation in Australia*, p.172; Peter Cowdroy, 'Dross into Gloss?' ibid., p. 187; David Evans, 'The Emperor's New Clothes', ibid., p. 192; Cynthia Coleman, 'Major Tax Simplification Begins' (1997) 35 *NSW Law Society Journal* (March), p. 46; Bin Tran-Nam, 'Tax Reform and Tax Simplification: Some Conceptual Issues and a Preliminary Assessment' (1999) 21 *Sydney Law Review*, p. 500. For views of the leaders of the tax project, see Brian Nolan and Tom Reid, 'Re-writing the Tax Act' (1994) 22 *Federal Law Review*, p. 448.

59 See papers from the 1996 Tax Drafting Conference (held in Auckland, New Zealand), published in (1997) 3 *New Zealand Journal of Taxation Law and Policy*, pp. 153 ff.

60 For some of the committee's activities, see M. Asprey, 'Trend Overwhelmingly in Favour of Plain Language, Survey Shows' (1994) *NSW Law Society Journal* (October), p. 70; M. Asprey, 'Lawyers Prefer Plain Language, Survey Finds' (1994) *NSW Law Society Journal* (November), p. 76.

61 Michele Asprey, *Plain Language for Lawyers*, 2nd edn (Sydney: Federation Press, 1996).

62 Law Society of New South Wales, *Style Manual for Lawyers* (Sydney, 1997).

63 Although why the heading of the new version ('Easement for drainage of sewage') was thought to be an improvement on the original ('Easement to drain sewage') remains a mystery.

Part 4   Easement to drain sewage

Full and free right for the body in whose favour this easement is created, and every person authorised by it, from time to time and at all times by means of pipes to drain sewage and other waste material and fluid in any quantities across and through the land herein indicated as the servient tenement, together with the right to use, for the purposes of the easement, any line of pipes already laid within the servient tenement for the purpose of draining sewage or any pipe or pipes in replacement or in substitution therefor and where no such line of pipes exists, to lay, place and maintain a line of pipes of sufficient internal diameter beneath or upon the surface of the servient tenement and together with the right for the body in whose favour this easement is created and every person authorised by it, with any tools, implements, or machinery, necessary for the purpose, to enter upon the servient tenement and to remain there for any reasonable time for the purpose of laying, inspecting, cleansing, repairing, maintaining, or renewing such pipe line or any part thereof and for any of the aforesaid purposes to open the soil of the servient tenement to such extent as may be necessary provided that the body in whose favour this easement is created and the persons authorised by it will take all reasonable precautions to ensure as little disturbance as possible to the surface of the servient tenement and will restore that surface as nearly as practicable to its original condition.

Part 6   Easement for drainage of sewage

1   The body having the benefit of this easement may:

    (a)   drain sewage, sullage and other fluid wastes in pipes through each lot burdened, but only within the site of this easement, and

    (b)   do anything reasonably necessary for that purpose, including:

       •   entering the lot burdened, and

       •   taking anything on to the lot burdened, and

       •   using any existing line of pipes, and

       •   carrying out works, such as constructing, placing, repairing or maintaining pipes and equipment.

2   In exercising those powers, the body having the benefit of this easement must:

    (a)   ensure all work is done properly, and

    (b)   cause as little inconvenience as is practicable to the owner and any occupier of the lot burdened, and

    (c)   cause as little damage as is practicable to the lot burdened and any improvement on it, and

    (d)   restore the lot burdened as nearly as is practicable to its former condition, and

    (e)   make good any collateral damage.

Panel 4 Examples of plain statutory drafting from New South Wales Conveyancing Act

The United States of America

In the United States, isolated plain English documents have been appearing since the mid-1970s.[64] To cite one example, the traditional form of eviction notice in Detroit formerly (and formally) began: 'PLEASE TAKE NOTICE, That you are hereby required to quit, surrender and deliver up possession to me of the premises hereinafter described ...'. The new version begins: 'Your landlord or landlady wants to evict you.'[65] Plain English contracts for sale and mortgages are used, though not as widely as in England and Australia.[66]

The year 1978 was a notable one for plain English in the United States. On 23 March, President Carter signed Executive Order No 12044, which (among other things) required federal agencies to ensure that regulations were written in plain English and could be understood by those who had to comply with them. Then on 1 November the New York State plain English law reached the statute book: see Panel 5. The law became known as the Sullivan law, after Assembly member Peter Sullivan who sponsored it through the legislature. While not itself a model of clarity and simplicity, the statute required residential leases and consumer contracts to be 'written in a clear and coherent manner using words with common and every day meanings'.[67] Other states later passed similar laws, and numerous states have regulations setting standards for plain English in insurance policies and consumer documents.[68]

Although some American lawyers supported the introduction of legislation 'mandating' plain English, others were less positive.[69] One leading

---

64 They include insurance policies, bank mortgages and promissory notes, contracts for the sale of land, wills, and leases. See R. W. Benson, 'The End of Legalese: The Game is Over' (1984–85) 13 *NYU Review of Law and Social Change*, pp. 564–5.

65 Ibid., pp. 566–7.

66 For the development of a mortgage, see Browne, 'Development of the FNMA/FHLMC Plain Language Mortgage Documents – Some Useful Techniques' (1979) 14 *Real Property Probate and Trust Journal*, p. 696.

67 For contemporary assessments of the New York law's success, see Walter Kretz, 'The Plain English Law' (1978) 23 *New York Law School Law Review*, p. 824; Richard Givens, 'The "Plain English" Law' (1978) 50 *New York State Bar Journal*, p. 479; Rosemary Moukad, 'New York's Plain English Law' (1980) 8 *Fordham Urban Law Journal*, p. 451.

68 For a comprehensive list (as at 1992), see Joseph Kimble, 'Plain English: A Charter for Clear Writing' (1992) 9 *Thomas M. Cooley Law Review*, pp. 31–7. See also James Dayananda, 'Plain English in the United States' (1986) 5 *English Today*, p. 14; G. Hathaway, 'An Overview of the Plain English Movement for Lawyers' (1983) 62 *Michigan Bar Journal*, p. 945.

69 Supporters included, Richard A. Givens, 'The "Plain English" Law' (1978) 50 *New York State Bar Journal*, p. 179; Walter A. Kretz Jr, 'The Plain English Law: "Let the Buyer Be Aware"' (1977–78) 23 *New York Law School Law Review*, p. 824; Stephen M. Ross, 'On Legalities and Linguistics: Plain Language Legislation' (1981) 30 *Buffalo Law Review*, p. 317. For a knee-jerk reaction, see Prather, 'In Defense of the People's Use of Three Syllable Words' (1978) 39 *Alabama Lawyer*, p. 394. For more insightful criticisms, see John Forshey, 'Plain English Contracts: The Demise of Legalese?' (1978) 30 *Baylor Law Review*, p. 765; Burt Leete, 'Plain Language Legislation: A Comparison of Approaches' (1981) 18 *American Business Law*

Senate and Assembly, do enact as follows:

5-702. Requirements for use of plain language in consumer transactions.

(a) Every written agreement entered into after November first, nineteen hundred seventy-eight, for the lease of space to be occupied for residential purposes, or to which a consumer is a party and the money, property or service which is the subject of the transaction is primarily for personal, family or household purposes must be:

1. Written in a clear and coherent manner using words with common and every day meanings;

2. Appropriately divided and captioned by its various sections.

Any creditor, seller or lessor who fails to comply with this subdivision shall be liable to a consumer who is a party to a written agreement governed by this subdivision in an amount equal to any actual damages sustained plus a penalty of fifty dollars. The total class action penalty against any such creditor, seller or lessor shall not exceed ten thousand dollars in any class action or series of class actions arising out of the use by a creditor, seller or lessor of an agreement which fails to comply with this subdivision. No action under this subdivision may be brought after both parties to the agreement have fully performed their obligation under such agreement, nor shall any creditor, seller or lessor who attempts in good faith to comply with this subdivision be liable for such penalties. This subdivision shall not apply to agreements involving amounts in excess of fifty thousand dollars nor prohibit the use of words or phrases or forms of agreement required by state or federal law, rule or regulation or by a governmental instrumentality.

(b) A violation of the provisions of subdivision (a) of this section shall not render any such agreement void or voidable nor shall it constitute:

  1. A defense to any action or proceeding to enforce such agreement; or

  2. A defense to any action or proceeding for breach of such agreement.

(c) In addition to the above, whenever the attorney general finds that there has been a violation of this section, he may proceed as provided in subdivision twelve of section sixty-three of the executive law.

2. This act shall take effect immediately.

Panel 5 New York plain English law

commentator, Reed Dickerson, saw its main value as symbolic and its main virtue as giving the legal profession and the law schools a 'solid legislative jolt'.[70] He pointed out that readability is not the same as clarity of substance. Also, the 'good faith' defence available under the New York law (and similar statutes) rendered it largely impotent, since most bad drafters operated in good faith. In his view, better drafting would only come with better law school education. Until then, legislation mandating plain English legislation was merely a useful temporary expedient.[71]

Another leading US commentator, Carl Felsenfeld, made the fundamental point that language is only one aspect of plain English. Speaking in 1978, he said that what really mattered was the *substance* of the document. This was particularly important where documents were built up, cumulatively, over a number of years. The process by which clauses were added was undisciplined: business people generally accepted a new phrase or paragraph on their lawyer's advice that it was desirable, and clauses once added tended to remain. In Felsenfeld's view, the plain English movement required a new approach. Documents should be analysed against the specific transaction and the protection required. Many traditional legal provisions might then be found to be unnecessary.[72]

Alan Siegel had spoken on the same theme two months before.[73] He had also urged the use of a number of devices now common in plain language documents: the active voice rather than the passive; shorter sentences; contractions; the 'we' and 'you' style; examples to clarify complex ideas; and good document design.

Since those early days, a number of Bar Associations have lent their support to the plain English movement. In 1989, the California Bar Association urged its members to use plain legal language.[74] Lest this be dismissed as a Californian eccentricity, the Bar Associations of Michigan and Texas established plain language committees, aimed at promoting clear drafting practices among lawyers. For some years the Texas committee published annual 'Legaldegook Awards' for delightfully atrocious

---

Journal, p. 511; David S. Cohen, 'Comment on the Plain English Movement' (1981–82) 6 *Canadian Business Law Journal*, p. 421; Gertrude Block, 'Plain Language Laws: Promise v Performance' (1983) 62 *Michigan Bar Journal*, p. 950; James Wetter, 'Plain Language in Pennsylvania: Fading Issue or Development on the Horizon?' (1985) 89 *Dickinson Law Review*, p. 441; Harold A. Lloyd, 'Plain Language Statutes: Plain Good Sense or Plain Nonsense?' (1986) 78 *Law Library Journal*, p. 683; Barbara Child, *Drafting Legal Documents*, 2nd edn (St Paul, Minnesota: West Publishing Co., 1992), ch. 8.

70 *Materials on Legal Drafting* (St Paul, Minnesota: West Publishing Co., 1981), p. 260.
71 Ibid., p. 262, originally in 'Should Plain English be Legislated?', *Plain English in a Complex Society* (The Poynter Center, Indiana University, 1980), p.19.
72 Reproduced in Dickerson, *Materials on Legal Drafting*, p. 266.
73 Conference of Experts in Clear Legal Drafting, National Center for Administrative Justice, Washington, DC (June 1978), reproduced in ibid., p. 294.
74 Resolution 135 of 1989.

legal writing.[75] The Michigan and Texas *Bar Association Journals* both published regular plain language columns. Under the leadership of Professor Barbara Child, the University of Florida established a compulsory course in plain language drafting for all law students, and many law schools now offer courses on the same subject.[76] American literature on plain legal language abounds.[77]

In August 1992 the Legal Writing Institute – the organisation of legal writing teachers in American law schools – formally resolved to urge its 950 members to work with their respective Bar Associations to establish plain language committees along the lines of those in Texas and Michigan. The institute also passed a 'Plain Language Resolution', which included the following:

1. The way lawyers write has been a source of complaint about lawyers for more than four centuries.
2. The language used by lawyers should agree with the common speech, unless there are reasons for a difference.
3. Legalese is unnecessary and no more precise than plain language.
4. Plain language is an important part of good legal writing.
5. Plain language means language that is clearly and readily understandable to the intended readers.[78]

Despite this activity, change has been slow in the United States compared with some other common law countries. Generally speaking, US lawyers have seemed reluctant to move to a plainer, more direct drafting style. Certainly they have lagged behind developments in countries such as the United Kingdom, Canada and Australia. That said, four recent developments may yet engender a willingness to consider change. First, in 1998 President Clinton issued an Executive Order requiring federal government documents to be in plain language.[79] Second, in the same

---

75 Its 1991 awards included: the 'Rise-of-the-Roman-Language Award' for pervasive use of Latin; the 'Serpentine Sentence Award' for a 174-word behemoth; and the 'Not Unnegative Award' for the most negatives confusingly placed. The 1992 awards included: the 'She-Sells-Seashells Award' for lilting legislative alliteration (citing the definition of 'reshippers' in the *Texas Administrative Code*: 'Reshippers – Persons who transship shucked shellfish in original containers, or shellstock, from certified shellfish shippers'); the 'Foggy Footnote Award'; the 'Save-the-Period-Award' for minimal use of full stops; and the 'Herculean Headnote Award'.
76 Professor Child's teaching materials are published as Child, *Drafting Legal Documents*.
77 Notable contributions include: Benson, 'The End of Legalese: The Game is Over' (1984–85) 13 *Review of Law and Social Change*, p. 519; Gopen, 'The State of Legal Writing: *Res Ipsa Loquitur*' (1987) 86 *Michigan Law Review*, p. 333; Benson and Kessler, 'Legalese v. Plain English: An Empirical Study of Persuasion and Credibility in Appellate Brief Writing' (1987) 20 *Loyola of LA Law Review*, p. 301; Kimble, 'Plain English: A Charter for Clear Writing' (1992) 9 *Thomas M. Cooley Law Review*, p. 1; Kimble, 'Answering the Critics of Plain Language' (1994–95) 5 *Scribes Journal of Legal Writing*, p. 51.
78 *The Second Draft* (Bulletin of the Legal Writing Institute), vol. 8, no. 1, 1992.
79 The text is in (1998) 42 *Clarity*, p. 2. The Plain Language Action Network was established as part of the initiative: its website is at <www.plainlanguage.gov>.

year, the Securities and Exchange Commission announced rules requiring some parts of prospectuses to be in plain language, and issued a handbook with guidelines for writing in plain language.[80] Third, for some years the Federal Court has been redrafting its rules of appellate procedure, under the guidance of one of the United States' leading exponents of plain language drafting, Bryan A. Garner.[81] And fourth, the American Bar Association resolved in August 1999 to urge agencies 'to use plain language in writing regulations, as a means of promoting the understanding of legal obligations'.[82]

Canada

For the past two decades Canadians have been active in promoting the use of plain language in law.[83] From the late 1980s to the mid-1990s, a number of Canadian organisations urged lawyers and those working in law-related fields to use plain language.[84] The Plain Language Institute in Vancouver and the Plain Language Project in Vancouver, both staffed by lawyers and funded by government and the legal profession, conducted substantial research into the use of plain language in law.[85] In Toronto for some years the Canadian Legal Information Centre had a Plain Language Centre, which maintained an extensive library and ran training courses across the country in plain language drafting.[86] Unfortunately, cuts in government funding later resulted in all three organisations closing.

At the professional level, the Law Society of Upper Canada published a book in 1990 urging the use of plain legal language.[87] In 1991 the

---

80 See T. Clyde, 'Plain Language Turns the Corner: New SEC Rules for Prospectuses' (1998) 42 *Clarity*, pp. 9–14. The handbook is available at <www.sec.gov/news/handbook.htm>.
81 See B. Garner, *Guidelines for Drafting and Editing Court Rules* (US Govt Printing Office, 1997). Garner's other leading texts include: *The Elements of Legal Style* (Oxford: Oxford University Press, 1991); *Dictionary of Modern Legal Usage*, 2nd edn (Oxford: Oxford University Press, 1995); *The Winning Brief* (Oxford: Oxford University Press, 1999).
82 Resolution of American Bar Association, adopted by House of Delegates, 9–10 August 1999.
83 Early articles include: Robert Dick, 'Plain English in Legal Drafting' (1980) 18 *Alberta Law Review*, p. 509; David Elliott, 'What is Plain English?' (1990) 11 *Statute Law Review*, p. 237, a response to Justice Crabbe, 'The Legislative Sentence' (1989) 10 *Statute Law Review*, p. 79; Susan Krongold, 'Writing Laws: Making Them Easier to Understand' (1992) 24 *Ottawa Law Review*, p. 495.
84 See David Elliott, 'Plain Language Initiative: A Canadian Trend' [1991] *International Legal Practitioner*, p. 19.
85 Notable publications of the Plain Language Institute included the following (all undated): *Legislating the Use of Plain Language: An Overview; Critical Opinions: the Public's View of Legal Documents; Language Issues for Service Agencies and their Clients; Editorial and Design Stylebook; Plain Language at City Hall; So People can Understand* (extracts published in *Clarity* 30 (1994) pp. 6–8, 13). An important publication of the Plain Language Project was its *Plain Language Wills* (undated).
86 See the centre's *Plain Language Resource Materials* (1990).
87 Perrin, *Better Writing for Lawyers* (1990).

Canadian Bar Association resolved (in incongruously archaic terms)[88] to encourage banks and other large organisations to use plain language, and urged law schools and Bar Associations to promote its use. The association also issued a report jointly with the Canadian Bankers Association, entitled *The Decline and Fall of Gobbledygook*, strongly recommending the use of plain language in banking documents.

In 1992 the Alberta Law Reform Institute released versions of several documents as part of its Plain Language Initiative. The initiative aimed to demonstrate to Albertan lawyers the advantages of drafting legal documents in plain language. Part of the aim was to overcome the legal profession's perception that plain legal language was a good idea but unworkable in practice.[89] The documents included a will, a bank guarantee, and an enduring power of attorney.

Canadian legislative drafters have long decried the traditional style of statutes,[90] although they appear to have had some difficulty in translating their progressive ideas into actual legislation. An early plain language statute was the *Financial Consumers Act* 1990 of Alberta. The purpose of the Act, as stated in s 1, is 'to encourage the use of readily understandable language in the financial marketplace'. Section 13 requires certain financial documents to be in 'readily understandable language and form'. The statute practises what it preaches, its language and layout ably illustrating plain language techniques.[91] In 1991, the Alberta Municipal Statutes Review Committee proposed a new *Muncipal Government Act* which, if adopted, would have broken new ground in Canadian statutory drafting.[92] The draft included devices such as purpose statements, headings as questions, notes and boxed information for readers, and flow charts. Sadly, many innovations in the committee's draft were dropped from the version as enacted[93] – although, paradoxically, they were adopted as the model for municipal legislation in Australia.[94]

---

88 Resolution M-08-91, 'Plain Language Documentation'. The text is available at
     <www.web.net/~raporter/English/LegalLanguage/cbares.html>.
89 Discussion Paper, 'Plain-Language Consumer Contracts: A Benefit for Consumers and
     Business Alike' (Alberta Consumer and Corporate Affairs, 1991).
90 Leading writers are Elmer Driedger, whose works include *The Composition of Legislation*
     (Ottawa: Dept of Justice, 1976); *A Manual of Instructions for Legislative and Legal Writing*
     (Ottawa: Dept of Justice, 1982); 'Legislative Drafting' (1949) 27 *Canadian Bar Review*, p. 291;
     and Robert C. Dick, *Legal Drafting in Plain Language*, 3rd edn (Toronto: Thomson Canada,
     1995).
91 The statute is discussed in David Elliott, 'Legislating Plain Language' (1992) 17 *Clarity*, p. 6;
     a fuller version of this article is at <www.compusmart.ab.ca/elliott>. See also David Elliott,
     'A Model Plain-Language Act' (1992) 3 *Scribes Journal of Legal Writing*, p. 51.
92 See the committee's report, *Municipal Government in Alberta: A Municipal Government Act for
     the 21st Century* (1991). The draft was largely the work of David Elliott, Barrister and
     Solicitor, Edmonton.
93 *Alberta Municipal Government Act* 1994 cM-26.1.
94 Notably, the *Local Government Act* 1993 (New South Wales), mentioned above, note 56.

What judges have said about plain English

We should not leave this survey of the movement towards plain legal English without mentioning the efforts of judges. Throughout history, many judges have praised the virtues of plain English. In times past, English judges such as Coke, Blackstone, Stephen, and Atkin (to name but a few) all spoke and wrote in clear, forthright terms. In modern times, judges such as Denning, Staughton, Hoffmann, Windeyer and Kirby (the last two being Australian) have shown the same qualities. A few judges have even extolled the virtues of plain language judgments.[95] Others, more restrained, have offered constructive comments on the thorny issue of how far to apply settled case law in interpreting plain English revisions of statutes and standard documents.[96]

Direct judicial advocacy of plain, modern English in legal writing as a central theme is, however, rare – at least in published material. This is odd, as judges appear to favour the use of plain English in documents that come before them in court. That at least is the evidence from the United States, where surveys have shown that, given the choice, over 80 per cent of American judges would prefer to see pleadings in plain English rather than in traditional form.[97]

Yet some judges have been openly hostile, their comments standing in uneasy contrast to the judicial criticisms of traditional drafting we outlined in Chapter 2. For example, an Australian appeal court judge recently described certain provisions of the Australian *Corporations Law* – which adopts a consciously plain English style – as being drafted 'in the language of the pop songs'. The judge's prime concern seemed to be the drafting technique of starting a section with 'However', followed by a comma. In his view, the quest for simplicity 'pays the price of vulgarity and ends in obscurity'.[98] Another Australian appellate judge decried the 'grotesque' use of 'must' in statutes, and especially the phrase 'must

---

95 Examples include F. M. Mester, 'Plain English for Judges' (1983) 62 *Michigan Bar Journal*, p. 978; A. L. Cohn, 'Effective Brief Writing: One Judge's Observations', ibid., p. 987; M. D. Kirby, 'On the Writing of Judgments' (1990) 64 *Australian Law Journal*, p. 691 (especially at 708: 'Brevity, simplicity and clarity are the watchwords for effective judicial writing.'); J. Doyle, 'Judgment Writing: Are there needs for change?' (1999) 73 ibid., p. 737.

96 See, for example, Justice G. Hill, 'A Judicial Perspective on Tax Law Reform' (1998) 72 *Australian Law Journal*, p. 685; Justice K. Lindgren, 'Interpretation of the Income Tax Assessment Act 1997' (1999) 73 ibid., p. 425; Justice D. Mahoney, 'A Judge's Attitude to Plain Language' (1996) 34 *NSW Law Society Journal* (September), p. 52.

97 R. Benson, 'Plain English Comes to Court' (1986) 13 *Litigation* 21; S. Harrington and J. Kimble, 'Survey: Plain English Wins Every Which Way' (1987) 66 *Michigan Bar Journal* 1024; J. Kimble and J. Prokop, 'Strike Three for Legalese' (1990) 69 *Michigan Bar Journal* 418; B. Child, 'Language Preferences of Judges and Lawyers: A Florida Survey' (1990) 64 *Florida Bar Journal* 32.

98 *G. M. & A. M. Pearce and Co. Pty Ltd v RGM Australia Pty Ltd* (1998) 16 ACLC 429 at 432 (Callaway JA).

not'.[99] Yet another appellate judge, criticising a clause in a plain English insurance policy, caricatured 'plain English' as 'confused thought and split infinitives'.[100] In the end, however, carping comments of this kind will not impede the relentless move towards plain legal language, for they overlook the substantial benefits of a plain language style in legal documents. To a consideration of those benefits we now turn.

---

99 *Halwood Corporation Ltd v Roads Corporation* [1998] 2 VR 439 at 445–6 (Tadgell JA). The judge's comments are trenchantly criticised by linguist Robert Eagleson in: 'Plain English: Changing the Lawyer's Image and Goals', paper delivered to Literature and the Law Seminar, Perth, Australia, 16 May 1998; extracts published in (1998) *Clarity* 42, p. 34.

100 *NRMA Insurance Ltd v Collier* (1996) 9 ANZ Insurance Cases 76,717 at 76,721 (Meagher JA).

4   Some Benefits of Drafting in Plain English

The previous chapter traced the development of the plain English movement, which arose out of the benefits perceived to arise from using plain language in legal documents. In this chapter, we consider some of those benefits in more detail.

The meaning of 'plain English'

We begin with a point of terminology: what is meant by the term 'plain English' or 'plain language' in the context of legal drafting? Various terms are used to describe the modern style of legal drafting, including 'modern English' and 'standard English'. 'Plain English' is the term that has achieved the most widespread use.

Some lawyers are reluctant to use the term 'plain English'. They assume that it denotes an oversimplified 'Dick and Jane' style – that its proponents employ a debased form of language, shorn of beauty, stripped of vocabulary, truncated in form and deficient in style. This, however, is a limited understanding of the true nature of plain English.[1] As the Law Reform Commission of Victoria (Australia) pointed out in its 1986 discussion paper *Legislation, Legal Rights and Plain English*, 'plain English' is a full, adult version of the language. Documents in plain English are rightly described as simplified, in the sense of being rid of entangled and convoluted language. But 'plain English' is more than that:

> Plain English is language that is not artificially complicated, but is clear and effective for its intended audience. While it shuns the antiquated and inflated word and phrase, which can readily be either omitted altogether or replaced with a more useful substitute, it does not seek to rid documents of terms which express important distinctions. Nonetheless, plain language documents offer non-expert readers some assistance in coping with these technical terms. To a far larger extent, plain language is concerned with matters of sentence

---

1 R. Eagleson, 'Plain English: Simple or Simplistic?' (1990) 4 *Vox*, p. 106.

and paragraph structure, with organisation and design, where so many of the hindrances to clear expression originate.[2]

The key lies in the phrase 'clear and effective for its intended audience'. Central to plain English is the assumption that the parties to the document, and not the lawyers, are the audience. Once that is established, the structure and language of the document take on a different form.

The National Consumer Council (UK) defines 'plain English' by reference to what it calls 'standard English'. The council has said (in a statement that owes something to the New York plain English law, discussed in Chapter 3):

> Plain English means standard English as currently used and understood, and any move which promotes the use of words in their ordinary, everyday meaning and deters the use of purple verbiage and fathomless grammar must only improve the whole quality of our language. There is not much literary merit in existing contracts.[3]

The nature of plain or standard English can be readily seen when set beside legalese or jargon, examples of which we saw in Chapter 2 and which we consider further in Chapter 5.

With this point of terminology behind us, we proceed to consider some of the benefits of using clear, modern English in legal documents.

Increased efficiency

The first benefit is increased efficiency. Plain language documents are easier to read and understand. Consider the following clauses, where traditional and plain language versions are juxtaposed. The plain language versions are more direct and more easily absorbed.

Traditional
The Builder shall at his own expense construct sewer level pave metal kerb flag channel drain light and otherwise make good (including the provision of street name plates in accordance with the requirements of the appropriate District Council and road markings and traffic signs in accordance with the requirements of the Council) the street.
Plain
The Builder must construct the street to Council specifications.

Traditional
Until the expiration of twenty one years from the death of the last survivor of the purchasers the trustees for the time being of this Deed shall have power

---

2 *Discussion Paper No. 1* (Melbourne, 1986), p. 3.
3 *Plain Words for Consumers* (London, 1984), p. 47.

to Mortgage Charge Lease or otherwise dispose of all or any part of the said property with all the powers in that behalf of an absolute owner.
Plain
For 21 years after the death of the last surviving purchaser, the trustees have all the powers of an absolute owner.

Traditional
That the Lessee will not without the previous consent in writing of the Lessor at any time fix or place any aerial wires poles or projections or any other articles notices signs pictures legend or advertisement or any other thing outside the Demised Premises nor any part thereof nor in the windows thereof on any part of the Property.
Plain
Except with the Landlord's written consent, that the Tenant must not put
• any aerial, wire, or sign, outside the property
• a sign in any window.

In all these examples, the plainer version is also shorter. This is usually the case, since plain language drafting omits unnecessary detail. Sometimes, however, a plain language version may be longer than the original: in resolving ambiguities or explaining hidden assumptions, material may have to be added, not subtracted.

The efficiencies achieved by using plain language in place of traditional legal language have been well-authenticated. This is so regardless of whether the document is a one-off, prepared for a particular transaction, or a standard form, prepared for transactions of a recurrent kind. Where a standard form is to be completed by a customer, plain language reduces customer queries about meaning; it also reduces customer errors in filling in the form. Staff formerly employed to handle enquiries and errors can be redeployed to more productive tasks. Staff can also more efficiently process forms that are drafted in plain language. In these ways, many businesses and government agencies have attested to saving substantial amounts by converting documents to plain language.[4]

Plain language is also more efficient for lawyers. For example, in a study for the Law Reform Commission of Victoria, lawyers read versions of the same statute, one written in plain language and the other in traditional language. On average, the time taken to understand the plain language version was one-third to one-half less than the time taken to

---

4 Many examples are documented in Joseph Kimble, 'Plain English: A Charter for Clear Writing' (1992) 9 *Thomas M. Cooley Law Review*, pp. 25ff; Joseph Kimble, 'Answering the Critics of Plain Language' (1994–95) 5 *Scribes Journal of Legal Writing*, p. 51; Joseph Kimble, 'Writing for Dollars, Writing to Please' (1996–97) 6 ibid., p. 1; G. Mills and M. Duckworth, *The Gains from Clarity: A Research Report on the Effects of Plain-language Documents* (Sydney: Law Foundation of NSW, 1996).

understand the traditional version.[5] This result has been confirmed in many other studies: they all show that lawyers find the plain language version easier to read than the traditional version, and that their comprehension of the content is markedly increased.[6]

Although the evidence for increased efficiency and understanding seems conclusive, some lawyers still have reservations on other grounds – reservations which they feel outweigh the benefits of increased efficiency. One (hardly meritorious) is the prospect of lower fees: if a document is more 'efficient', in the sense of taking less time to digest, then lawyers' fees might be reduced proportionately. Of course, given its unethical nature, this reservation is unlikely to be expressed so starkly. But in any case, efficiency of this kind is not the threat to income that it might seem, for there is no direct correlation between expertise and efficiency. As we saw in Chapter 1, time is only one factor in assessing the lawyer's fee.

A related reservation might be the time taken to draft plain language documents. For many lawyers, especially those new to the techniques, drafting in plain language may take longer than drafting in the traditional style. While the reader receives the benefit of the drafter's efforts, the drafter may have spent considerably more time preparing the document than if it had been lifted from the word processor.

Several responses can be made to this reservation. First, the drafter one day is a reader the next. Lawyers are not always drafters, any more than clients are always sellers. Roles change. If plain language documents become the norm, the legal profession as a whole benefits. Second, the drafter's task is not finished when the draft is prepared and sent out. The other party may propose amendments. If the draft is in plain language, the drafter can absorb and deal with amendments more easily than if the document is in traditional form.[7] Of course, the drafter might be working from a standard precedent which is already in plain English. The advent of plain English will not negate the usefulness of precedents. In a pressured world, precedents fulfil a need. They are an efficient tool in turning out documents. To advocate that every document should be created anew every time is to fly in the face of reality. Even so, the plain

---

5 Robert Eagleson, 'Plain English: A Boon for Lawyers' [1991] *The Second Draft* (Legal Writing Institute), p. 12.
6 For examples, see Kimble, 'Answering the Critics of Plain Language' pp. 62–5, 69–70; Kimble, 'Writing for Dollars, Writing to Please', p. 25; Cutts, *Lucid Law* (Stockport: Plain Language Commission, 1994), pp. 22–6 (law students).
7 The experience of plain drafters, it must be said, is that amendments to plain language documents are often proposed in traditional language. This produces an uneven document (which can sometimes be improved by the original drafter exercising a little judicious and unannounced editing). Until plain drafting becomes universal, or virtually universal, amendments in an alien style may have to be absorbed.

English precedent can be adapted more easily to the needs of each transaction than can its traditional counterpart, because its meaning is more transparent.

Fewer errors

A related bonus of a plain language style is the potential for reducing mistakes.[8] Traditional legal language tends to hide inconsistencies and ambiguities. Errors are harder to find in dense and convoluted prose. Removing legalese helps lay bare any oversights in the original. This can benefit not only the client for whom the document is drawn, but also the drafter, for it forces the drafter to reappraise the text and consider what the client really intended. And by exposing the contents of the document, plain language reduces the likelihood of a professional negligence claim against the drafter. Clients who sign a document which is plainly expressed and easily understood will be hard-pressed to convince a court that they did not understand it – and so may well find it hard to prove a case in professional negligence based on misinterpreted instructions.

Logically, if plain language helps reduce errors it should also help reduce litigation about the meaning of documents. Anecdotal evidence suggests that this is indeed the case. For example, the company solicitor for NRMA Insurance (one of Australia's first plain language insurance companies) has written:

> When our first Plain English policy wording was released, Mr Justice Reynolds in an address to the Australian Insurance Institute suggested that the reduction of insurance policy wordings to Plain English might be at the expense of legal inexactitude [sic] or, put in another way, might give rise to litigation over particular wordings which would not have arisen had traditional wordings been used. No such increase has occurred – on the contrary litigation has been reduced in this regard.[9]

This is not to say that plain language documents will never produce litigation about meaning: indeed, cases have already arisen.[10] But it seems

---

8 For some examples, see Robert Eagleson, 'Efficiency in Legal Drafting', in *Essays on Legislative Drafting in Honour of J. Q. Ewens*, ed. D. St Kelly (Adelaide University Press, 1990), p. 25.

9 Neville King, 'An Experience with Plain English' (1985) 61 *Current Affairs Bulletin* (January), p. 21. To similar effect, in its submissions to the Australian Parliamentary Inquiry into Commonwealth Legislative and Legal Drafting (18 September 1992), the NRMA stated: 'The NRMA has not experienced any adverse court decisions by reason of the "Plain English" and subsequent "user friendly" documents.'

10 For example, *Ciampa v NRMA Insurance Ltd* (unreported, Supreme Court of NSW, Bryson J, 23 October 1989); *NRMA Insurance Ltd v McCarney* (1992) 7 ANZ Insurance Cases 61–146; *Ross v NRMA Life Ltd* (1993) 7 ANZ Insurance Cases 61–170; *NRMA Insurance Ltd v Collier* (1996) 9 ANZ Insurance Cases 76,717. For reasoned discussions of the possibilities

unlikely that plain language documents will produce court lists as lengthy as those in which judges are asked to discern meaning from documents drafted in the traditional style. As long ago as 1941, an American study showed that, of 500 contract cases decided the previous year, about 25 per cent were traceable to incomplete negotiation by the parties and to poor draftsmanship by the parties or their lawyers.[11]

Image of the legal profession

Another benefit of plain English is its effect on the legal profession's public image. Lawyers have never had a good press; writers frequently lampoon them. A chief source of ridicule is the way in which lawyers draft documents. Lawyers use a language that can only be described as alien: alien to the general public; alien to clients of all kinds; and alien to the educated user of English.[12] Paradoxically, it is also alien to lawyers themselves. Australian surveys show that, given the choice, most practising lawyers prefer plain language.[13] So do most American lawyers, as we saw in Chapter 3.

Legal language has a unique tendency to be wordy, unclear, pompous and dull.[14] It is also impersonal, lacking warmth.[15] Yet, of all professionals, lawyers should have a special affinity with language. Words are the tools of their trade.[16] Nevertheless, a Canadian survey shows that readers find legal language 'seriously incomprehensible'[17] and find legal documents 'difficult/very difficult' to read. It also shows that the general public believes that, of all professionals, lawyers care least about communicating clearly.[18] English research produces similar results.[19]

---

of increased litigation from plain language insurance policies, see L. Squires, 'Autopsy of a Plain English Insurance Contract: Can Plain English Survive Proximate Cause?' (1984) 59 *Washington Law Review*, p. 569; N. Risjord, '"Plain Language" Permission Clauses Spelling Trouble for Insurers' [1990] *Defense Counsel Journal* (January), p. 77; U. Procaccia, 'Readable Insurance Policies: Judicial Regulation and Interpretation' (1979) 74 *Israel Law Review*, p. 74.

11 Harold Shepherd, Book Review, (1948) 1 *Journal of Legal Education*, p. 154.

12 See, for example, Law Reform Commission of Victoria, *Report No. 9: Plain English and the Law*, vol. 1, paras 17 ('barely intelligible to many lawyers') and 24 ('lawyers themselves are sometimes misled').

13 Bron McKillop, 'What Lawyers Think about Plain Legal Language' (1994) 32 *NSW Law Society Journal* (May), p. 68; Michele Asprey, 'Lawyers Prefer Plain Language, Survey Finds', ibid. (November), p. 76. There are exceptions: see, for example, W. O. Caldwell, 'Be Conservative or Risk It?', ibid. (July), p. 66.

14 David Mellinkoff, *The Language of the Law* (Boston: Little, Brown & Co., 1963), ch. III.

15 See Mark Adler, *Clarity for Lawyers*, p. 1.

16 See Glanville Williams, 'Language and the Law' (1945) 61 *Law Quarterly Review*, p. 71.

17 Robert Benson, 'The End of Legalese: the Game is Over' (1984–85) 13 *Review of Law and Social Change*, p. 532.

18 Survey carried out by the Plain Language Institute of British Columbia: see its *Preliminary Report, 'Critical Opinions: the Public's View of Legal Documents'* (1992), pp. 18, 26.

19 Mark Adler, 'Bamboozling the Public' [1991] *New Law Journal*, p. 1032.

The image of the legal profession would be greatly enhanced if lawyers used plain language. As a former president of the Law Society of England and Wales said in his presidential address to the society's 1984 national conference:

> Few things have done more to drive people from our doors than our inability both in documents and in letters and speech to express ourselves in clear simple English. As Professor Felsenfeld has said 'Lawyers have two common failings. One is that they do not write well, and the other is that they think they do.' It is not the mark of a learned man to express himself in language which others cannot understand; it is the sign of a fool who cannot think clearly.[20]

Marketing

Related to issues of image, plain language can be a valuable marketing tool. Many businesses such as insurance companies and banks now treat comprehensible language as a virtue, to be trumpeted in public advertising: 'come to us because you can understand our documents'. Lawyers too can market their plain language skills. Many of the larger law firms already do so, with partners publishing widely in law-related journals.[21]

Compliance with statutory requirements

Chapter 3 discussed some of the US laws compelling the use of plain language in certain documents. Many other jurisdictions have passed laws requiring specified documents to be in plain language. Whatever the jurisdiction, these laws illustrate a phenomenon that does no credit to the legal profession: parliamentary intervention to compel recalcitrant lawyers to depart from their traditional style in favour of plainer, more accessible drafting.

Here we consider briefly some of the legislation in the United Kingdom and Australia requiring the use of plain language in some contexts. In these countries, as in others which have passed similar laws, the legislation brings with it drafting opportunities for those skilled in plain language techniques.

---

20 Arthur Hoole (1984) 81 *Law Society's Gazette*, p. 2817. The Felsenfeld quotation is from 'The Plain English Movement in the United States' (1981–82) 6 *Canadian Business Law Journal*, p. 413, originally a paper delivered at the University of Toronto in 1981.
21 Australian examples include: E. Kerr, 'Plain Language: Is it Legal?' (1991) 29 *NSW Law Society Journal* (June), p. 52; David Colenso, 'Plain English Leases – Clearly Better Leases' (1996) 26 *Queensland Law Society Journal* (April), p. 157; David Kelly, 'Plain English: An Underestimated Task?' (1999) 43 *Clarity*, p. 5; Steve Palyga, 'Is it Safer to Use Legalese or Plain English? What the Judges Say', ibid., p. 46.

The United Kingdom

An example in the United Kingdom is the Unfair Terms in Consumer Contracts Regulations 1999,[22] implementing a directive of the European Commission. Essentially, the regulations provide that a consumer is not bound by a standard term with a seller or supplier if that term is unfair. By regulation 7:

(1) A seller or supplier shall ensure that any written term of a contract is expressed in plain, intelligible language.
(2) If there is doubt about the meaning of a written term, the interpretation which is most favourable to the consumer shall prevail ...

This provision, which may have been inspired in part by the plain language movement in English-speaking countries,[23] is not without its difficulties – in particular, the word 'intelligible'. 'Intelligible to whom?', one may ask.[24]

By regulation 10, the Office of Fair Trading is primarily responsible for enforcing the regulations. The head of the office's Unfair Contract Terms Unit has written that that the office is yet to find a legal concept that defies translation into plain language.[25] The office urges:

- the use of ordinary words
- a transparent style and structure
- legibility
- abandoning cross-references to statutes and the consumer rights under them
- jettisoning general phrases like 'this does not affect your statutory rights' and exclusions like 'to the greatest extent permitted by law'.

The office publishes regular bulletins on cases where traders have dropped or amended terms as a result of enforcement action.[26]

Given the limited wording of the regulations, their application to documents creating or transferring interests in land is open to doubt.[27]

---

22 SI 1999 No. 2083, revoking and replacing SI 1994 No. 3159.
23 See Ewoud Hondius, 'EC Directive on Unfair Terms in Consumer Contracts: Towards a European Law of Contract' (1994) 7 *Journal of Contract Law*, p. 42.
24 Meryll Dean, 'Unfair Contract Terms: The European Approach' (1993) 56 *Modern Law Review*, p. 5581. See also Francis Bennion, 'Opposites Attract' [1997] *New Law Journal*, p. 684 (commenting on a discussion of the regulations by Tracey Reeves, 'Opposites Attract: Plain English with a European Interpretation', ibid., p. 576).
25 Ray Wooley, 'Plainly Unfair' (1998) 68 *Adviser*, p. 36.
26 Some of these are detailed in Sheila Bone and Steve Wilson, 'Contract terms, fairness and the consumer' [1998] *Solicitors Journal*, p. 346. See also J. E. Adams, 'Unfair Contract Terms – The Conveyancer and the Regulations' [1999] Conv 8.
27 See, for example, Rex Newman and Clive Halperin, 'Fair Enough?' (1995) 139 *Solicitors Journal*, p. 632.

However, whether as the result of the regulations or not, a shift to plain language is evident in a number of important conveyancing documents used in England. These include:

- the Standard Conditions of Sale
- the Law Society's business leases
- mortgage conditions of several large lenders
- the Standard Commercial Property Conditions (1999)
- the British Property Federation's short-term commercial lease (1999).

The Standard Commercial Property Conditions follow the same pattern as the earlier Standard Conditions of Sale. Both are logically ordered, written in a style that is plain and direct, and reject *shall*. (The similarity is perhaps to be expected, as both result from a joint endeavour between the Law Society of England and Wales and Oyez Forms Publishing.) Likewise, the British Property Federation's lease is a bold attempt to provide industry-standard documentation. It is in simple form, to ensure comprehension by a wide audience. While not as radical as the Law Society's business lease or Aldridge's *Practical Lease Precedents*,[28] it shares many of the same features: clear layout, direct language, and no superfluous provisions.

Finally, on the subject of leases, since 1995 there has been a Code of Practice for commercial property leases in England and Wales. Endorsed by a number of major organisations,[29] it states that

as far as possible leases should:
(a) be written clearly in plain language and in a manner which can be understood by people other than lawyers;
(b) be concise and relevant;
(c) link the various parts of the document ... by a proper system of page numbering and cross-referencing so that they can be easily and quickly assimilated;
(d) state explicitly (consistent with the need to be concise) any important legal position relevant to the transaction, for example, that certain consents cannot be unreasonably withheld, even where this is already covered by statute.

Australia

A number of Australian statutes prescribe plain language in certain areas. For example, the New South Wales *Legal Profession Act* requires

---

28 Trevor Aldridge, *Practical Lease Precedents* (London: Sweet & Maxwell, looseleaf).
29 London: RICS Business Services, 1995, Association of British Insurers, British Council for Offices, British Property Federation, British Retail Consortium, Confederation of British Industry, Federation of Small Businesses, Incorporated Society of Valuers and Auctioneers, Law Society, Property Market Reform Group, Royal Institution of Chartered Surveyors.

fee disclosures by lawyers to 'be made in writing and be expressed in clear plain language'.[30] Consumer credit legislation in all states requires contracts and notices by credit providers to be 'easily legible' and 'clearly expressed'.[31] Commonwealth insurance legislation requires insurers to 'clearly inform' prospective insured persons of their duty of disclosure when taking out insurance,[32] a requirement that has been held to require not only that the information be clearly expressed but also that it be adequately brought to the insured's attention.[33] The Queensland *Workplace Relations Act* 1997, s 348, requires the Queensland Industrial Relations Commission to ensure that its written decisions are 'in plain English' and 'structured in a way that makes a decision as easy to understand as the subject matter allows'. And the Commonwealth *Industrial Relations Reform Act* 1993 requires the Commonwealth Industrial Relations Commission to vary industrial awards that are not 'expressed in plain English', or are not 'structured in a way that is as easy to understand as the subject matter allows', or that prescribe matters 'in unnecessary detail'.[34]

Less directly, consumer protection legislation both at Commonwealth and state level empowers courts to vary or set aside contracts that are unconscionable or unjust. For example, ss 51AB and 51AC of the *Trade Practices Act* 1974 (Cth) proscribe conduct in trade or commerce that is 'unconscionable'. Under both sections, in deciding whether conduct is 'unconscionable', the court may have regard to (among other matters) 'whether the consumer was able to understand any documents relating to' the transaction. Similarly, under s 7 of the *Contracts Review Act* 1980 (NSW), a court may vary or set aside contracts that are 'unjust' in the circumstances in which they are made. Under s 9, in considering a contract that is wholly or partly in writing, the court may have regard to (among other things) 'the physical form of the contract, and the intelligibility of the language in which it is expressed'. The case law which has developed under these and comparable provisions indicates that courts look closely at the language in which contracts are couched, and particularly take into account the impediments to understanding posed by documents drafted in the traditional style.[35]

---

30 1987 (NSW), s 179(1).

31 For example, Consumer Credit (NSW) Code, s 162.

32 *Insurance Contracts Act* 1984 (Cth), s 22(1).

33 *Suncorp General Insurance Ltd v Cheihk* (1999) 10 ANZ Insurance Cases 61–442 at 75,024.

34 *Industrial Relations Reform Act* 1993 (Cth), s 17, inserting a new provision, s 150A, into the *Industrial Relations Act* 1988 (Cth). Compare Lord Diplock's lament in *Merkur Island Shipping Corporation v Laughton* [1983] AC 570 at 612, that the law 'should be expressed in terms that can easily be understood by those who have to apply it even at shop floor level'.

35 Cases include: *National Australia Bank Ltd v Nobile* (1988) ATPR 40–855; *Bridge Wholesale Acceptance (Australia) Ltd v GVS Associates Pty Ltd* [1991] ASC 57,116; *Goldsbrough v Ford Credit Australia Ltd* [1989] ASC 58,583; *National Australia Bank Ltd v Hall* [1993] ASC 56–234. Compare J. Goldring, 'Certainty in Contracts, Unconscionability and the Trade Practices Act: The Effect of Section 52A' (1986) 11 *Sydney Law Review*, p. 529, arguing that, since the *Contracts Review Act* requires all the circumstances to be taken into account, this provision should not be taken as a general injunction to use plain English documentation.

Indeed, even in the absence of statutory provisions of this kind, it can be argued that the law has evolved to the point that courts take factors such as these into account in deciding whether to set aside contracts on the equitable ground of unconscionability.[36] If correct, this argument gives the lie to the premise (discussed in Chapter 1) that safety lies in retaining traditional forms of legal drafting. US courts have held that elements in establishing unconscionability include:

- hiding clauses which are disadvantageous to one party in a 'mass of fine print trivia' or in places which are inconspicuous to the party signing the contract
- phrasing clauses in language that is incomprehensible to a lay reader or that divert the lay reader's attention from the problems they raise or the rights they extinguish.[37]

Conclusion

A legal document has several functions. The primary one is to carry out a legal purpose, but there are others: to communicate, to inform, and to persuade. A legal document creates a private law for the parties, governing their relationship for a specified time and for a specified purpose. In laying down that private law, there is no good reason to use any language other than plain, modern English.

The traditional legal document is a communication from lawyer to lawyer. The reform movement in legal drafting reminds us that it is also a communication from lawyer to client. Specialists can talk to specialists in special language if they wish. An expert in heraldry may describe an armorial bearing to another expert in language which is precise and unambiguous, and unintelligible to the uninitiated; nothing much turns on the unintelligibility of their coded language to outsiders. But law is different. Law is involved with the whole world, with life and with people. Legal language should no more be confined to coded messages than language generally.

Modern, plain English is as capable of precision as traditional legal English. It can cope with all the concepts and complexities of the law and legal processes. The few technical terms that the lawyer might feel compelled to retain for convenience or necessity can be incorporated without destroying the document's integrity. The modern English of a legal document will never read like a good novel, but it can be attractive and effective in a clean, clear, functional style.

---

36 Examples include: *Commercial Bank of Australia Ltd v Amadio* (1983) 151 CLR 447; *Creswell v Potter* [1978] 1 WLR 255, especially at 260.

37 *Willie v Southwestern Bell Telephone Company* 549 P 2d 903 at 907 (1976).

5   What to Avoid when Drafting Modern Documents

In the preceding chapters we examined the influences that tend to perpetuate the traditional style of legal drafting. We also considered the ways in which legal documents are interpreted. We traced the move towards plain legal language and explored some of the benefits of using modern, standard English. Now we move to examine more closely the techniques of drafting in modern, standard English: the 'how to'. The best way to begin is by considering what *not* to do – the techniques the drafter should *avoid*. And so this chapter highlights those aspects of the traditional style that should be shunned by the legal drafter who wants to move to a clear, modern style.

It is not difficult to identify the characteristics of traditional legal documents that are to be avoided. Here are some of the more common:

* wordiness and redundancy
* overuse of the modal verb 'shall'
* obscure language
* unusual word order
* constantly litigated words and phrases
* foreign words and phrases
* unduly long sense-bites
* legalese and jargon
* peculiar linguistic conventions
* use of noun phrases in place of verbs
* overuse of the passive
* deeming
* poor use of definitions
* overuse of capitals
* careless use of provisos.

This list of characteristics is not exhaustive. But all are found, to a greater or lesser degree, in traditionally drafted legal documents. We will consider each in turn.

Wordiness and redundancy

Wordiness is the legal profession's most recognisable characteristic, redundancy its strongest point. Lawyers really do go on. Their motto might be: 'Never use one word where you can use two; and the more you use, the better.' As an American judge has put it: 'The legal mind finds magnetic attraction in redundancy and overkill.'[1]

These characteristics of wordiness and redundancy give legal writing its distinctiveness. Yet they are almost always unnecessary, both linguistically and legally. They serve only to dull the reader. They are seen most often in common doublets like 'null and void', 'goods and chattels', 'fit and proper', 'storm and tempest', 'well and sufficiently', 'agreed and declared'. (The tautological nature of some of these doublets was discussed in Chapter 1.) But they are also seen in forms of repetition that are longer and more ambitious. Consider, for example, the following typical lease provision, setting out some of the tenant's rights:

> TOGETHER WITH the right in common with the Landlord and all others having the like right to use for the purpose of ingress to and egress from the Flat the pathway leading thereto from Grenville Road and also the right to use the yard at the rear of the Flat and the washing line situate therein
>
> TOGETHER WITH the free and uninterrupted use of all gas water electricity and other pipes wires flues drains passing in through or under any part of the property but excepting and reserving to the Landlord and the person or persons for the time being occupying any other part or parts of the property (a) the free and uninterrupted use of gas water electricity drainage telephone supply and other pipes wires flues conduits and drains in through and under the Flat (b) the right to install or renew any such services causing as little disturbance as possible and making good any damage forthwith.

This wordiness springs from a spurious attempt at precision. The drafter hopes, by piling word on word, to cover every conceivable circumstance, as if to ensure exactitude by sheer weight of verbiage. But the reality is that the tenant's rights could have been expressed much more simply and just as efficaciously:

> With the right to use (along with other users)
> - the path between the flat and Grenville Road
> - the yard behind the flat
> - the washing line in the yard

---

1 *Coca Cola Bottling Co. v Reeves* 486 So 2d 374 at 383–4 (Miss. 1986; Robertson J).

- all service conduits and wires running in any part of the property

but reserving[2] to the landlord and occupiers of other parts of the property

- the use of all service conduits and wires running in the flat
- the right to install or renew any service conduits and wires serving the flat, but causing as little disturbance as possible and repairing any damage straight away.

This would reduce the original 150 words to about 90, gaining clarity without losing precision.

Repairing covenants in leases also commonly exhibit the same excessive wordiness. The following clause was the subject of litigation in England:

> When where and so often as occasion shall require well and sufficiently to repair renew rebuild uphold support sustain maintain pave purge scour cleanse glaze empty amend and keep the premises and every part thereof (including all fixtures and additions thereto) and all floors walls columns roofs canopies lifts and escalators (including all motors and machinery therefor) shafts stairways fences pavements forecourts drains sewers ducts flues conduits wires cables gutters soil and other pipes tanks cisterns pumps and other water and sanitary apparatus thereon with all needful and necessary amendments whatsoever (damage by any of the insured risks excepted so long as the lessor's policy or policies of insurance in respect thereof shall not have become vitiated or payment of the policy moneys be refused in whole or in part in consequence of some act or default of the lessee) and to keep all water pipes and water fittings in the premises protected from frost and to be responsible in all respects for all damage caused to the premises or to the said buildings or any part thereof or to the neighbouring property or to the respective owners or occupiers thereof through the bursting overflowing or stopping up of such pipes and fittings occasioned by or through the neglect of the lessee or its servants or agents.

This clause is replete with tautology, both linguistic and legal. No doubt its verbosity was prompted by a desire for precision. Yet despite all its words, the parties ended up in court disputing the extent of the obligation to 'repair'.[3]

Often a repairing covenant spells out that the tenant must not only 'repair' but must also 'put into repair'. This is strictly unnecessary, for an obligation 'to repair' generally includes an obligation to put into repair.[4] Likewise, a repairing covenant generally includes an obligation to rebuild

---

2 The original uses 'excepting and reserving'. Chapter 1 noted the technical distinction between an 'exception' and a 'reservation'. The indiscriminate conjunction of the terms here shows that the drafter is unlikely to have appreciated the distinction.

3 *Ravenseft Properties Ltd v Davstone (Holdings) Ltd* [1980] QB 12.

4 See *Foster v Day* (1968) 208 EG 495.

following wilful neglect or destruction by the party obliged to 'repair', to decorate where necessary, and to keep clear of vermin. But these also are strictly unnecessary, being comprehended by a general obligation to 'repair'.[5] So, although most current repairing covenants are much more fulsome than merely requiring the tenant to 'repair', the extra words usually add nothing. Indeed, by expressing the tenant's duties in over-particular ways, added words can be counterproductive, since they may serve to exclude what would otherwise be implied (see the discussion of the *expressio unius* rule in Chapter 2).

Excessive wordiness is also commonly found in grants of rights of way. The grantee is given 'the full right to pass and repass on foot or with or without vehicles along and over the footpaths and roads respectively of the said Estate'. Is this any different from 'a right of way, on foot or with vehicles, over the footpaths and roads of the Estate'?[6]

Overuse of 'shall'

Shall is the hallmark of traditional legal writing. Whenever lawyers want to express themselves in formal style, *shall* intrudes. The word litters most precedent books, and finds its way into wills, conveyances, leases, and all types of contracts.

In traditional legal documents, *shall* serves many purposes. They include the following (with examples drawn from documents drafted in the traditional style):

- To impose a duty: 'The Distributor *shall* keep in good and saleable condition a stock of the Goods.'
- To grant a right: 'A purchaser *shall* have the right to cancel the purchase transaction until midnight.'
- To give a direction: 'The receipt of a person who appears to be a proper officer of the charity *shall* be a discharge to my Trustees.'
- To state circumstances: 'The said restrictions *shall* be binding on the property hereby assured and the owner of owners thereof from time to time but the Purchasers *shall* not be personally liable for any breach thereof occurring after they *shall* have parted with all interest in the land in respect of which the breach *shall* occur.'

---

5 *Manchester Bonded Warehouse Co. v Carr* (1880) 5 CPD 507 at 512 (obligation to rebuild on wilful neglect or destruction); *Proudfoot v Hart* (1890) 25 QBD 42 at 53–5, 56 (obligation to decorate when necessary). See also *Jones v Joseph* (1918) 87 LJKB 510 (obligation to keep clear of vermin).

6 Even here, the reference to access 'on foot' is strictly unnecessary, since a right of vehicular use includes a right of pedestrian use, permitting the grantee to walk along the roads as well as the footpaths: *Davies v Stephens* (1836) 7 C & P 570.

- To create a condition precedent (a 'precondition'): 'If the Vendor *shall* within one month of the receipt of such notice give written notice ...'.
- To create a condition subsequent: 'If in any circumstances my said intended marriage *shall* not have been solemnised within the period of six months from the date hereof then at the end of that period this my said will *shall* become void.'
- To express the future: 'The waiver of the observance and performance of the said covenant *shall* terminate on the disposal of the said property.'
- To negate a duty or discretion: 'The Vendor *shall* not be bound to show any title to boundaries fences ditches or walls.'
- To negate a right: 'Such statement *shall* be deemed to be correct and *shall* be binding on the Client.'
- To express intention: 'The said wall when erected *shall* be deemed to be a party wall.'

This list is not exhaustive. Like the categories of negligence, the categories of *shall* are not closed. Often, in the one document, *shall* serves a number of purposes. There may be a primary purpose, with subsidiary purposes; or two or three purposes may carry equal weight.

To the lawyer, a chief attraction of *shall* is its flexibility. But this flexibility is also a source of danger, for it may lead to legitimate argument about which use of *shall* was intended. And so the primary objection to *shall* is not merely that it is archaic and marks out formal legal English from modern standard English, but that its use can lead to confusion – which in turn can lead to disaster for client and lawyer alike.

Judicial authority on *shall* centres on two prime areas. The first concerns the difference between futurity and a precondition. The second concerns the difference between an obligation and a direction.

Futurity or precondition?

The issue here is the relationship of a triggering event to the date of the document: can a triggering event already have taken place by the time the document is written, even though the document may not come into effect until much later? On one line of authorities, typified by *Re Walker*,[7] the answer is 'no', because *shall* necessarily implies futurity. On this view, a *shall* provision relates only to the period after the document's date; it speaks only of events occurring after the document comes into existence. But on a contrary line of authorities, based on *Loring v Thomas*,[8] the answer is 'yes', because a *shall* provision is a mere description of a state of

---

7 [1930] 1 Ch 469.
8 (1861) 30 LJ Ch 789.

affairs at a later date, setting out a precondition to some other occurrence. On this second view, something which has already happened before the document's date can be a triggering event.

To illustrate the different approaches, consider the following clause from a partnership deed:

> If any partner shall become bankrupt, the other partners may terminate the partnership.

Can the partnership be terminated on the ground that a partner was already bankrupt at the date of the partnership agreement? According to *Re Walker*, 'no', because *shall* indicates that the parties have in mind a bankruptcy occurring *after* the date of the partnership deed. According to *Loring v Thomas*, 'yes', because the precondition to termination is bankruptcy, *whenever* it occurs.

The problem is acute in the case of wills, which come into effect not when they are signed but when the testator dies. Wills commonly contain references such as 'who shall die in my lifetime' or 'who shall predecease me' or the like – as in a bequest to the children of those 'who shall die in my lifetime' or to the children of those 'who shall predecease me'. On the first line of authorities, the phrase does not encompass the children of persons already dead at the date of the will.[9] Likewise, the phrase 'who shall be born' would usually exclude persons born before the date of the will.[10]

In *Re Walker*, Lord Hanworth MR said that the 'natural meaning' of *shall* was 'as a word of futurity'.[11] However, that 'natural meaning' clearly did not commend itself to the judges in the *Loring v Thomas* line of cases.[12] An example is *Metcalfe v Williams*,[13] which concerned a substitutionary gift drafted in these terms: if a child of the testator 'shall die in my [that is, the testator's] lifetime', then that child's share should pass to that child's children. A son of the testator had died before the testator made his will. Were the children of that son entitled to the share which

---

9 See, for example, *Christopherson v Naylor* (1816) 1 Mer 320; 35 ER 693; *Gorringe v Mahlstedt* [1907] AC 225; *Re Cope* [1908] 2 Ch 1, CA; *Re Brown* [1917] 2 Ch 232; *Re Walker* [1930] 1 Ch 469 (Eve J and CA); *Re McPherson* [1968] VR 368; *Re Rowlands* [1973] VR 225. See also *Bateman's Will Trusts* [1970] 3 All ER 817 (Pennycuick V-C) ('as shall be stated by me').

10 *Gibbons v Gibbons* (1881) 6 App Cas 471.

11 *Re Walker* [1930] All ER Rep 392 at 395, CA. This passage did not find its way into the authorised report, [1930] 1 Ch 469; but it appears in other reports of the case: (1930) 99 LJ Ch 225 at 228; (1930) 142 LT 472 at 474.

12 *Loring v Thomas* (1861) 30 LJ Ch 789; *Re Birchall* [1940] 1 All ER 545, CA; *Re Lambert* [1908] 2 Ch 117; *Barraclough v Cooper* [1908] 2 Ch 121n, HL; *Re Metcalfe* [1909] 1 Ch 424; *Re Sheppard* (1855) 1 K & J 269; 69 ER 459; *Re Rayner* (1925) 134 LT 141; *Re Halliday* [1925] SASR 104; *Re Sewell* [1929] SASR 226; *Re Booth's Will Trusts* (1940) 163 LT 77.

13 [1914] 2 Ch 61, CA.

their father would have taken had he survived the testator? The court held 'yes'. Likewise, a surrender of copyhold land[14] to such uses as a certain person (the testator) 'shall' by will direct was held to apply to a will executed before the surrender, since the court considered that the surrender referred to whatever will was in existence at the testator's death.[15] So also a clause in a trust deed divesting property from the donee if the donee 'shall become bankrupt' was held to mean simply 'being bankrupt'; it was immaterial whether the bankruptcy occurred before or after the date of the trust deed.[16] And in a recent Australian case, a statute provided that where an insurance policy indemnified a person against liability, the amount of the liability 'shall ... be a charge' on the insurance moneys payable in respect of that liability. The insurer argued that *shall* here required a construction that the charge arose only where the event insured against arose after the policy came into existence: that is, *shall* required an element of futurity. The court rejected this argument, holding that the charge arose even where the event insured against occurred before the policy was taken out: that is, *shall* here did not import any element of futurity, but merely described an existing legal result.[17]

These differing conclusions on the effect of *shall* point up the dangers in its uncritical use. They illustrate the folly in assuming that *shall* is a word of legal precision, with a certain and sure meaning. Ultimately, whether *shall* is read as importing a necessary element of futurity or merely a precondition (whether occurring before or after the date of the document) depends entirely on context, each case turning on its own particular circumstances – a factor introducing easy potential for litigation. As Lord Greene MR said in *Re Donald*, concerning the use of *shall*:

> A number of cases have been cited. I find no assistance in scrutinising the exact language of those cases and comparing it with the language used in this case. In cases dealing with the construction of wills a comparison in, so to speak, parallel columns between the language used in wills which have been the subject of decided cases and that used in the will before the court does not often lead to a useful result. On the contrary, it very often tends to confuse.[18]

---

14 The appropriate way of transferring copyhold land (which is now obsolete) was by surrendering the land to the lord of the manor, followed by a regrant to the intended transferee.

15 *Spring v Biles* (1783) 1 TR 435n at 437 (99 ER 1182n at 1184), Lord Mansfield: 'A will speaks at different times for different purposes; to many purposes from the date; to other purposes from the testator's death.'

16 *Manning v Chambers* (1847) 1 De G & Sm 282 (69 ER 1069), interpreted in *Seymour v Lucas* (1860) 29 LJ Ch 841 (Kindersley V-C). See also *Re Akeroyd's Settlement* [1893] 3 Ch. 363.

17 *FAI General Insurance Co. Ltd v McSweeney* (1997) 73 FCR 379 (Fed Ct, Australia, Lindgren J).

18 [1947] 1 All ER 764 at 766, CA.

If it is necessary to express the future, what word should be used? Most modern drafters, seeing the difficulties in *shall*, use *will* instead. But of course, this is not without difficulties of its own. *Will* carries as many problems as *shall*, for although normally denoting futurity it can also denote compulsion,[19] an issue to which we now turn.

Direction or obligation?

Courts usually construe *shall* as creating an obligation. Sometimes, though, they construe it as giving a mere direction.[20] To illustrate: in *Halley v Watt*,[21] a Scottish statute provided (in a section headed 'Jury trial in Sheriff Court') that in an employee's action for damages against an employer either party could require that 'the cause shall be tried before a jury'. This provision was held to give a *right* to that mode of trial, regardless of the court's view about the suitability of the case for trial by jury: in effect, *shall* was mandatory. In contrast, in *R v Craske, ex parte Metropolitan Police Commissioner*,[22] a provision that 'the court shall proceed to the summary trial' (that is, a trial without a jury) was held to be directory only, and did not deprive the court of the power to allow the accused to elect for trial by jury instead of summary trial.

Shall has even been found in the same section of a statute both to impose a duty and to grant a right.[23] This result has been called curious,[24] but it is far from unknown.[25] For example, in *Hatton v Beaumont* the Australian High Court held that paragraph (a) of a liquor licensing regulation, which stated that an appellant 'shall lodge ... a notice of his intention to appeal ... within twenty-one days' of the decision appealed against, was mandatory. Yet the court also held that paragraph (e) of the same regulation, which stated that the appellant 'shall within seven days of lodging his notice of appeal deposit the sum of ten pounds or enter into a recognisance with one surety in the sum of ten pounds', was directory only, the appeal not being vitiated by its non-observance.[26]

---

19 See *Rayfield v Hands* [1958] 2 All ER 194 ('will' imposes obligation); *Hector Steamship Co. Ltd v VO Sovfracht Moscow* [1945] KB 343 ('will' equals 'is bound to').
20 For examples, see *Stroud's Judicial Dictionary*, 5th edn, ed. John S. James (London: Sweet & Maxwell, 1986), pp. 2403–11.
21 [1956] SLT 111.
22 [1957] 2 QB 591.
23 *Cooke v New River Co.* (1888) 38 Ch D 56, CA; on appeal (1889) 14 App Cas 698 at 699 (Lord Herschell): 'My lords, it has been my lot to construe many Acts of Parliament which were obscurely worded, but I do not think I ever met with one upon which it was more impossible to put a satisfactory construction than the statute with which we have to deal in the present case.'
24 By the editor of *Stroud's Judicial Dictionary*, at p. 2409.
25 See George Coode, *On Legislative Expression*, 2nd edn (1852), pp. 17, 31; reprinted in E. Driedger, *The Composition of Legislation* (Ottawa: Department of Justice, 1976).
26 (1978) 20 ALR 314.

Here too, the differing senses of *shall* point up the dangers inherent in its uncritical use. As with the futurity/precondition dichotomy, so also the obligation/direction dichotomy serves as a warning to those who assume that *shall*, so hallowed by usage, is necessarily precise. We return to the obligation/direction dichotomy in Chapter 6, where we consider whether *shall* has any place in a modern legal document.

Obscure language

Obscure language should be an anathema in all legal writing, yet it abounds in legal documents. Lawyers may defend the language they use on the ground that it is necessary for legal efficacy, but legal efficacy and obscurity are strange bedfellows indeed. So too are obscurity and precision. Almost always, simple language has just as much legal effect as obscure language, and it can be just as precise.

To illustrate, consider this description of leased property, drawn from an actual lease:

> ALL THOSE offices and toilet on the second floor of the building at Mill Lane shown for the purpose of identification only edged red on the plan annexed hereto (hereinafter called 'the Building')

This language is simply the product of habit. It is justified neither by legal necessity nor by precision. The words are intended to describe the leased property, which was the whole of the second floor in the building, and nothing more than the second floor. The drafter apparently inserted the references to 'the Building' and 'edged red on the plan' because, from a bird's-eye view, the boundaries of the building and of the floor to be let were identical. But it would surely have been clearer to say:

> ALL THOSE offices and toilet (on the second floor of 'the Building' at Mill Lane) shown for the purpose of identification only edged red on the plan annexed hereto.

Once this stage is reached, unnecessary words and phrases could have been deleted in an attempt to write literate, modern English. Unnecessary words and phrases are: 'All those', 'the purpose of', 'hereto'. The word 'only' is also strictly unnecessary, because 'shown for identification' surely means shown for identification and not for any other purpose; and in any case, the whole phrase 'shown for identification' can be replaced with 'shown'. Also, we could define 'the building' and 'the plan' elsewhere. We could then describe the property as:

The offices and toilet on the second floor of the building and shown edged red on the plan.

Unusual word order

Lawyers often adopt an unusual word order. Here are some typical examples taken from traditionally drafted documents:

- 'title absolute'
- 'for the time being entitled'
- 'from time to time and at all times during the said lease well and substantially to repair'
- 'such documents as the vendor is required by legislation to furnish'
- 'as well before as after any judgment'
- 'as in this deed provided'
- 'that the tenant paying the rents hereby reserved and performing and observing the several covenants on its part herein contained shall peaceably hold and enjoy the leased property'
- 'the title above mentioned'
- 'therein appearing'
- 'will at the cost of the borrowers forthwith comply with the same'
- 'and may thereafter upon the demised premises or on some part thereof in the name of the whole re-enter'
- 'being then a licensed moneylender'.

Examples such as these cause little trouble for lawyers, for whom inverting word order becomes second nature. But they trouble the non-lawyer, unfamiliar with such linguistic eccentricities.

Separating parts of a verb

A particular source of difficulty is the device of widely separating two parts of a verb. Sense may well be lost, as in this clause:

> In the event of any breach by the Cardholder of this agreement the Bank *may* in circumstances where the Principal Cardholder fails to comply or to procure compliance with the terms of a notice served by the Bank upon the Principal Cardholder *require* repayment in full of the outstanding balance on the Account.

The verb combination here is 'may require', but the modal auxiliary 'may' is separated from its associated main verb 'require' by twenty-seven words. The whole passage contains only fifty-three words, so the verb is split by more than half the total words – no wonder the reader is thrown.

It would have been better first to state what the bank has power to do, and then to specify the circumstances in which it is entitled to exercise that power. The result would look something like this (stripping out the unnecessary capitals):

> The bank may require repayment in full of the balance on the account if the cardholder breaks this agreement and the principal cardholder fails to comply with the terms of a notice served by the bank.

Consider also this example, cited in Gowers, *The Complete Plain Words*,[27] involving a split infinitive. The 'rule' against splitting the infinitive is not followed as strongly today as it once was. But in this example the crescendo of splitting is so extreme that it hinders comprehension:

> The tenant hereby agrees:
> (i) *to pay* the said rent;
> (ii) *to* properly *clean* all the windows;
> (iii) *to* at all times properly *empty* all closets;
> (iv) *to* immediately any litter or disorder shall have been made by him or for his purpose on the staircase or landings or any other part of the said building or garden *remove* the same.

Constantly litigated words and phrases

Chapter 2 discussed the dangers in over-reliance on precedent as an aid to interpretation. Traditional legal drafters tend to assume that well-litigated words and phrases should be retained, in the belief that documents benefit from this judicial exegesis on meaning. However, it would be more logical to be suspicious of constantly litigated words and phrases, for the very fact of litigation suggests an inherent problem with meaning. Any word or phrase that has produced frequent litigation should surely be shunned. Let us consider two examples, familiar to all legal drafters: 'best endeavours' and 'forthwith'.

'Best endeavours' is commonly used by contracting parties who promise to use their 'best endeavours' to carry out a particular act. Sometimes the use of the phrase suggests a compromise, neither party being willing to accept a clear and unambiguous statement of their respective obligations.[28] This can been seen in the following example, taken from an English case:

> The sellers will use their best endeavours to secure delivery of the goods on the estimated delivery dates from time to time furnished, but they do not

27 Rev. edn (London: Penguin, 1987), p. 145.
28 M. D. Varcoe-Cocks, 'Best Endeavours' (1986) 83 *Law Society Gazette*, p. 1992.

guarantee time of delivery, nor shall they be liable for any damages or claim of any kind in respect of delay in delivery.[29]

The phrase is not confined to contracts. It is used in various contexts, including letters, statutes, and professional undertakings. Drafters who use it should recognise its inherent vagueness. Goff J put it plainly in 1972, when he asked rhetorically whether anything could be less specific or more uncertain than an exhortation to use 'best endeavours'; in his view, there was absolutely no criterion by which best endeavours were to be judged.[30] The numerous cases on the meaning of the phrase support this view.[31] In professional undertakings its use is particularly dangerous, given the inherent vagueness and open-endedness it introduces into the obligation undertaken. For this reason, the Law Society of England and Wales has warned solicitors against giving a 'best endeavours' undertaking.[32]

The word 'forthwith' has also led to a great deal of litigation. It is too open-ended to admit of certainty. Some of the many judicial discussions are mentioned in the footnote.[33]

---

29 This was the contractual term considered in *Monkland v Jack Barclay Ltd* [1951] 1 All ER 714, CA.

30 *Bower v Bantam Investments Ltd* [1972] 3 All ER 349 at 355.

31 Judicial discussions of 'best endeavours' and similar obligations over a two-decade period include the following: *Secured Income Real Estate (Australia) Ltd v St Martins Investments Pty Ltd* (1979) 53 ALJR 745; *Kathopoulos v Bjelica Investments Pty Ltd* (1979) 26 ALR 309; *Heel v Bicknell* (1975) 1 SR (WA) 11; *Steiner v EHD Investments Ltd* (1977) 78 DLR (3d) 449; *Gollin & Co. Ltd v Karenlee Nominees Pty Ltd* [1982] VR 493; *Booker Industries Pty Ltd v Wilson Parking (Qld) Pty Ltd* (1982) 56 ALJR 825 at 826–7; *Meehan v Jones* (1982) 56 ALJR 813 at 821 (considered in *Crumblin v Progress & Properties Pty Ltd* (1983) NSW ConvR 55–142); *Eggins v Tassone* (1983) NSW ConvR 55–120; *Hedlow Holdings Pty Ltd v Manjalda Pty Ltd* (1984) NSW ConvR 55–186; *Laidlaw Pty Ltd v Cleverley* (1972) 25 LGRA 196 at 203; *Glen Ayr Pastoral Pty Ltd v Terry Scott Pty Ltd* (1974) 2 BPR 9215; *Fileman v Liddle* (1974) 2 BPR 9192; *Spencer v Hanson Pastoral Co. Pty Ltd* (1979) 2 BPR 9151; *Wilsher v Flatford Investments Pty Ltd* (1981) 2 BPR 9211; *Great Georgian Realty Group v Genesis Marketing Organization Ltd* (1977) 76 DLR (3d) 592; *Dynamic Transport Ltd v OK Detailing Ltd* (1978) 85 DLR (3d) 19; *Munro v French* (1979) 10 RPR (Can) 179; *Commercial Bank of Australia Ltd v G. H. Dean & Co. Pty Ltd* [1983] 2 Qd R 204; *GR Securities Pty Ltd v Baulkham Hills Private Hospital Pty Ltd* (1986) 40 NSWLR 631 at 635; *CSS Investments Pty Ltd v Lopiron Pty Ltd* (1987) 76 ALR 463; *Contarino v Sciacca* (unreported, Qld FC, 30 October 1987); *IBM United Kingdom Ltd v Rockware Glass Ltd* [1980] FSR 335 at 343 (Buckley LJ), applied in *Hawkins v Pender Bros Pty Ltd* [1990] 1 Qd R 135 at 152; *Parland Pty Ltd v Mariposa Pty Ltd* (1995) 5 Tas R 121 at 132; *Hospital Products Ltd v United States Surgical Corporation* (1984) 156 CLR 41 at 64 (Gibbs J).

32 Nicola Taylor (ed), *The Guide to the Professional Conduct of Solicitors*, 8th edn (London: The Law Society, 1999), p. 355.

33 *Staunton v Wood* (1851) SC 15 Jur 1123 (delivery 'forthwith' could be within 14 days); *Re Southam; ex parte Lamb* (1881) 19 Ch D 169 (notice entered on a Friday and given the following Monday not given 'forthwith'); *Bontex Knitting Works Ltd v St John's Garage* (1943) 60 TLR 253 (one hour's delay in delivery not delivery 'forthwith'); *R v Secretary of State for Social Services; ex parte Child Poverty Action Group*, The Times, 10 October 1988 (duty to submit a social security claim 'forthwith' did not arise until the department was in possession of the basic information to enable a claim to be determined).

To these two examples we could add many more. All give the lie to the belief that judicial exposition of the meaning of a word or phrase demands retention of the word or phrase. In reality, the opposite is often the case. Drafters should beware of constantly litigated words or phrases, lest they incorporate into their documents the very uncertainty that led to the litigation.

Foreign words and phrases

More commonly than ordinary writers, lawyers delight in foreign words and phrases – usually Latin or law-French. Many of these words and phrases have long since disappeared from ordinary English speech and writing. Lawyers themselves may only half-understand them. Examples are:

- *de bene esse*: for the time being (said of something which suffices for now but may be replaced by something better)
- *en ventre sa mere*:[34] conceived but not born
- *force majeure*: an event which can neither be anticipated nor controlled
- *inter alia*: among other things
- *inter se*: among themselves
- *inter vivos*: between living people
- *mutatis mutandis*: with the necessary changes made
- *per stirpes*: by the stocks of descent
- *pro tanto*: to that extent
- *res ipsa loquitur*: the reason is self-evident
- *toties quoties*: as often as required
- *ultra vires*: beyond the powers.

Phrases of this kind are best abandoned, for two reasons. One is that the average reader will not understand them. The second is that their foreign origins convey a sense of precision and technicality which they simply do not possess.[35] Almost always they can be discarded for an equivalent in modern English.

Long sense-bites

Another characteristic of traditional legal drafting is long slabs of unbroken text – long 'sense-bites'. When combined with a deliberate absence of

---

34 A phrase condemned as long ago as 1840 as 'repulsive': Gael, *A Practical Treatise on the Analogy between Legal and General Composition* (Butterworths: London, 1840), p. 29. For a modern parody, see R. Atherton, 'En Ventre sa Frigidaire' (1999) 19 *Legal Studies*, p. 139.

35 For example, see *Delnorth Pty Ltd v State Bank of New South Wales* (1995) 17 ACSR 379 (NSW Sup Ct, Cohen J) on the inherent uncertainty of *mutatis mutandis*; *Schellenberg v Tunnell Holdings Pty Ltd* (2000) 74 ALJR 743, on the precise scope of the doctrine of *res ipsa loquitur*.

punctuation and a lack of paragraphing and indentation, this produces impenetrable text, confounding comprehension. Although not currently in use, an excessive example can be seen in Panel 6, a leviathan clause taken from a standard-form mortgage used by a leading New Zealand bank.

To some extent, old-style documents helped to signal their contents and to guide their readers by putting whole words or phrases in capital letters. Located appropriately, this did much to break up dense text. Typical examples include:

- NOW THIS DEED WITNESSETH
- ALL THAT
- TO HOLD
- PROVIDED THAT
- AND IT IS HEREBY AGREED AND DECLARED
- IN WITNESS.

A typical block of type broken up like this can be seen in Panel 7. Use of capitals in this way (along with the occasional use of brackets) reduced enormously long sentences to a series of shorter passages which, in context, could be digested more easily.

Matters have improved somewhat in recent years. Nowadays, legal documents exhibit much more paragraphing, sub-paragraphing and indentation. Even so, lengthy slabs of text still appear, particularly in conveyancing documents. These formidable blocks of type should be broken up, if not into shorter sentences then certainly into shorter sense-bites. We return to this topic in Chapter 6.

Legalese and jargon

Legalese is more than merely the 'language of lawyers'. Rather, it is the language that lawyers would not use in ordinary communication but for the fact that they are lawyers.[36] Consider the following extract from a letter from one lawyer to another:

> We have now seen our client as regards preliminary enquiries and accordingly return replies to the same herewith together with any enclosures referred to therein.

'Herewith' and 'therein' are pure legalese. So is 'the same', a phrase for which lawyers have a fondness verging on the pathological. ('As regards' is not strictly legalese, since its use is not specific to the legal profession;

---

36 Stanley Robinson, 'Drafting – Its Substance and Teaching' (1973) 25 *Journal of Legal Education*, p. 516.

33. Where the mortgaged property or any part thereof consists of a stratum estate created pursuant to the provisions of the Unit Titles Act 1972 and any amendment thereto (in this clause referred to as "the Act") then without in any way (except as provided in this clause) limiting any of the other provisions of this security all sums properly levied on or recoverable from the Mortgagors in respect of the mortgaged property by the Body Corporate and all and every requirement imposed on the Mortgagors by virtue of the Act or the rules of the Body Corporate or pursuant to any resolution whether unanimous or otherwise of the Body Corporate to be paid observed or performed have been paid observed and performed up to the day of the date of this Mortgage, and the Mortgagors will at all times during the continuance of this security pay all sums properly levied on or recoverable from the Mortgagors in respect of the mortgaged property by the Body Corporate and will observe and perform all and every requirement imposed on the Mortgagors by virtue of the Act or the rules of the Body Corporate or pursuant to any resolution whether unanimous or otherwise of the Body Corporate to be paid observed or performed on the part of the Mortgagors and will keep the Bank indemnified against all actions suits proceedings costs damages claims and demands which may be incurred or sustained by reason of the non-payment of the said sums or any part thereof or by the breach or non-observance or non-performance of the said requirements or any of them and upon any breach or non-observance or non-performance of this covenant the Bank shall be at liberty (but without any obligation so to do) at any time and from time to time to make and do all or any of such payments acts and things as aforesaid on behalf of the Mortgagors AND the Mortgagors shall make all reasonable endeavours to procure that the Body Corporate shall observe and perform all and every requirement imposed on it by the provisions of the Act and by its rules and pursuant to any resolution whether unanimous or otherwise of the Body Corporate. During the continuance of the security it shall be lawful for but not obligatory upon the Bank to exercise the voting rights of the Mortgagors at any meeting of the Body Corporate in accordance with the provisions of the Act and where such voting rights are not exercised by the bank they shall be exercised by the Mortgagors in accordance with such directions as the Bank may give from time to time to the Mortgagors in writing not less than twenty-four hours prior to the meeting or adjourned meeting at which such voting rights are capable of being exercised and if no such direction be given within the time so limited the Mortgagors may exercise such voting rights in such manner subject to the covenant conditions or agreements herein contained or implied as the Mortgagors may think fit. The Mortgagors shall forthwith on receiving notice of any such meeting furnish the Bank with a copy of the notice. The Mortgagors shall during the continuance of this security give to the Bank such information relating to the affairs of the Body Corporate as the Bank shall reasonably require. The Mortgagors will not at any time during the continuance of this security without the previous consent in writing of the Bank signed by any of the Officers of the Bank join in any resolution of the Body Corporate to approve any transfer lease or easement or other dealing affecting the common property or land that is to become part of the common property. The Mortgagors will not at any time during the continuance of this security join in any resolution with the Body Corporate to forgo the insurance to be effected by the Body Corporate pursuant to the Act and if such resolution is now in effect the Mortgagors shall forthwith give written notice to the Body Corporate that the Mortgagors require such insurance cover paid and provided that for the purpose of construing Clause 5 of this security any insurance effected by the Body Corporate in respect of the mortgaged property pursuant to the Act shall be deemed to have been effected by the Mortgagors notwithstanding that it is not in the name of the Bank and that the bank alone may not have the power to settle compromise and recover any claim against the insurance company with which the insurance has been effected. The Mortgagors will not during the continuance of this security without the previous consent in writing of the bank signed by any of the Officers of the Bank either alone or together with the other proprietors of Units make any application to the District Land Registrar pursuant to the Act to cancel the unit plan and will (unless the Bank otherwise requests) make all reasonable endeavours to procure that the Body Corporate or the administrator will not make the application to the High Court for an order cancelling the unit plan pursuant to the Act and the making of any such application without such consent as aforesaid shall be deemed to constitute a default in the performance or observance of the terms of these presents AND the Mortgagors will not during the continuance of this security without the previous consent in writing of the bank signed by any Officers of the Bank make any application to the District Land Registrar for the deposit of a plan of redevelopment pursuant to the Act or join in making such application or in any resolution of the Body Corporate to make such application. The Mortgagors will not during the continuance of this security without the previous consent in writing of the Bank signed by any of the Officers of the Bank make any application to the High Court for the appointment of an administrator pursuant to the Act and will unless the Bank otherwise requests make all reasonable efforts to procure that the Body Corporate shall not make such application. In any case where the High Court makes an order pursuant to Section 42 or Section 43 of the Act and the Mortgagors did not in the case of an order made pursuant to Section 42 support the resolution or act or in the case of an order made pursuant to Section 43 did support the resolution or act then the making of such order shall be deemed to constitute a default in the performance or observance of the terms of these presents.

Panel 6 Extract of bank mortgage

NOW THIS DEED WITNESSETH as follows:-

1.   IN consideration of the sum of Nineteen thousand seven
hundred and fifty pounds (£19,750) paid to the Lessor by
the Tenant on or before the execution hereof (the receipt
whereof the Lessor hereby acknowledges) and of the rents
and covenants hereinafter reserved and contained and on the
part of the Tenant to be paid observed and performed the
Lessor hereby demises unto the Tenant ALL THAT the upper
maisonette being 25 Anyroad Derrytown
(hereinafter called "the maisonette") forming part of the
said property known as Numbers 25 and 27 Anyroad
Derrytown Plymouth aforesaid (hereinafter called "the
building") including one half part in depth of the
structure between the floors of the maisonette and ceilings
of the lower maisonette and (subject to clause 7(1) hereof)
the internal and external walls of the maisonette to the
same level and the land and structure of the building above
the maisonette including the roof space gutters downpipes
windows and window frames TOGETHER WITH the front garden
and a portion of the rear garden which is delineated on the
plan annexed hereto and thereon edged in green AND TOGETHER
ALSO with the pathway (including the gate and gateway)
edged blue on the said plan AND TOGETHER ALSO with the
easements rights and privileges mentioned in the second
schedule hereto subject as therein mentioned but EXCEPTING
AND RESERVING as mentioned in the third schedule hereto TO
HOLD the maisonette hereby demised unto the Tenant from the
first day of April One thousand nine hundred and eighty for
the term of ninety nine years paying therefor yearly during
the said term the rent of Thirty pounds (£30) by equal
yearly payments (in advance) on the twenty fifth day of
December in every year free of all deductions whatsoever
the first payment thereof being a proportionate part of the
said annual sum calculated from the date hereof to the
twenty fifth day of December next to be paid upon the
signing hereof

Panel 7 Use of capitals to break up text

it is merely ugly English.) The sentence could have been written more simply:

> We have seen our client about preliminary enquiries and so can return replies to them together with the enclosures referred to.

Even better would be:

> We return replies to your preliminary enquiries.

The concept of 'returning replies' reflects the English practice by which preliminary enquiries were usually made on a two-column form, with the left column for the enquiries and the right column for the replies. Even so, no misunderstanding would be caused by an even shorter version:

> We reply to your preliminary enquiries.

Of course, legalese is not confined to letters between solicitors. It spills over into documents and letters that lawyers draft for clients. It is also rife in standard forms printed by publishers for use in legal offices. Here is an extract from a standard form of executor's oath:

> To the best of my/our knowledge information and belief there was no land vested in the said deceased which was settled previously to his/her death and not by his/her Will and which remained settled land notwithstanding such death.

This bears many of the marks of legalese. 'Knowledge', 'information' and 'belief' are synonyms or near-synonyms. They could have been deleted and replaced with: 'so far as I/we know'. The double negative ('no land ... not by his/her Will') occurs frequently in legal documents, despite being a well-known hindrance to understanding. 'The said deceased' has an impersonal tone – a tone which is typical and seemingly inevitable in legal forms. 'Notwithstanding' is a word rarely seen in everyday communication between lay writers. The paragraph could have been written:

> So far as I/we know, the deceased owned no settled land which remained settled land after his or her death.

Allied to legalese is jargon, by which we mean language peculiar to a profession. Jargon abounds in legal and quasi-legal documents. Consider the following clause in a will:

> I hereby revoke all Wills made by me at any time heretofore. I appoint my Wife, Jean Heath, and Robert High, of Denton Road, Wolverhampton, aforesaid, Plumber, to be my Executors, and direct that all my Debts and Funeral Expenses shall be paid as soon as conveniently may be after my decease.

'Hereby', 'at any time heretofore', and 'aforesaid' are pure jargon. All are unnecessary (as is the description 'Plumber'). They give the clause a legal feel without serving any legal purpose. Legal feel is further heightened in this example by jargon-like techniques. There is an over-use of capitals, as though virtually every noun needed one. Also, the direction to pay debts and funeral expenses 'as soon as conveniently may be' employs quaint language but adds nothing, since personal representatives have a duty to pay debts and funeral expenses. It would have been simpler and clearer to write:

> I revoke all previous wills.[37] I appoint as my executors my wife Jean Heath, and Robert High of Denton Road, Wolverhampton.

Jargon may be acceptable in a document which a lawyer drafts solely for another lawyer, but it is not acceptable in a document which a lawyer drafts for a lay client. Almost certainly the lay client will find the language stilted, and may well have difficulty understanding it. Rarely can there be any justification in drafting a document which the client finds difficult to understand.

Terms of art

To be distinguished from the unthinking and unnecessary use of jargon is the appropriate use of technical terms – 'terms of art'. Like other professions, law contains an irreducible minimum of terms of art, that is, terms which have a peculiar and fixed technical meaning, unmodified by context, and which are difficult and sometimes impossible to express in any other way.[38] Examples are *bailment, hearsay, deed* (in contrast to an agreement not under seal), *delivery* (in the sense of the act which brings a deed into operation), and *certiorari* (as in an order of certiorari). But there are relatively few genuine legal terms of art in this narrow sense.[39] More often than not, supposed terms of art are mere jargon. One writer has implied that the phrase 'term of art' is merely lawyers' jargon for lawyers' jargon.[40]

---

37 Strictly, 'previous' is tautologous, since a person can hardly revoke a will that is not yet made. But it probably helps to clarify meaning to a non-lawyer.

38 In *Skerrits of Nottingham Ltd v Secretary of State for the Environment, Transport and the Regions* [2000] 3 WLR 511 at 518, Robert Walker LJ described a 'term of art' as being 'an expression which is used by persons skilled in some particular profession, art or science, and which the practitioners clearly understand even if the uninitiated do not'. The court held that 'curtilage' (as in the curtilage of a building) is not a term of art.

39 Research in the United States suggests that in property documents the proportion of judicially defined terms is less than 3 per cent: B. Barr, G. Hathaway, N. Omichinski and D. Pratt, 'Legalese and the Myth of Case Precedent' (1985) 64 *Michigan Bar Journal*, p. 136.

40 David S. Levine, in the chapter '"My Client Has Discussed Your Proposal to Fill the Drainage Ditch with his Partners": Legal Language', in *State of the Language*, ed. Leonard Michaels and Christopher Ricks (Berkeley: University of California Press, 1980), p. 403.

Many familiar legal words and phrases which bear the illusion of terms of art would be better abandoned, for two chief reasons. First, the illusion would disappear. Second, other words and phrases are better suited to the task. To illustrate: is 'moiety' more certain than 'half', or 'dwelling-house' more certain than 'house' or 'dwelling'? Or is the following standard description

> 'ALL THAT piece or parcel of land together with the messuage or dwelling-house erected thereon or on some part thereof situate at and known as No. 3 St Andrew Street'

any more precise than the simple description 'No. 3 St Andrew Street'?

A typical example of jargon in the guise of term of art is the phrase 'without prejudice to'. The phrase is commonly used to preserve the force of one provision while expressing another contrasting or overlapping provision. Here is an example from a tenant's covenant in a lease:

> *Without prejudice to* sub-clause (c) hereof not to create any interest in the Premises or any part thereof derived out of the Term howsoever remote or inferior and in particular but *without prejudice* to the generality of the foregoing not to underlet the Premises or any part thereof.

In this context, 'without prejudice to' has no legal magic demanding its use. Where it first appears in this example, it can be replaced by a simple English word such as 'despite'; where it second appears, it can be replaced by a phrase such as 'without affecting' or 'without limiting'.

'Without prejudice' also has an entirely different written usage – to introduce a letter written in an attempt to settle a dispute. In this context, its purpose is to claim a form of privilege, to ensure that the letter cannot be used as evidence in court if the attempted settlement fails. It is legal shorthand for 'without prejudice to the position of the writer of the letter if the negotiations ... propose[d] are not accepted'.[41] But this usage, too, is jargon in the guise of term of art. It also confuses readers. An English survey shows that a large percentage of non-lawyers misunderstand the phrase and are liable to be misled about its intended effect.[42] Moreover its use does not guarantee privilege for the letter. Privilege depends on the rules of evidence that apply to the letter in the context in which it was written, not on the knee-jerk addition of 'without prejudice'. Lord Griffiths has said:

---

41 *Walker v Wilsher* (1889) 23 QBD 335 at 337 (Lindley LJ). For a recent application, see *Unilever plc v The Procter & Gamble Co.* [1999] 1 WLR 1630.

42 Mark Adler, 'Bamboozling the Public' [1991] *New Law Journal*, p. 1032: only 10 out of 77 people with some experience of lawyers 'clearly understood' the meaning; and of those who did not understand, '33 (or 43%) were under a misapprehension which seriously threatened their rights'.

A competent solicitor will always head any negotiating correspondence 'without prejudice' to make clear beyond doubt that in the event of the negotiations being unsuccessful they are not to be referred to at the subsequent trial. However, the application of the rule is not dependent upon the use of the phrase 'without prejudice' and *if it is clear from the surrounding circumstances* that the parties were seeking to compromise the action, evidence of the content of those negotiations will, as a general rule, not be admissible at the trial.[43]

Peculiar linguistic conventions

Legal writing exhibits lingustic quirks that set it apart from other kinds of writing. These quirks are easily recognisable, and are almost always unnecessary. To take a simple illustration, lawyers habitually use words that have long since disappeared from ordinary speech. Examples are: *hereby, herein, hereunder, hereinafter, heretofore, herewith, wherein, whereas* (but still standard English when used to introduce a contrast), *thereof, thereto, therein, therefor,* and *thereunder.* These words – like other examples considered earlier in this chapter – give legal writing a distinctive voice, but are quite unnecessary for legal efficacy. Usually they can be discarded entirely, or at least replaced by more modern equivalents.

In addition, lawyers often adopt linguistic conventions that have no basis in law, logic or modern usage. Examples are:

- 'of even date herewith', instead of 'dated the same as this document'
- 'these presents', instead of 'this document'
- 'the date hereof', instead of 'today'
- 'situate at', instead of 'at' or 'in'
- 'the county of Devon', instead of 'Devon'
- 'my said mother', instead of 'my mother'
- 'for the purpose of identification only more particularly delineated',[44] instead of 'for identification only' or 'more particularly delineated'
- 'jointly and severally' instead of 'separately and together'.

In all these examples, the modern idiomatic equivalent is just as legally effective as its quirky counterpart.

Sometimes more radical treatment is required than merely substituting a modern equivalent. Examples are the formulas customarily used to begin and end the operative part of a deed: 'now this deed witnesseth'[45]

---

43 *Rush & Tompkins Ltd v Greater London Council* [1989] AC 1280 at 1299 (our emphasis).
44 A phrase which is self-contradictory and should not be used: *Neilson v Poole* (1969) 210 EG 113 (Megarry J.). See further discussion of the use of plans in Chapter 6.
45 Verbs ending in -*th* endings remain prevalent in legal documents to this day, though the usage was regional even in Shakespeare's day: Robert McCrum, William Cran and Robert McNeil, *The Story of English* (London and Boston: Faber & Faber and BBC Publications, 1986), p. 101.

and 'in witness whereof the parties hereto have hereunto set their hands and seals the day and year first hereinbefore written'. Both these formalisms can be discarded without threat to the legal efficacy of the deed (see Chapter 6).

Another quirk is the insistence on spelling dates in words, rather than simply using figures: thus, 'one thousand nine hundred and ninety-nine', instead of '1999'. Yet another, doubtless retained out of a sense of excessive caution, is the insistence on using both words and figures when referring to sums of money, as in the following: 'in consideration of fifty thousand pounds (£50,000)'. This legal convention is unnecessary. Words alone, or figures alone, will suffice; and figures, being more instantly recognisable to the eye, should be preferred. The convention may also be counterproductive if there is a discrepancy between the words and figures. Where a commercial document displays a discrepancy between words and figures, on the face of it the words prevail.[46] Yet this general rule yields to context,[47] a sure invitation to litigation.

Linguists have long known of these and other oddities of legal language. Two leading linguists, David Crystal and Derek Davy, in their 1969 analysis *Investigating English Style*, were intrigued by the rarity in legal documents of substitute words like *he, she, they, this, that* and *it*.[48] (They might also have pointed out the corresponding rarity of the possessive forms of these words.) The most notable omission they found to be *it*: where used in phrases like 'It is agreed', *it* is the subject rather than a substitute for something mentioned before. Crystal and Davy also highlighted other characteristics:

- Adverbs and adverbial phrases or clauses are placed next to the verbs they modify. This results in oddities such as 'a proposal to effect with the Society an assurance' (rather than 'a proposal to effect an assurance with the Society') .
- Sentences are unduly long. Sequences of connected information are put into complex sentences capable of standing alone, instead of in short sentences with linking devices to show continuity.
- Postmodifying elements are inserted at those points in a group where they will most clearly give the required sense. Though the aim is precision, the practice produces oddities such as 'the payment to the owner of the total amount' (rather than 'the payment of the total

---

46 *Saunderson v Piper* (1839) 5 Bing (NC) 425; 132 ER 1163 (a case involving a discrepancy between words and figures in a bill of exchange but pre-dating the legislation by which words prevail over figures in negotiable instruments); *Re Hammond* [1938] 3 All ER 308; *Coote v Borland* (1904) 35 SCR (Can) 282 at 284.

47 *Re Hammond* [1938] 3 All ER 308 at 309.

48 David Crystal and Derek Davy, *Investigating English Style* (London: Longmans, 1969), p. 202.

amount to the owner') and 'any instalments then remaining unpaid of the rent' (instead of 'any instalments of the rent then remaining unpaid').[49]

Nouns instead of verbs

Another linguistic convention is the use of noun phrases instead of verbs – the practice of 'nominalisation'. This convention is not peculiar to legal writing; it infects all bureaucratic and official language. But it is endemic in legal documents. For example, parties to legal documents don't 'decide' to do something; instead, they 'make a decision'. They don't 'resolve', but 'pass a resolution'. They don't 'sever' a joint tenancy, but 'effect a severance'. This practice of nominalisation might be thought to achieve a certain formality of tone, but it is at the expense of effective communication. Verbs, especially strong verbs, communicate more effectively. They help make writing more direct.

Overuse of the passive

Traditional legal drafters slip easily into the passive voice, instinctively feeling more at home with the indirect, formal style it exudes. Yet all writing texts – including legal writing texts – say that the active voice communicates more effectively. The active is more direct, driving home the message. The passive is less direct. It can also obscure who is to do something; and so may cause the drafter to overlook important matters. For example, the constitution of a company may provide: 'A meeting of the Board *is to be called* each month.' Who is to call the meeting? If this clause had been drafted in the active voice, that question would have been obvious to the drafter.

Some texts imply that drafters should *never* use the passive, but that is going too far. On occasions the passive is convenient – for example, where the doer of an act is intentionally left unstated. The point is that lawyers tend to write in the passive instinctively. It is better to avoid the passive, except where the drafter makes a reasoned decision to use it.

Deeming

'Deeming' is common in legal documents. It is generally used to create a legal fiction: a thing is deemed to be something else, or an event is deemed to have occurred, despite evidence to the contrary. To a lay reader, the device must seem contrived. To a lawyer, however, it is second

---

49 Ibid., p. 204, 201, 213, 205.

nature; indeed, the more openly fictional a statement, the more readily lawyers accept deeming. So a lawyer can draft, with hardly a second thought, 'In this contract, black is deemed to be white', even though in the real world the statement is patent nonsense. The deeming makes it acceptable.

The main problem with 'deeming' is the artificiality it produces.[50] This impairs comprehension. In words befitting a Lewis Carroll character, Cave J said in 1891:

> Generally speaking, when you talk of a thing being deemed to be something, you do not mean to say that it is that which it is to be deemed to be. It is rather an admission that it is not what it is to be deemed to be, and that, notwithstanding it is not that particular thing, nevertheless ... it is to be deemed to be that thing.[51]

Lawyers also use 'deemed' to mean 'considered to be', or 'adjudged to be', or simply 'is'. Here the usage is not so much to create a legal fiction as to satisfy a state of fact. For example, a lease may provide that a tenant 'shall be deemed to be in default' if the rent is in arrears for seven days. What is meant is that the tenant is in default if the rent is in arrears for seven days. The 'deeming' could be discarded.[52]

Definitions

Stretched definitions

Often found with deeming provisions are stretched definitions. By 'stretched', we mean definitions that give a word a meaning beyond what the reader would expect. This unhelpful technique is particularly pernicious where the word has a well-understood lay meaning. Sometimes, the technique produces unintended humour, as in Australian statutes that define 'fish' to include beachworm and 'fingerprint' to include toeprint.[53]

The dangers of stretched definitions, whether or not in conjunction with 'deeming' provisions, are well documented.[54] They can impair communication between drafter and reader. They can trap the drafter as well as the reader. And they are an easy source of ridicule, inviting caricature

---

50 See *Burrell & Kinnaird v Attorney-General* [1937] AC 286, HL.
51 *R v Norfolk County Council* (1891) 60 LJ QB 379 at 380.
52 See *Barclays Bank Ltd v Inland Revenue Commissioner* [1961] AC 509 at 541 (Lord Denning).
53 *Fisheries Management Act* 1994 (NSW), s 5; *Crimes Act* 1958 (Vic), s 464.
54 See E. L. Piesse, *Elements of Drafting*, 9th edn (Sydney: LBC Information Services, 1995), p. 48; Robinson, *Drafting*, p. 58; Dickerson, *Fundamentals of Legal Drafting*, p. 140.

as typical of lawyers' language.[55] Stanley Robinson and Reed Dickerson call stretched definitions 'Humpty Dumptyisms', echoing Humpty-Dumpty's scornful assertion: 'When I use a word, it means just what I choose it to mean – neither more nor less.'[56]

Stretched definitions overlook the reality that language is a form of communication based on convention and habit. To succeed, communication must evoke a response in the person to whom it is addressed. That response depends on the addressee's existing store of usage, and that store of usage varies from person to person: for as Richard Robinson pointed out in his book *Definition*,[57] a word is a human contrivance, and its meaning can only be what some person means by it. Words do not have an inherently correct meaning; there is no natural relationship between a word and what it refers to. To quote Justice Holmes's famous aphorism, 'a word is not a crystal, transparent and unchanged', but rather is 'the skin of a living thought and may vary greatly in color and content according to the circumstances and the time in which it is used'.[58] Nevertheless, most words in everyday usage convey a common core of understanding, and the reader's task is made more difficult when a word with an accepted core of meaning is stretched to mean the unexpected.

Over-defining

Over-defining bedevils modern legal documents. It is a comparatively recent phenomenon. Drafters feel compelled to define every term, even terms that are used once only or in one clause only. The result is page after page of definitions. The document becomes long and unwieldy. The reader is forced to keep jumping between substantive provisions and definitions.

A definition is unnecessary if the meaning of the word or phrase is clear or can be readily ascertained from the context. A word or phrase need not be defined merely because it is technical or unusual. Also, to define a word that is used only once (the 'one-shot' definition) is generally superfluous.[59] Sometimes definitions are used to define words or phrases which appear only in other definitions, an incestuous device that eases the drafter's task at the cost of irritating the reader.

---

55 As in the spoof case of *R v Ojibway* (1965) 8 *Criminal Law Quarterly*, p.137 ('small bird' defined to include horse); *Nada Shah v Sleeman* (1917) 19 WALR 119 (a camel is a 'domestic animal').
56 Lewis Carroll, *Through the Looking Glass* (Chicago: Wellington Publishing, 1989), p. 127. For a legal analysis of this passage, see Lord Hoffmann in *Investors Compensation Scheme Ltd v West Bromwich Building Society* [1998] 1 WLR 896 at 914, HL.
57 (Oxford: Clarendon Press, 1950), p. 37.
58 *Towne v Eisner* 245 US 418 at 425 (1918).
59 See Dickerson, *Fundamentals of Legal Drafting*, p. 150.

To help reduce dependence on definitions, more use could be made of the parliamentary drafter's device of describing rather than defining. To take an example from England and Wales, s 28 of the *Crime and Disorder Act* 1998 states:

An offence is racially aggravated if – .

The private drafter would almost certainly be drawn in a dictionary-type definition, such as:

'Racially aggravated' means … .

Some commonly encountered definitions are strictly redundant because they are supplied by statute. For example, most common law jurisdictions have statutory provisions along the following lines:

* *month* means calendar month
* *person* includes a corporation
* the masculine includes the feminine and vice versa
* the singular includes the plural and vice versa.[60]

Subject to a qualification mentioned below, to repeat the effect of these provisions is legally superfluous.

In like vein, most common law jurisdictions have statutory provisions to the effect that the benefit of a covenant made with more than one person is joint and several.[61] To state this in the document is also superfluous. In contrast, however, statute says nothing about the *burden* of a covenant made by more than one person. Hence it is common to see provisions spelling out the position for both the benefit and the burden. This achieves a nice symmetry, which can hardly be open to much criticism.

To qualify what we have just said, sometimes it is desirable for the drafter to indicate the intended meaning of words and phrases, even if they are enshrined in statute. Lay readers cannot be presumed to know the statutory provisions. A document ought to be as comprehensible as possible on its face, and as complete in itself as it can reasonably be. As so often, this calls for fine judgment by the drafter. Documents can be so cluttered with legally superfluous material that they verge on the absurd.

---

60 In England and Wales, the provision is found in s 61 of the *Law of Property Act* 1925.
61 In England and Wales, the provision is found in s 81 of the *Law of Property Act* 1925. For the meaning of 'joint and several', see Chapter 7.

Disguise of an operative element

A deviant form of definition is the 'stuffed' definition.[62] By stuffed, we mean a definition that carries some operative element. An example, taken from a contract for the sale of land, is:

> 'Completion date' means 30 June 2000, and on that date the purchaser must pay the purchase price and relieve the vendor of liability for all rates and taxes payable on the property.

This goes further than merely defining the term 'completion date'. In the guise of a definition, it imposes contractual obligations. The result is to hide operative obligations in a part of the document where the reader does not expect to find them. Time is wasted in locating an important contractual obligation. The technique does not render the document invalid, but it irritates the reader and hinders efficient understanding.

Again, consider the following definition from a trust deed:

> 'The specified period' means a period beginning at the date of execution of these presents and enduring for eighty years and the said number of years shall be the perpetuity period applicable hereto.

The purpose here is to define the perpetuity period applying to the document as the 'specified period'. It would be better to declare in a main clause simply that the 'specified period' is the perpetuity period, and then to define the specified period as '80 years beginning today'. Better still would be to remove the reference to 'specified period' altogether, and simply say:

> The perpetuity period applicable to this deed is 80 years beginning today.

Excessively detailed definitions

Not content merely with incorporating definitions of questionable necessity, many drafters attempt to extend them to cover every conceivable circumstance. This results in definitions of excessive length and detail.

Excessively long and detailed definitions can be counterproductive. In attempting to be all-inclusive, the drafter may unintentionally omit something which should have been included. The courts might then apply the maxim *expressio unius exclusio alterius* (the expression of one thing excludes another; see Chapter 2) and treat the exclusion as deliberate. The drafter's excessive zeal has then served only to create loopholes. Lord

---

62 A Reed Dickerson phrase: *Fundamentals of Legal Drafting*, p. 151.

Wilberforce alluded to this risk in *Seay v Eastwood*, a case dealing with legislation to control gambling. In the context of a statutory definition of 'bookmaker', he said that it was impossible to frame definitions to cover every variety of gambling activity: 'attempts to do so may indeed be counter-productive, since each added precision merely provides an incentive to devise a variant which eludes it'.[63]

'Unless the context requires otherwise'

An unfortunate drafting technique in definitions is the insertion of the cautionary rider 'unless the context requires otherwise', or 'where the context so admits', or the like. The purpose is clear enough: to prevent difficulties of interpretation if the drafter inadvertently uses a defined word in an undefined sense. But, to state the obvious, drafting lapses of this kind should not occur – particularly in an era of word processors with search facilities, where every occurrence of a word can be hunted down and checked for consistency of use. The rider should be unnecessary in thoughtfully drafted documents.[64] And, of course, its presence does not preclude litigation over meaning, because it leaves open the question whether the context in fact 'requires' or 'admits' a meaning different from the defined meaning.[65]

We return to the topic of definitions in Chapter 6, where we consider their proper use in modern documents.

Overuse of capitals

Overuse of capital letters is another mark of legal writing. The reason is primarily historical: see the ancient examples in Panel 8.

Today, initial capital letters are commonly used in legal documents to identify defined terms. This convention is so well-established that it may be difficult to discard, but care should be taken not to carry the practice to excess. We consider the convention further in Chapter 6.

---

63 [1976] 1 WLR 1117 (HL) at 1121.

64 See David Mellinkoff, *Legal Writing: Sense and Nonsense* (St Paul, Minnesota: West Publishing Co., 1982), p. 24: 'The formula abandons the client for whom the writing was prepared and the reader to whom it was addressed. It leaves them to the tender interpretation of strangers. If you define, you create an important part of the context. It is your responsibility to adjust your definition to fit your context, or your context to fit your definition, or to forget about definition as a route to precision.' For other objections, see Giles A. Morgan, 'Interpretation Clauses: a Cautionary Tale' (1996) 140 *Solicitors Journal*, p. 838 ('where the context otherwise requires').

65 As in *Blue Metal Industries Ltd v Dilley* [1970] AC 827 (PC); *Floor v Davis* [1980] AC 695 (PC).

31. *Eliz. in the Common Pleas.*

161   BUCKHURST's Case.

L Essee for ten years granted a rent charge unto his Lessor for the years: Afterwards the Lessor granted the Remainder in Fee to the Lessee. It was the opinion of the Court that the rent was gone and extinct, because the Lessor who had the rent, is a party to the Destruction of the Lease, which is the ground of the Rent.

29. *Eliz. In the King's Bench.*

162   ALLEN and PATSHALL's Case.

A Copy-holder doth surrender unto the use of a Stranger for ever; and the Lord admits the Surrendree to have and to hold to him and his Heirs. It was adjudged in this Case; That if it were upon a devise, that such a one should have the Copyhold in Fee; and afterwards a surrender is made unto the Lord to grant the Copyhold according to the Will; and he grants it in Fee to him and his Heirs, that the Grant is good. But *quære* in the first Case, for it was there but a bare Surrender only.

Mich. 27,28. *Eliz. in the King's Bench.*

163   STRANGDEN and BARNELL's Case.

A N Action of Trover and Conversion was brought of Goods in *Ipswich*; the Defendant pleaded, That the Goods came to his hand in *Dunwich* in the same County; and that the Plaintiffe gave unto him the goods which came to his hands in *Dunwich*, *absq̃, hoc* that he is guilty of any Trover, and Conversion of Goods in *Ipswich*. And by the opinion of the Court, the same is a good manner of Pleading by reason of the speciall Justification. *Vide* 27. *H.* 6. But when the Justification is generall, the County is not traversable at this day. *Vide* 19. *H.* 6.6, & 7.

T

Panel 8 Historic use of capitals

There are two main objections to excessive use of capitals: the effect on the reader, and the influence on interpretation.

Effect on the reader

Words are recognised as shapes.[66] Readers absorb words because they have learned what words look like, in the same way that they recognise trees, cars, crockery and faces.[67] Modern readers, unused to the historical practice of frequent capitals, may find them irritating. Further, overuse of capitals offends the principle that legal writing is simply a version of ordinary writing; it should follow the rules and conventions of literate English.[68]

Reed Dickerson said that the legal drafter should use initial capital letters only where required by good usage, as for proper nouns.[69] Other writers, though, have advocated the (sparing) use of capitals. Piesse, for example, suggests that although the undue use of capital initial letters is 'inelegant', the device may actually help the careful reader.[70] Thus, if a party to a document is a company, it can be referred to throughout as 'the Company', leaving 'company' without a capital for use if a company in general is meant. The device of using a capital letter is particularly helpful when (as in that example) the descriptive word is likely to be used also in a different sense: the capital letter warns the reader that for the purpose of the document the word bears a particular meaning. A better practice, though, would be to avoid the misunderstanding by calling the party something altogether different, such as 'the supplier'.

In traditionally drafted documents, as we have seen, capitals are sometimes used for complete words, to break up blocks of text: common examples are WHEREAS, TOGETHER WITH, PROVIDED THAT, ALL THAT, and the like. However, overuse of capitals in whole words or passages hinders fluent readers.[71] This is because the shape of a whole word in capitals is less distinctive than its counterpart in lower case.[72] There is no

---

66 Frank Smith, *Writing and the Writer* (London: Heinemann, 1982), p. 145.

67 Frank Smith, *Reading*, 2nd edn (Cambridge: CUP, 1985), p. 107.

68 David Mellinkoff, *Legal Writing: Sense and Nonsense*, p. 44. See also Robert C. Dick, *Legal Drafting in Plain Language*, 3rd edn (Toronto: Thomson Canada, 1995), p. 112: 'Capital letters should be used only where necessary. In so many documents words such as Grantor, Grantee, Guarantor and Corporation are capitalized. Most of these capitalizations are completely unnecessary and are in fact visually disconcerting. In writing a letter to a friend, a lawyer would omit almost all capitals, except for words at the beginning of sentences. Much the same procedure should be followed in drafting.'

69 *Fundamentals of Legal Drafting*, p. 189.

70 *Elements of Legal Drafting*, pp. 48–9.

71 National Consumer Council, *Plain English for Lawyers* (London, 1984), p. 25.

72 Martin Cutts and Chrissie Maher, *Writing Plain English* (Stockport: Plain English Campaign, 1980), p. 21.

justification for continuing the practice in modern documents, particularly as other devices exist for breaking blocks of text into manageable chunks.

Influence on interpretation

For readers unused to the convention, to define a term and then to draw attention to it by capital initial letters when it is used in the text may downgrade other expressions that do not receive the same treatment. Conversely, to use capital letters for terms that have *not* been defined tends to elevate them to a status they do not merit. Consider this clause:

> This Mortgage incorporates the National and Provincial Building Society Mortgage Conditions 1983 Edition and the Rules and the Borrower (and the Guarantor (if any)) have received copies of the said Mortgage Conditions and the Rules.

In the building society mortgage from which this example was taken, the only defined terms were 'the Borrower', 'the Guarantor,' and 'the Society'. Neither 'Mortgage' nor 'the Rules' was defined. (The word 'mortgage' also occurred later, in the phrase 'by way of legal mortgage'). The indiscriminate capitalisation produces a clause which at best is hard to read, and at worst may prove difficult to interpret.

In short, excessive capitalisation creates a wholly artificial atmosphere in a document, without appreciably increasing the reader's understanding. Significantly, modern parliamentary drafters rarely if ever assign capital letters to defined words or phrases in statutes or regulations. Private legal drafters could do well to follow their lead.

Provisos

'Provisos' have a long legislative history. For centuries in England, the term *provided* or *provided that* was used to introduce substantive provisions in legislation, as a contraction of the enacting formula *it is provided [that]*. This use has long ceased, but the term *provided* or *provided that* has survived, unique to legal writing. It has degenerated to a 'legal incantation … an all-purpose conjunction, invented by lawyers but not known to or understood by grammarians'.[73]

Properly used in modern legal drafting, provisos serve the useful purpose of limiting or qualifying what has gone before. In practice, however, they are typically introduced by formalistic phrases such as *provided that,*

---

73 E. Driedger, *The Composition of Legislation*, 2nd edn (Ottawa: 1976), ch. IX and p. 96.

or *provided however that*. No legal precision would be lost by replacing these phrases with simple English words, like *if* or *but* or *however*.

To illustrate, a will might say:

I give my property to my children *provided that* they marry.

The drafter could dispense with *provided that* and use *if* or *when*. Indeed, it would be better to do so. As the will stands, it is unclear whether the proviso introduces a condition precedent or a condition subsequent; that is, it is unclear whether the gift is initially contingent, with marriage being a condition precedent to vesting, or initially vested but subject to divesting in the case of children who do not marry.[74] An alert drafter could have used *if* to introduce a contingent gift; or could have used *to be paid over when* to introduce a vested gift ('to be paid over to them when they marry').[75]

This is not to deny that a true proviso has its place. But in practice the technique is often abused. Rather than qualify or limit the width of what has gone before, the self-styled 'proviso' in fact introduces material of equal force; it adds a parallel provision, inserting material that should have been drafted as a stand-alone clause. At best, this can cause difficulty of comprehension, for the reader is uncertain whether to assume that the proviso is intended to limit the preceding covenant (its proper function) or to introduce a separate covenant; at worst, it can lead to litigation.[76] Where the purpose is to introduce new material, the words introducing the proviso – *provided that*, or *provided however that* – should be struck out, and a new sentence begun.

Provisos are frequently a product of the negotiation process. The document is drafted by A, the lawyer for one side in the transaction. The other side's lawyer, B, needs to make a substantive amendment but does not want to renumber all the existing clauses. So B inserts a proviso, which by its nature is tacked onto an existing clause. A feels constrained by professional comity to leave the amendment as a proviso. Hence the proviso slips in when, by all the principles enunciated here, it should be put somewhere else.

To illustrate the points just discussed, consider the following clause from a lease of property in an earthquake zone:

---

74 As in *Re Cohn* [1974] 3 All ER 928 (CA); *Nicholls v Public Trustee (South Australia)* (1945) 72 CLR 86.

75 *Hume v Perpetual Trustees Executors and Agency Co. of Tasmania* (1939) 62 CLR 242. See F. V. Hawkins and E. C. Ryder, *The Construction of Wills* (London: Sweet & Maxwell, 1965), pp. 303–8; *Barclays Bank Trust Co. Ltd v McDougall* (2000) *Law Society's Gazette* 3 August 39 (Rimer J).

76 As in *Hely v Sterling* [1982] VR 246.

The tenant must repaint the premises *provided that* if there has been an earthquake the tenant must repair any structural damage.

Here the drafter has used the technique of proviso, not to qualify what has gone before, but to introduce an entirely new obligation. It would be better to delete the proviso and divide the clause into two independent parts:

1. The tenant must repaint the premises.
2. If there is an earthquake, the tenant must repair any structural damage.

Again, consider the following provision:

All fixtures installed during the term of the lease by the tenant become the property of the landlord upon the expiry of the term PROVIDED THAT the tenant may remove its fixtures at the end of the term.[77]

The meaning, or the purpose, of this clause is almost impossible to discern. The first half (up to the proviso) seems merely to reflect the common law assumption that fixtures which a tenant affixes to the property are the landlord's property unless and until the tenant removes them,[78] and that a tenant who wishes to do so must remove them before the lease expires, otherwise they remain the landlord's property.[79] The second half (the proviso) seems to give the tenant an unfettered right to remove fixtures at the end of the term: but this also merely reflects the common law right of tenants to remove their fixtures at or before the end of the lease.[80] Probably, the drafter intended the proviso – despite being cast as a proviso – to be the main head of tenant's right, and the opening words to limit the time in which the tenant could exercise that right. If so, it would have been much better to avoid the use of a proviso altogether, and reverse the order of provisions, thus:

1. The tenant may remove its fixtures at the end of the term.
2. Any fixtures not so removed remain the landlord's property.

Conclusion

This chapter has highlighted some of the practices which modern drafters should shun. All the practices considered in the preceding pages

---

77 Adapted from Dick, *Legal Drafting*, p. 104.
78 *Bain v Brand* (1876) 1 App Cas 762 at 770 (Lord Cairns).
79 *New Zealand Government Property Corporation v HM & S Ltd* [1982] QB 1145.
80 Ibid.

have been developed and sustained over many generations, even centuries; they are stocked in plentiful supply in the arsenal of traditional legal drafters. But all are practices which non-lawyers find disconcerting, and which therefore hinder comprehension. They can be discarded without threat to precision or legal effect.

6   How to Draft Modern Documents

In the previous chapter we considered some of the techniques to avoid when drafting modern legal documents. The emphasis was on the negative – what *not* to do. Now we turn to the positive – what to *do*. That is, we consider some of the techniques to be adopted when drafting legal documents in the modern style.

Modern, standard English

We begin with a proposition that underlies all we have said so far in this book: legal documents should be written in modern, standard English – that is, in standard English as currently used and understood.[1] Identifying modern, standard English is not difficult. It can be found in articles in the more serious newspapers, in popular and academic books on many subjects, and in reports of governments and public authorities. Its hallmark is a style that is direct, informative and readable.

For many traditional lawyers, the move to modern, standard English is difficult. It forces them to rethink, and rethinking takes time. Also, more is required than simply a process of translation. While merely updating terminology will help, a well-drawn document goes further. It takes into account matters of structure, layout, word order, and design. It also takes into account the issues of substantive law that will almost certainly arise.

To illustrate some of the difficulties in this process, consider the following clause from a traditionally drafted sublease:

> Not to affix or exhibit or permit or suffer to be affixed or exhibited to or upon the external walls windows or other external parts of the demised premises any name flag placard sign poster signboard nameplate sunblind (for advertising purposes only) or other advertisement whatsoever without the prior consent in writing of the Landlord.

---

1 National Consumer Council, *Plain Words for Consumers* (London: 1984), p. 47; David Mellinkoff, *Legal Writing: Sense and Nonsense* (St Paul, Minnesota: West Publishing Co., 1982), p. 44.

Before altering the wording, the modern drafter asks a number of questions. These include:

- What is the purpose of the clause?
- How can that purpose best be expressed?
- Is there a difference between *doing* something and *permitting* something?
- Is there a difference between *suffering* and *permitting*?
- What is the most effective word order?
- Can I be bold, or should I err on the side of caution?

The purpose of the clause seems to be to prevent advertising on the outside of the leased property. That can be expressed in direct, modern English, thus:

> Not to put any advertisement on the outside of the property or in the windows, except with the Landlord's written consent.

The original used the phrase 'not to permit or suffer to be affixed'. Conceptually, of course, there is a distinction between doing something directly and allowing it to be done by someone else. In legal documents, however, the distinction (though often found) is frequently unimportant. Persons subject to a direct prohibition will usually be in breach if they allow another person to do the prohibited act, in the sense of directly or indirectly sanctioning it to be done.[2] In any case, disputes over possible differences between *permit* and *suffer* can be circumvented by using *allow*, for *allow* is at least as wide as *permit*, if not wider.[3] And if (despite these arguments) the drafter feels it necessary to preserve the distinction between direct and indirect breach, this can be achieved by a paragraph within the interpretation clause, such as:

> A prohibition on an activity includes a prohibition on allowing that activity.

This at least removes the need to repeat the distinction in each substantive provision.

As for the most effective word order: if an act is to be prohibited, but with qualifications, it is best to begin with the prohibition and then to add the qualifications afterwards. Legal documents often reverse this order, putting the qualifications first. But to start with a qualification – 'Except with the Landlord's written consent' – tends to obscure the

---

2 *Hardcastle v Bielby* [1892] 1 QB 709; *Massey v Morris* [1894] 1 QB 412; *Ferrier v Wilson* (1906) 4 CLR 785.
3 See *Barton v Reed* [1932] 1 Ch 362 at 375 (Luxmoore J); *De Kupyer v Crafter* [1942] SASR 238 at 243–4.

main purpose of the clause. Putting the prohibition first helps the reader assimilate the message.

To repeat these processes for each clause in a long lease might seem both time-consuming and difficult. At first it may be. But once the drafter becomes attuned to a new way of thinking, the process becomes much easier. Nor need the process be undertaken unaided. The lawyer drafting in modern, standard English may still use precedents as an *aide-mémoire* – not following them willy-nilly, but adapting them to the requirements of the particular transaction.

Document structure

The contents of a legal document should be ordered logically, to enable the document to be read and used quickly and effectively. As we explain below, by 'logically' we mean logically from the reader's perspective. Each clause and paragraph should be presented in a way that is both sensible and comprehensible to the user. More important clauses should come before less important clauses. To illustrate, the general pattern of a contract might be:

- heading
- date
- parties
- definitions
- the heart of the deal
- things associated with the heart of the deal
- general housekeeping, such as
  - duration
  - assignment
  - effect of death or dissolution
- what happens if things go wrong, such as
  - bankruptcy or insolvency
  - rescission for breach
  - liquidated damages
  - dispute resolution
- standard provisions ('boilerplate'), such as
  - effect of extraneous events ('force majeure')
  - service of notices
  - governing law.

Of course, these divisions are not hard and fast. For example, the definitions might be better located towards the end of the document (see below). What is crucial, though, is to identify the heart of the deal and things associated with the heart of the deal, and to place them up front.

The clause containing the heart of the deal then acts as a kind of purpose or object clause, governing the rest of the document. It should be kept separate from matters that are relevant to the transaction but are not at its heart.

When considering whether a document flows logically, the aim is an order which is comfortable for the client rather than necessarily comfortable for the lawyer. Traditional documents are cast in a framework familiar to the lawyer. But legal efficacy does not require the lawyer's framework. There is no legal impediment to presenting a document in a way that reflects the client's thought processes about the deal. The drafter should try to anticipate those thought processes and build the document around them.

As a general rule, each main clause should be limited to a single core concept. Combining two or more core concepts in a single clause adds unnecessary complexity. For example, leases traditionally combined the demise (that is, the formal grant of the lease) and the reddendum (the obligation to pay rent), but the client would understand the transaction better if the grant of the lease and the rent obligations were in separate clauses. Similarly, it is helpful to separate concepts such as dispute resolution from notices relating to breach.

Examples

To illustrate issues of structure, consider a deed creating a partnership. The heart of the deal is the establishment of the partnership itself. Things associated with the heart of the deal are the nature of the business, the location of the activity, and the name of the firm. In a short document creating a straightforward relationship, the heart of the deal and things associated with it can be run together in one clause, thus:

> The partners will carry on business in partnership as solicitors under the name Castle & Co., at 113 High Street Hurstpierpoint West Sussex, beginning on 1 January 1999 and continuing until brought to an end in accordance with this deed.

General, but essential, housekeeping matters should follow straight afterwards – matters such as the sharing of profits or losses, the provision of capital, and the accounting year. Less crucial (but still important) matters might appear next – the keeping of bank accounts, who can sign cheques, and what drawings can be made. Boilerplate comes last, for it may never have to be referred to if the agreement is performed in accordance with its terms. With a contract structure of this kind, the parties can rapidly see what they are trying to achieve and how they are expected to achieve it.

Other types of document call for different provisions, but should be structured on the same principles. For example, a lease might take this form:

- the grant of the lease (the heart of the deal)
- rent and rent review (things associated with the heart of the deal)
- tenant's covenants
- landlord's covenants
- general housekeeping (for example, relating to services)
- early ending (for example, on damage or destruction)
- forfeiture for breach
- boilerplate, such as
  - service of notices
  - resolution of disputes
  - interest on late payments.

Wills, too, can be structured in a way that regulates administration and distribution in a natural sequence. The structure could be:
- revocation of earlier wills
- appointment of executors
- gifts of particular items
- gifts of money
- distribution of residue
- powers of executors
- charging clause.

Layout and design

The use of modern, standard English and a logical structure, are complemented by user-friendly layout and design. As long ago as 1978, Alan Siegel said:

> Just as important as clear language is careful layout and design. If a document looks terrifying it does not matter how easy the words are: they will never be read. Good design sets the tone for the document. It communicates the document's intent as much as words do. It also makes the document more useful, by guiding the reader's eye to the information he or she wants to know.[4]

Layout and design are more than merely cosmetic. They improve understanding by helping readers find their way around the document, aiding assimilation of the contents. They may also provide an incidental

---

4 Conference of Experts in Clear Legal Drafting, National Center for Administrative Justice, Washington, DC, 2 June 1978, reproduced in Reed Dickerson, *Materials on Legal Drafting* (St Paul, Minnesota: West Publishing Co., 1981), p. 294).

benefit for the drafter: readers presented with a document which looks good, reads logically, and encourages them to move forward, are less likely to amend the document than would readers disgruntled with the document's presentation.

There are many ways to improve the layout and design of traditional legal documents. Set out below are suggestions. Some are no more than common sense; others are the result of research into document design. But all help improve the accessibility of legal documents.

White space

Use plenty of white space. This presents readers with an uncluttered page, encouraging progress through the document. In particular:

- Break up slabs of text.
- Use generous margins all round, including at the top and bottom of the page. Have a generous margin on the left, to allow for notations at the draft stage.
- Double-space all text (or at least use 1.5 spacing). Single spacing is too crowded; it also makes it harder to mark amendments on drafts.
- Use generous spacing between clauses.

Headings

Use plenty of headings. They are useful signposts for the reader. In particular:

- Use a bold central heading at the beginning of the document to identify its nature (for example, 'Mortgage' or 'Transfer'), followed by bold headings (lower case and flush left) to introduce the various divisions of the document (see Panel 9).
- Give each main clause a heading (bold, lower case). If possible, also give each subsidiary clause a heading (but in italics, to distinguish from main clause headings).
- Ensure that headings are not 'orphaned' at the bottom of a page, isolated from the words to which they relate.

Navigation and ease of reading

- If possible, use signposting techniques such as running headings (headers) on each page, shoulder headings, lists of contents and indexes. These techniques are now beginning to appear in legislation.[5]

---

5 For a study of their benefits in legislative design, see Centre for Plain Legal Language, *Discussion Paper: Review and Redesign of NSW Legislation* (1994). For applications, see *Retirement Villages Act* 1999 (NSW); UK Inland Revenue Tax Law Rewrite, Exposure Draft No. 9 (February 2000), vol. 2 (Draft Capital Allowances Bill).

DISTRIBUTION AGREEMENT

Date   2001

Parties

A.   John Jones & Company Limited whose registered office is at 3 Acacia

Avenue, Anytown, Shropshire ("the manufacturer").

B.   Jack Smith Limited whose registered office is at 96 High Street,

Bockhampton, Dorset ("the distributor").

1.   Background

(1)   The manufacturer makes widgets and other products, and in relation to

widgets has registered a patent and maintains all other intellectual property

rights.

(2)   The distributor is a distributor of goods from its principal base in Southampton.

(3)   The parties have agreed that the distributor is to have the right to distribute and

sell widgets throughout Hampshire, Dorset and the Isle of Wight.

Panel 9 Document layout

Realistically, however, busy lawyers may not have time to see that they are constructed well in the beginning and remain in proper order after the document has been heavily amended.
• Indent subsidiary paragraphs.[6] Use indents consistently, and ensure all text within an indented passage is kept to the same indentation.

---

6 In *Re Gulbenkian's Settlement* [1970] AC 508 at 526, Lord Donovan said that he had never understood why some conveyancers regarded it as beneath their dignity to use paragraphing techniques to make their meaning plain: had that been done on the facts of the case, 'much trouble and expense would have been avoided'.

- Use a serif typeface. Studies generally show that a font with serifs is more readable than one without (sanserif).[7] For contrast, use sanserif for headings.[8]
- Use a generous type size. The literature on typography and design agrees that a type size of between 9 and 12 point is the most legible for general reading purposes.[9] Judges have condemned the use of too-small type in legal documents,[10] although it seems unlikely that a court would absolve a contracting party from liability purely on the ground that the type was so small that it was practically illegible.[11]
- Don't justify the right margin. Although readability seems generally unaffected by whether the right margin is justified or unjustified (ragged), an unjustified right margin gives a document a more relaxed feel.[12]
- Use a cover sheet for a document of any length (say, more than five or six pages). Like the cover of a book, it shows the nature of the document at a glance. For a document that will be folded lengthwise, a backsheet can also be useful. But don't put too much information on the cover sheet or backsheet, lest it be used to qualify the content of the body of the document.[13]

---

7 C. Wheildon, *Communicating: or Just Making Pretty Shapes* (1986; a study for the Newspaper Advertising Bureau of Australia Ltd), pp. 16, 17; Centre for Plain Legal Language, *Discussion Paper*, p. 14. However, some studies are less adamant about the advantages of serif over sanserif: for example, James Hartley, *Designing Instructional Text*, 3rd edn (London: Kogan Page, 1994), ch. 4. The apparent preference for serif may be due to familiarity, serif being the norm in newspapers.

8 A technique recommended in the study by the Centre for Plain Legal Language, *Discussion Paper*, and now adopted in New South Wales legislation.

9 Ibid., pp. 16–17; Hartley, *Designing Instructional Text*, pp. 23–4; Document Design Project, *Guidelines for Document Designers* (American Institutes for Research, 1981), pp. 77–8.

10 For example, *Goldsbrough v Ford Credit Aust Ltd* [1989] ASC 55-946 at 58,584; *George T. Collings (Aust) Pty Ltd v H. F. Stevenson* [1991] ASC 56-051.

11 *Koskas v Standard Marine Insurance Co. Ltd* (1927) 27 Ll L Rep 59 at 62, where Scrutton LJ said: 'I am rather afraid of the doctrine that you can get out of clauses by saying that they are difficult to read. There may be extreme cases. I have in mind the bill of a well-known shipping line printed on red paper which was calculated to produce blindness in anyone reading it. I am not saying that in no case can you get out of it on the point of illegibility, but this case does not appear to me to be a case in which that doctrine should be applied.'
See also *Lezam Pty Ltd v Seabridge Australia Pty Ltd* (1992) 35 FCR 535. But compare the South African case of *Fourie v Hansen* [2000] JOL 5993(W), where the small font used throughout a document was a factor in holding an exemption clause unenforceable.

12 Hartley, *Designing Instructional Text*, p 37; Document Design Project, *Guidelines for Document Designers*, pp. 37, 38. Wheildon, *Communicating: or Just Making Pretty Shapes*, p. 35, concludes that justified text promotes readability more than unjustified.

13 For a case where the judge took account of the contents of a backsheet, see *Meadfield Properties Ltd v Secretary of State for the Environment* [1995] 1 EGLR 39 at 41 (Warner J).

Numbering systems

Legal documents exhibit a variety of numbering systems. Some examples are shown in Table 1. A variant is to use bullet points to enumerate items in a list.

Table 1 Numbering systems

Arabic/Roman	Decimal	Partial combination
1.	1.	1.
2.	2.	2.
3. (1)	3.1	3.1
(2)	3.2	3.2
(3) (a)	3.3.1	3.3 (a)
(b)	3.3.2	(b)
(c) ...	3.3.3	(c) ...
(i)	3.3.3.1	(i)
(ii)	3.3.3.2	(ii)
(iii) ...	3.3.3.3	(iii) ...
(A)	3.3.3.3.1	(A)
(B)	3.3.3.3.2	(B)
(C)	3.3.3.3.3	(C)

The choice of numbering system is a matter of personal preference. No one system is best, although the modern trend is towards the decimal system. Whichever system is chosen, however, two matters must be kept in mind. First, all numbering systems become cumbersome when they descend to more than about three levels. Drafters who find themselves subdividing further than this should reconsider the structure of their document. Second, consistency in numbering is crucial; having chosen a system, the drafter should apply it remorselessly.

Short sense-bites

In Chapter 5 we discussed the excessive wordiness and the unduly long 'sense-bites' that characterise traditional legal drafting. These peculiarities modern drafters take care to avoid.

Modern drafters are often exhorted to write short sentences. But a better exhortation would be: write short sense-bites. Blind adherence to a policy of short sentences is not always appropriate. For example, sentences that list a series of obligations or events are inevitably long. Consider the tenant's covenants in a lease: they are usually structured in the form of a single sentence, introduced by such words as 'The tenant covenants with the landlord: ...'. Each covenant then appears as a separate sub-sentence, thus: 'to pay the rent', 'to pay outgoings', and the like. To insist that each covenant be a separate sentence beginning 'The tenant covenants with the landlord to ...' would be irritating and silly. Much better to use sub-paragraphs and indentation to reduce each covenant to manageable sense-bites, so that the reader can quickly grasp the meaning.

Example

To illustrate the advantages of short sense-bites, here are two versions of an easement to drain water, taken from the New South Wales *Conveyancing Act* 1919. (For similar examples, see p. 76.) The first version is the traditionally drafted form of easement:

> Full and free right for the body in whose favour this easement is created, and every person authorised by it, from time to time and at all times to drain water (whether rain, storm, spring, soakage, or seepage water) in any quantities across and through the land herein indicated as the servient tenement, together with the right to use, for the purposes of the easement, any line of pipes already laid within the servient tenement for the purpose of draining water or any pipe or pipes in replacement or in substitution therefor and where no such line of pipes exists, to lay, place and maintain a line of pipes of sufficient internal diameter beneath or upon the surface of the servient tenement and together with the right for the body in whose favour this easement is created and every person authorised by it, with any tools, implements, or machinery, necessary for the purpose, to enter upon the servient tenement and to remain there for any reasonable time for the purpose of laying, inspecting, cleansing, repairing, maintaining, or renewing such pipe line or any part thereof and for any of the aforesaid purposes to open the soil of the servient tenement to such extent as may be necessary provided that the body in whose favour this easement is created and the persons authorised by it will take all reasonable precautions to ensure as little disturbance as possible to the surface of the servient tenement and will restore that surface as nearly as practicable to its original condition.

This is all one single sentence of 256 words. Contrast the following version of the same easement, incorporated into the Act in 1995. As a matter of strict grammar, each clause is a single sentence. But each is broken down into smaller, more digestible, sense-bites:

1. The body having the benefit of this easement may:
   (a) drain water from any natural source through each lot burdened, but only within the site of this easement, and
   (b) do anything reasonably necessary for that purpose, including:
      • entering the lot burdened, and
      • taking anything on to the lot burdened, and

- using any existing line of pipes, and
- carrying out work, such as constructing, placing, repairing or maintaining pipes, channels, ditches and equipment.

2. In exercising those powers, the body having the benefit of this easement must:

(a) ensure all work is done properly, and

(b) cause as little inconvenience as is practicable to the owner and any occupier of the lot burdened, and

(c) cause as little damage as is practicable to the lot burdened and any improvement on it, and

(d) restore the lot burdened as nearly as is practicable to its former condition, and

(e) make good any collateral damage.

Punctuation

Traditional legal drafting uses punctuation sparingly. This has been the practice from the earliest times. As late as 1860, Davidson wrote in the introductory notes to his highly regarded *Precedents in Conveyancing*:

> The writing of a legal instrument is without punctuation; such stops and marks of parenthesis must be supplied by the reader as will give effect to the whole. Marks of parenthesis are, indeed, usually inserted, but it seems that they are to be regarded, in the construction of the deed, only when they are consonant with the sense, and required by the context. The Precedents in this and other collections are pointed by the printers, according to the usual practice; but no attention is to be paid to the punctuation.[14]

This approach probably reflects a belief among lawyers that statutes were largely unpunctuated when they left the drafter, and that any punctuation later added was done at the behest of the printer, not the author. This belief David Mellinkoff has convincingly shown to be misconceived.[15] It did lead, however, to the attitude, once prevalent judicially, that punctuation played little or no part in construing legal documents. For example, in *Sandford v Raikes*, Sir William Grant MR said that the sense of legal writing should be gathered from the words of the document and their context, rather than from punctuation.[16] Other judges have said the same thing.[17]

---

14 3rd edn (London: William Maxwell, 1860), p. 30 (citations omitted).

15 *The Language of the Law*, p. 152. See also V. Crabbe, 'Punctuation in Legislation' (1988) 9 *Statute Law Review*, p. 87; R. Wydick, 'Should Lawyers Punctuate?' (1990) 1 *Scribes Journal of Legal Writing*, p. 7.

16 (1816) 1 Mer 646 at 651; 35 ER 808 at 810.

17 For example, Lord Kenyon CJ in *Doe d Willis v Martin* (1790) 4 TR 39 at 65, 66; 100 ER 882 at 897.

But that is no longer the prevalent view. The modern style of legal drafting uses punctuation for the same reason as any other careful prose uses punctuation – to give guidance about meaning. As Lord Shaw pointed out in *Houston v Burns*, punctuation is part of the composition of language, and is sometimes quite significant; he saw no reason to deprive legal documents of the significance attached to punctuation in other writings.[18]

So, for example, brackets can be used in legal documents to mark off parenthetical material, in the same way as in normal prose. This technique is used widely in statutes,[19] and is equally applicable to private legal documents. The only disadvantage – practical, not legal – is that the reader may skip the material in parenthesis, considering it less significant than the surrounding material.[20]

Inverted commas can be used in the same way as in normal prose. Indeed, they are now common in definition clauses, often in combination with brackets. For example, a lease might set out the tenant's details, followed by the parenthetical phrase: (called 'the tenant').[21]

So too, commas can be used in the same way as they are in ordinary prose – as an aid to understanding. Indeed, they *should* be used where necessary, to clarify meaning. For example, in an Australian case, a workers insurance policy described the employer's business as 'Fuel Carrying and Repairing'. Did the policy cover an employee who was injured when driving the employer's vehicle carrying bricks? The New South Wales Court of Appeal held that it did, over-ruling the trial judge. The court interpreted the policy as if it read either 'Fuel, Carrying, and Repairing' or 'Fuel Carrying, and Repairing' (the first alternative being sufficient to cover the facts). The insertion of a comma would have prevented the need for litigation to clarify meaning.[22] Similarly, in an Ohio case a statute allowed a prosecutor to 'introduce the evaluation report or present other evidence at the hearing in accordance with the Rules of Evidence'. At issue was whether the introduction of an evaluation report had to comply with the rules of evidence. A comma between 'report' and 'or' would have given one meaning; but a comma between 'hearing' and 'in' would have given the opposite meaning. In the end, the court construed the provision as if there were a comma between 'report' and 'or', applying the somewhat arbitrary rule that a modifying phrase

---

18 [1918] AC 337 at 348, HL.
19 For example, *Retirement Villages Act* 1999 (NSW).
20 As pointed out by Lord Lloyd of Berwick in *Investors Compensation Scheme Ltd v West Bromwich Building Society* [1998] 1 WLR 896 at 902–3, 904.
21 Many modern drafters would now omit the inverted commas, along with the word 'called', leaving the parenthetical phrase to read simply: (the tenant).
22 *Manufacturers' Mutual Insurance Ltd v Withers* (1988) 5 ANZ Insurance Cases 60–853.

applies only to the words or phrase that immediately precede it ('the last antecedent' principle); but here too the presence of a comma in the legislation would have prevented litigation.[23]

For the possessive also, modern legal usage follows ordinary English usage. Common examples are: *landlord's fixtures, surveyor's fees, tenant's covenants, claimant's case* and *executor's oath*. On the other hand, if it seems more idiomatic to say 'the fixtures of the landlord' or 'the fees of the surveyor', then that construction is adopted.

The dash is also common in legal documents, though its usage differs. Parliamentary drafters use a dash after a lead-in or introduction, to indicate that material is to follow, thus:

In this Part of this Act –

Private drafters rarely use a dash for this purpose. The prefer the traditional but curious hybrid mark combining both colon and dash, thus:

In this Lease, unless the context otherwise requires, the following expressions have the following meanings:–

The modern trend is towards replacing this hybrid mark with a simple colon. This conforms with current practice in ordinary writing, where the colon has acquired the function of pointing to information that is to follow.[24]

Normal punctuation techniques, then, apply as much to legal drafting as they do to ordinary prose. Properly employed, they are useful aids to comprehension. However, their usefulness is subject to one over-riding qualification: judges retain the right to ignore punctuation if they think that by doing so the parties' meaning is better deduced. For example, several leading Australian judges have said that a court is entitled to take notice of commas but is not to be controlled by them if the context requires otherwise.[25] And Sir Robert Megarry has said of punctuation generally:

one must remember that punctuation is normally an aid, and no more than an aid, towards revealing the meaning of the phrases used, and the sense that they are to convey when put in their setting. Punctuation is the servant and not the master of substance and meaning.[26]

---

23 *State of Ohio v Bowen* (Court of Appeals, First Appellate District of Ohio, 28 July 2000).
24 *Fowler's Modern English Usage*, 3rd edn, ed. R. W. Burchfield (Oxford: Clarendon Press, 1996), p. 159. The combination of colon and dash is referred to by printers as 'a full set'.
25 *Committee of Direction of Fruit Marketing v Collins* (1925) 36 CLR 410 at 421 (Isaacs J); *Chew v The Queen* (1992) 173 CLR 626 at 639 (Dawson J).
26 *Marshall v Cottingham* [1982] 1 Ch 82 at 88.

Perhaps for fear of judicial attitudes, there survives a style of modern legal writing which rejects almost all punctuation, leaving much of the sense of a document to be gleaned from layout, particularly from spacing and indentation. This style of drafting offends the principle that legal documents should follow the rules of English composition.[27] Even so, it has received some sort of professional recognition.[28] There is, however, no logical need to deprive legal writing of the benefits of punctuation.

Definitions

In Chapter 5 we discussed aspects of the unsatisfactory use of definitions. But of course definitions have a proper role to play in legal documents. The main one is to give a precise meaning to words and phrases used in the document. Used this way, definitions provide a shorthand method of referring to a particular word or phrase that crops up repeatedly in the document. This can help reduce the length of a document. For example, here is a clause from a traditionally worded mortgage:

> The mortgagee, for himself, *his heirs, executors, administrators and assigns,* covenants with the mortgagor, *his heirs, executors, administrators and assigns,* that if the mortgagor, *his heirs, executors, administrators and assigns,* pays on time all instalments of interest and observes all the covenants to be performed by the mortgagor, *his heirs, executors, administrators and assigns,* then the mortgagee, *his heirs, executors, administrators and assigns* will not call up the principal sum until [*date*]; and it is also agreed that the mortgagor, *his heirs, executors, administrators and assigns,* will not call upon the mortgagee, *his heirs, executors, administrators and assigns,* to accept repayment of the principal sum until [*date*].

The length of this clause could easily be reduced by appropriate definitions, thus:

- 'The mortgagor' includes the mortgagor's heirs, executors, administrators and assigns.
- 'The mortgagee' includes the mortgagee's heirs, executors, administrators and assigns.

Even without further revision (which would be beneficial), the clause can now be shortened to:

> The mortgagee covenants with the mortgagor that if the mortgagor pays on time all instalments of interest and observes all the covenants to be performed

---

27 David Mellinkoff, *Legal Writing: Sense and Nonsense,* p. 44.
28 Piesse, *Elements of Drafting,* pp. 102–3.

by the mortgagor, then the mortgagee will not call up the principal sum until [*date*]; and it is also agreed that the mortgagor will not call upon the mortgagee to accept repayment of the principal sum until [*date*].

Location

Where should definitions be placed in the document? The traditional technique is to put them at the start. There is, of course, some logic to this. The reader encounters the defined meanings early, before meeting the substantive provisions of the document, and so can proceed knowing that particular words and phrases are to be understood in a particular way. But the drawback – at least in a complex document – is the daunting thicket of definitions which are apparently to be conquered before even beginning to wrestle with the substantive provisions. For the lay reader, the document becomes unnecessarily intimidating – for, in contrast to the lawyer, the lay reader is unlikely to proceed directly to the substantive provisions and then return to the definitions to fill out meaning where necessary.

Another technique, increasingly evident in legislative drafting, is to place definitions at the end of the document. This too has some logic to it. The reader begins with the substantive provisions, coming to the definitions later, by which time some feeling has been obtained for the thrust of the document.

A third technique, aiming to capture the best of both worlds, is to begin the document with a bare list of the defined terms, explaining that they are defined at another (specified) point in the document. This technique is now appearing in legislation.[29] It allows the reader to move fairly directly to the substantive provisions, forewarned that certain words and phrases have defined meanings but not yet burdened with the detail of those meanings.

Highlighting defined terms

Most lawyers highlight defined terms where they appear in a document. Readers, alerted that the term is used in a special sense, can then check the definition. In traditional legal documents, the conventional way to highlight a defined term is to capitalise the initial letter of the word (or of each word, if the term comprises more than one word). This convention may well disconcert lay readers, who are unfamiliar with it. As we mentioned in Chapter 5, the convention is so entrenched that it will be difficult to overturn. But that is no justification for preserving it. Other

---

29 For example, in the *Native Title Act* 1993 (Cth).

methods of highlighting defined terms are available, and should be considered. One way is to print them in italics, a convention that some Australian parliamentary drafters now use. Another is to mark them with an asterisk, perhaps adding a running footer along the following lines: 'Asterisked terms have defined meanings, to be found in clause X'.

Whichever method is chosen, it should not unduly interrupt the reader's flow. Highlighting techniques draw attention to themselves, offending the principle that legal documents should follow the ordinary rules of composition. For this reason, the legislative drafting convention – still used in many countries, including England – of leaving defined terms unhighlighted, may have something to commend it. In legal drafting, as in writing generally, lack of clutter is a desirable attribute.

Tables, plans and formulas

Modern legal documents exhibit a growing trend towards the use of tables, plans and formulas. In the hands of the adept drafter, these are indispensable tools for conveying information more efficiently than mere words ever can.

Tables

Tables and tabulation can be used to illustrate the order of steps in a transaction, or to set clauses side-by-side for easy comparison, or to show lists of figures. Their usefulness can be seen in Table 2, taken from an agreement to sell a piece of land and to build a house on it.

Table 2 Use of a table in a contract

Payment table
(a) The Purchaser will pay the Smiths:

Stage	Amount (£)	Triggering event	Date due in 2001
1	60,000	Completion of transfer	3 July
2	30,000	At damp proof course	24 July
3	50,000	At wall plate level	1 September
4	50,000	When the roof of the dwelling is on and the dwelling is plastered out	30 September
5	60,000	Upon satisfactory finish of the works	22 October

(b) The dates for stages 2, 3, 4 and 5 are estimates only, but the date at stage 1 is the contractual date for completion of the transfer.

Plans

Plans can often convey information more effectively than words. They are traditionally used to identify land in conveyances,[30] leases, and transfers of part of the land in a registered title. But they are suitable for all kinds of legal documents, including pleadings (where they are used occasionally) and wills (where they are virtually never used).

Of course, plans should be used only if they are accurate. Inaccurate plans are a fertile source of litigation. So too are plans that are accurate enough for some purposes, but lack sufficient precision for the particular task in hand. Conveyancing plans in England and Wales are often insufficiently accurate to describe the property being conveyed.[31] The English Court of Appeal in *Scarfe v Adams* reminded conveyancers of the consequences of inadequate plans. After stating that a small-scale Ordnance Survey map would be wholly inadequate in ordinary conveyancing, Cumming-Bruce LJ warned:

> I hope that this judgment will be understood by every conveyancing solicitor in the land as giving them warning, loud and clear ... [It] is absolutely essential that each parcel conveyed shall be described in the conveyance or transfer deed with such particularity and precision that there is no room for doubt about the boundaries of each, and for such purposes if a plan is intended to control the description, an Ordnance map on a scale of 1:2500 is worse than useless. The plan or other drawing bound up with the deed must be on such a large scale that it clearly shows with precision where each boundary runs. In my view the parties to this appeal are the victims of sloppy conveyancing for which the professional advisers of vendor and purchasers appear to bear the responsibility.[32]

A common source of difficulty in conveyancing transactions is discrepancy between the words used to describe a property and the plan used to describe the same property. Which prevails: the verbal description or the plan? Sometimes the answer can be gleaned from the document. Thus if the plan is said to be 'for the purposes of identification only' – a phrase we criticised in Chapter 5 – the verbal description prevails.[33] Conversely, if the verbal description proclaims that the property is more

---

30 A buyer cannot insist on a plan where the contract description is clear: *Re Sharman's Contract* [1936] Ch 755. However, the buyer can compel the seller to convey by reference to a plan where it is impossible to describe the property sufficiently without one: *Re Sparrow and James' Contract* [1910] 2 Ch 60.
31 Theodore B. F. Ruoff and others (eds), *Ruoff and Roper on the Law and Practice of Registered Conveyancing* (looseleaf, London: Sweet & Maxwell, 1996), para 4-01.
32 [1981] 1 All ER 843 at 845, CA.
33 *Hopgood v Brown* [1955] 1 WLR 213, 228, CA; *Webb v Nightingale* (1957) 107 LJ 359; *Neilson v Poole* (1969) 20 P&CR 909; *Wigginton and Milner Ltd v Winster Engineering Ltd* [1978] 1 WLR 1462, CA.

particularly described in the plan, the plan prevails.[34] But at other times
the answer is far from clear, as where the following unhelpful (and all
too common) phrases are used: 'for the purposes of identification only
more particularly delineated'[35] or 'for identification more particularly
described'.[36]

Judges take a realistic approach to the role of plans, particularly in
conveyancing transactions. For instance, a plan has been held decisive
in showing that a conveyance passed the entire building within the area
delineated on the plan, even though that building included a room
projecting from a neighbouring property.[37] On the other hand, where a
plan in a conveyance of a 'dwelling-house' showed a wall abutting the
boundary but did not show that the footings supporting the wall pro-
jected slightly beyond the coloured portion of the plan, the conveyance
was held to include the footings; this was because a conveyance of a
'dwelling-house' means all the parts of the dwelling-house, including the
eaves and the footings and any projections of the house.[38]

Graphs and similar techniques

Graphs and similar techniques – flow charts, bar charts, pie charts,
sketches – can be useful in presenting or interpreting legal ideas. They are
already seen in some commercial documents as technical annexes or
schedules, where specialists (such as structural engineers, scientists and
architects) set out their own message in their own way. But they could
be used much more in legal documents generally. Indeed, graphs and
diagrams are sometimes the only way to give information with sufficient
precision. For example, in the field of patents, they are considered

---

34 *Eastwood v Ashton* [1915] AC 900 at 920, HL.
35 See *Neilson v Poole* (1969) 20 P & CR 909 at 916, where Megarry J roundly condemned the
    phrase; *Alan Wibberley Building Ltd v Insley* [1999] 1 WLR 894 at 899, where Lord Hoffmann
    described the phrase as 'fairly inconclusive'.
36 These phrases have echoes in 'as joint tenants in equal shares', another nonsense phrase which
    strings together two conflicting notions. See *Martin v Martin* (1987) 54 P & CR 238 ('as
    beneficial joint tenants in common in equal shares' held to create a tenancy in common); and
    Re Barbour [1967] Qd R 10 ('share and share alike as joint tenants' held to create joint
    tenancy). See also comments by J. E. Adams, 'What's Mine is Mine and What's Yours is Ours'
    [1987] Conv 405.
37 *Laybourn v Gridley* [1892] 2 Ch 53; *Grigsby v Melville* [1974] 1 WLR 80, CA.
38 *Truckell v Stock* [1957] 1 WLR 161, CA. However, the conveyance does not include the
    column of air between the projecting eaves and the projecting footings (ibid. at 163, Lord
    Denning LJ), nor, presumably, the airspace above the projecting eaves or the ground below
    the projecting footings. In the 19th century and early 20th century, it was common to describe
    land 'as the same is now in the occupation of [John Smith] as tenant thereof'. In *Corbett v Hill*
    (1870) 9 LR Eq 671 this type of wording was held to convey a projecting room but not the
    column of air above it. This form of description has now died out, a happy circumstance given
    its inadequate nature.

essential. They are also particularly useful in road traffic regulations, as Panel 10 illustrates.[39]

Formulas

Properly used, mathematical formulas can replace words – reducing length, aiding comprehension, and preventing ambiguity.[40] The formulas themselves can be quite simple. Take this example from the English *Rent Act* 1977, designed to work out what part of a premium lawfully paid on the grant or assignment of a tenancy can be recovered on a later assignment:

The fraction is $\frac{X}{Y}$ where –

X is the residue of the term of the tenancy at the date of the assignment, and Y is the term for which the tenancy was granted.

Another example is the calculation of the price in an option to purchase land:

The price is
$[(A - B) \times 80\%] - OF$
where
- A = open market value
- B = the costs
- OF = the option fee

To express these concepts accurately by way of formula is relatively easy. To express them unambiguously in words would be difficult.

Sometimes, a mathematical formula can express a concept precisely where a verbal formula would be ambiguous. Thus, the relatively simple and unambiguous mathematical formula

$$\sqrt{\frac{250}{3}} + 7$$

---

39 Good examples are *Road Traffic Regulations 1991* (Law Reform Commission of Victoria, Discussion Paper, 1991), and *Proposed Australian Road Rules* (National Road Transport Commission, 1995). Both combine plain English with coloured diagrams.

40 For example, Casen and Steiner have shown that by use of the Heaviside unit step function (invented by Oliver Heaviside and used in engineering applications), potentially ambiguous words can be replaced by a precise mathematical formula which caters for varying conditions. The formula and its associated definitions ran to nearly three typed pages. See M. Casen and J. M. Steiner, 'Mathematical Functions and Legal Drafting' (1986) 102 *Law Quarterly Review*, p. 585.

Riding a bicycle in a bicycle lane

1406   If there is a bicycle lane on a *carriageway*⁺ you must ride
       in it if it is practicable to do so.

Fig.115 a,b,c,d.
Bicycle lane signs.

Penalty : 1 penalty unit

Riding a bicycle on a separated footpath

1407   If you are riding a bicycle on a *separated footpath*⁺, you
       must not ride it on the side of the *footpath*⁺ that is
       reserved for *pedestrians*⁺.

Fig.116 a,b,c,d.
Separated footpath signs.

Penalty : 1 penalty unit

> Similarly, a pedestrian must not use a bicycle path or that
> part of a separated footpath that is reserved for bicycles (See
> Reg.1710).

Riding a bicycle on a shared footpath

1408   If you are riding a bicycle on a *shared footpath*⁺, you
       must *give way*⁺ to a pedestrian who is either on, or
       entering, the footpath.

Fig.117 a,b,c,d.
Shared footpath signs.

Penalty : 1 penalty unit

Panel 10 Regulatory signs

can be expressed verbally as 'the square root of two hundred and fifty divided by three plus seven'.[41] But those words, used alone, are ambiguous, since they can also mean:

$$\sqrt{\frac{250}{3+7}}$$

$$\text{or } \sqrt{200} + \frac{50}{3} + 7$$

$$\text{or } \sqrt{200} + \frac{50}{3+7}$$

Drafters should not fear that judges are hostile to the use of mathematical formulas. Quite the contrary: judges have encouraged their use in legal documents. For example, in *London Regional Transport v Wimpey Group Services*, Hoffmann J concluded his judgment:

> Finally, I might be allowed to offer a word of advice to both surveyors and conveyancers. I doubt whether the mistakes which gave rise to this litigation would have happened if the surveyors' formula had been expressed algebraically instead of verbally, either in the original correspondence or the agreement. Rent formulae can often be expressed more simply and unambiguously in algebraic form and this case shows that a very modest degree of numeracy can save a great deal of money.[42]

Notes and examples

There is a growing trend in legislation to insert notes and examples to help readers understand the effect of provisions.[43] These devices can also be useful in private legal documents. For example, a rent review provision in a lease may contain a working example of the way in which the valuer is to take into account the various factors that are relevant to calculating the revised rent; or a clause in a mortgage may end with a 'Note' pointing readers to other clauses in the mortgage that deal with related material. In practice, examples or notes are sometimes qualified by a provision to the effect that they are for information only, and are not intended to affect the construction of the document – though such a provision might be thought to suggest that the drafter is somewhat

---

41 See David Crystal, *The Cambridge Encyclopedia of Language* (Cambridge: Cambridge University Press, 1987), p. 381.

42 [1986] 2 EGLR 41. This case is discussed in Chapter 2.

43 The devices are not new: examples can be found in the *Indian Evidence Act* of 1872, cited in Law Reform Commission of Victoria, *Report No. 33: Access to the Law: The Structure and Format of Legislation* (1990), pp. 54–5.

insecure about the effect of the document. But in any case, the drafter should of course take care to ensure that the examples are correct, for nothing is more apt to confuse than an example in conflict with its accompanying text.[44]

'Shall' and the modern document

In Chapter 5 we dealt with some of the interpretational difficulties caused by the word *shall*. We mentioned particularly the potential for imprecision the word raises in two contexts: the futurity/precondition dichotomy, and the obligation/direction dichotomy.

Some modern writers still feel that *shall* has a place in legal documents. They distinguish between provisions that express a *command* and provisions that are merely *directory*. By *directory* they mean provisions requiring a certain course to be taken but imposing no sanction for breach – provisions that deprive the subject of an opportunity or right, but whose breach gives rise to no legal consequences. In the view of these writers, *must* should be used for directory provisions but *shall* should be retained to impose a command (mandatory).[45] Thus, for example, a former Chief Parliamentary Counsel for England and Wales has written:

> I would as a rule expect to find 'shall' in provisions expressing a command and either 'shall' or 'must' in directory provisions such as 'notice of appeal shall/must be given within thirty days'. There are of course also provisions of other kinds in which either of those words may occur. We have nothing in the nature of guidelines. The word chosen depends on the nature of the provision and on ordinary usage.[46]

This view seems to be based on the premise that to use *must* for obligation leaves nothing distinctive for direction. Yet to prescribe *shall* for obligation and *must* for direction seems unnecessarily pedantic and as a practical matter invites trouble.[47] It also overlooks the linguistic reality that in common speech *shall* is now used only rarely, and where it is used

---

44 As in *Whittaker v Comcare* (1998) 28 AAR 55.
45 See Dickerson, *Fundamentals of Legal Drafting*, 2nd edn (Boston and Toronto: Little, Brown and Co., 1986), p. 214; R. W. Ramage, 'Will or Shall?' (1970) 120 *New Law Journal*, p. 402; Dick, *Legal Drafting*, p. 93; Robinson, *Drafting*, p. 40.
46 C. H. de Waal in a letter to Richard Castle, 20 March 1987.
47 Some exemplars of the modern style such as Garner and Kimble see some benefits in preserving this use of *shall*, although conceding as a practical matter that *must* is preferable: B. Garner, *Dictionary of Modern Legal Usage*, 2nd edn (Oxford: Oxford University Press, 1995), pp. 939–42; J. Kimble, 'The Many Misuses of *Shall*' (1992) 3 *Scribes Journal of Legal Writing*, p. 61 (cf M. Asprey, 'Shall Must Go' ibid., p. 79, and Kimble's rejoinder, ibid., p. 85).

it can have two quite different senses: to indicate compulsion ('You shall shut the door') or futurity ('Tomorrow I shall shut the door'). To use it in legal documents can give rise to the same ambiguity.

The modern trend is to eliminate *shall* altogether and replace it with something more appropriate – usually *must*. As long ago as 1985 the Attorney-General of Victoria, in a ministerial statement on legislative drafting, stipulated that in future legislation *must* was to replace *shall* wherever *shall* was used to impose an obligation.[48] The Law Reform Commission of Victoria recommended the same approach in its report on plain language.[49] These pioneering views received a degree of judicial criticism – especially when used in the negative form, *must not*[50] – and some professional resistance.[51] However, the move to *must* is now seen in the legislation of many jurisdictions, including most Australian states, New Zealand, and Canada.[52] *Must* is also now finding favour in the United Kingdom.[53] Lawyers who draft private legal documents could well follow this lead.

Of course, drafters must use *must* consistently. In careless hands, *must* can be as ambiguous as *shall*.[54] Judges have always felt free in appropriate circumstances to interpret *shall* as creating a mere direction or discretion – that is, to read *shall* as *may*.[55] So too they will feel free to construe *must* as *may*. There is one difference, however: unlike *shall*, there is as yet no established line of authority to comfort a judge who is tempted to adopt such a flexible construction of *must*. Judicial statements to date all support the view that *must* is to be read as mandatory. For example, as long ago as 1979, the Ontario Divisional Court said that 'must' has to be considered mandatory, and that it is not an equivocal word like 'shall',

---

48 Victorian Parliament, *Plain English Legislation* [Melbourne, 1985], p. 6; also in *Victorian Parliamentary Debates*, vol. 377, pp. 432–7. See also Canada's *Uniform Interpretation Act 1967–68*, c 7, ss 10 and 28.

49 *Report 9: Plain English and the Law* (1987), vol. 1, p. 61.

50 *Halwood Corporation Ltd v Roads Corporation* [1998] 2 VR 439 at 445–6 (Tadgell JA).

51 See correspondence in the *Australian Law Journal*: (1989) 63, pp. 75–8, 522–5, 726–8; (1990) 64 ALJ 168–9.

52 See A. Watson-Brown, 'Shall Revisited' (1995) 25 *Queensland Law Society Journal* (June), p. 263; New Zealand Law Commission, *Legislation Manual* (Wellington, 1996), paras 171–3. In Canada, since 1992 the statutes of British Columbia use *must* to impose obligation, bolstered by s 29 of the *Interpretation Act* (RSBC, 1996, ch. 238) requiring *must* to be construed as imperative.

53 See *Human Rights Act* 1998, a quiet about-turn in English parliamentary drafting.

54 John Lyons, *Introduction to Theoretical Linguistics* (Cambridge: Cambridge University Press, 1968), p. 309.

55 See, for example, *Balabel v Mehmet* [1990] 1 EGLR 220 (CA), where a clause in a contract for purchase of a leasehold entitled the purchaser to go into possession before completion, but provided that if the landlord's consent to assignment was refused within a stated time, then 'the Purchaser shall vacate the premises'. In the context, it was held that 'shall' meant 'shall be entitled to', or 'may'. See also Chapter 5.

which courts had held could be either mandatory or directory.[56] More recently, a British Columbia judge (construing a statute which formerly provided that 'the Court *shall* make' an order restraining a person from disposing of matrimonial assets, but which had been amended to provide that 'the Court *must* make' the order) said that 'must' entails a 'more mandatory obligation, admitting of less discretion in the Court'.[57] And an Australian judge has expressly recognised that 'must' is quite sufficient to impose an obligation.[58]

Some drafters shun *must* because they see it as too harsh or heavy-handed for the tone of their document. This attitude should not be dismissed out of hand as precious. The tone of a document may be important. For instance, where parties have worked hard to develop a relationship of mutual co-operation and respect, an overuse of *must* in the document which regulates their relationship might introduce an unnecessarily adversarial attitude. In such a case, the drafter might try *is to*, an alternative now quite acceptable as a means of creating compulsion – for example: the tenant '*is to* keep the premises in repair' or the landlord '*is to* provide a set a keys'.[59] Here too, however, consistency of terminology is important: it would be unwise to use both *must* and *is to* in the same document, lest it be thought that the drafter intended to distinguish between them.[60]

Handling generality and vagueness

Sometimes, lawyers must draft in generalities. Detail may not be possible. An example is where the parties to a document have settled heads of agreement and wish to bind themselves contractually without waiting for fine detail to be worked through. Usually, this does not cause any problem. Generality is only to be condemned where it produces ambiguity – something that is open to two or more different meanings.

Sometimes, too, lawyers must use expressions that are inherently vague, for nothing more precise is available. Examples are: *reasonable, as soon as possible, as soon as may be, as soon as practicable, immediately,*

---

56 *Re Agricultural Union and others v Massey-Ferguson Industries Ltd* (1979) 94 DLR (3d) 743. But see *Brygel v Stewart-Thornton* [1992] 2 VR 387 at 379–99 (followed in *Re Phillip Andrew Balyl* (1994) 75 A Crim R 575), holding that a statutory provision that a document 'must' contain specified material was satisfied if the document contained substantially that material.
57 *Lovick v Brough* (unreported, Sup Ct of BC, Spencer J, 4 March 1998).
58 *South Australian Housing Trust v Development Assessment Commission* (1994) 63 SASR 35 at 38.
59 An example is the English Standard Conditions of Sale of Land; see Richard Castle, 'Standard Conditions of Sale: a Milestone' (1990) 16 *Law Society Gazette*, p. 24.
60 For an example of lapses of this kind, see s 133D of the *Real Property Act* 1900 (NSW), where *is to* and *must* are used interchangeably in the one section; and s 85 of the *Retirement Villages Act* 1999 (NSW), where *will* and *must* are used interchangeably in the one sentence.

whenever, reputable, satisfactory, usual, material, fair, proper. The import of
these and similar words varies with the context. Here, too, condemnation
is appropriate only where the vagueness leads to ambiguity.

In some contexts, vagueness can be a benefit.[61] David Mellinkoff
praises what he calls 'calculated' ambiguity, equating it with flexibility
and the use of vague words like *necessary, reasonable, substantial, satisfactory* and *proper*.[62] Consider, for example, the following right of way,
granted on the sale of a council house. It exhibits elements of vagueness,
but it is not ambiguous:

> The right to pass and repass at all times with or without vehicles over that part
> of the vehicular access as is shown coloured brown on the plan annexed hereto
> subject to the payment to the Council ... of a proportion of the cost of
> maintenance and upkeep thereof.

The precise 'proportion' to be paid is not specified (nor would the
obligation be any more precise if the drafter had employed a more commonly used phrase: 'a proper proportion', 'a fair proportion', 'a proper
proportion according to use', or the like). In reality, the parties will use
their common sense to calculate a figure as the question arises from time
to time. Specifying a more precise formula is not a central issue in the
document, and the risk that the clause will be tested in court is so remote
that it can be discounted. Provisions of this kind rarely prove a problem.
They demonstrate the adage that drafters should ask themselves 'Will it
work?' rather than 'What will a judge think of it?', which in turn reflects
Professor J. E. Adams's distinction between 'planning for performance'
and 'planning for risk'.[63]

Again, consider the following extract from a franchise agreement for a
milk round:

> The Franchisor undertakes ... :
> (a) To supply sufficient Liquid Milk and Milk Products ... as the Franchise
>   Operator may require to enable him to provide a regular and efficient
>   service to retail customers in the Franchise Area.

The words 'sufficient', 'regular', and 'efficient', are incapable of precise
definition. But the parties can see quite well what is meant, and given
that each side gains advantages from the contract, it works. The writing,
though fuzzy, is adequate for the occasion.

---

61 Reed Dickerson, *Fundamentals of Legal Drafting*, pp. 35, 39.
62 *Language of the Law*, p. 450.
63 J. E. Adams, Address to the Commerce and Industry Group of the Law Society of England
   and Wales, reported at (1982) 72 *Law Society Gazette*, p. 1582. Professor Adams is the
   precedents editor of the leading English journal, *The Conveyancer and Property Lawyer*.

Of course, some legal documents demand more precision than others. For example, in conveyances of land it is important to be precise in describing the property being conveyed (the 'parcels clause'). But even here some flexibility may be allowed. An example is the parcels clause from the conveyance set out below. Although hardly a model of crisp drafting, the description of the width had to be vague because the strips of land in question were hundreds of yards long:

> ALL THOSE four strips of land varying in width between one and two feet adjoining on the northern and southern side of the public highway, all which said strips of land form part of the holding known as Cowleaze Farm, ... all which four lengths of such strips being identified on the plan marked A annexed hereto by red lines.

To cite another example: as a general rule, undertakings should set out clearly what is undertaken to be done. This is particularly the case with undertakings given by lawyers, for they must be susceptible to judicial enforcement as part of the courts' supervisory jurisdiction over their officers.[64] But with some other kinds of undertakings, a degree of woolliness may be excused. The following is a borrower's undertaking to a building society:

> I undertake that I will carry out the following work to the above property within six months of completion of your mortgage advance to me on the security of the above property namely:–
> 1. Replace few roof slates (house and garage).
> 2. Repair gutter joints.
> 3. Repair plumbing joints at base of hot water cylinder.
> 4. Remedy dampness to chimney-breast in bedroom (boiler flue may need lining) – check damp roof timbers above.
> 5. Examine very slight woodworm attacks to floorboards in loft and under the staircase – treat if still active

Some of the borrower's obligations are expressed vaguely. Yet as long as both sides acknowledge the vagueness (which they can be taken to have done), no harm is caused. Undertakings like these rarely have to be enforced, for in all probability the borrower will make sure the work is done.

Generality and vagueness, then, have a proper place in legal documents. But they should be used sparingly, for excessive use of either can

---

64 *Re a Solicitor* [1966] 1 WLR 1604; *Wade v Licardy* (1993) 33 NSWLR 1 at 7–9; *Re C (a solicitor)* [1982] 1 NZLR 137.

be counterproductive. Yet so too can excessive particularity. The problem lies in knowing on which side of the line to go.[65]

To illustrate the problems of excessive particularity, take the following example of a tenant's covenant in a commercial lease:

> Not at any time on or after [*date*] to bring keep store stack or lay out upon the land any materials equipment plant bins crates cartons boxes or any receptacle for waste or any other item which is or might become unsightly or in any way detrimental to the Premises or the area generally.

Does the covenant preclude the tenant from bringing onto the land any barrels or tins? On one view, no. The maxim *expressio unius est exclusio alterius* (the inclusion of one thing is the exclusion of the other; see Chapter 2) suggests that the omission of barrels and tins from the list of prohibited items is deliberate. But on another view, yes. The maxim *eiusdem generis* (where a list of items belonging to the same category is followed by general words, the general words are construed as confined to the same category; see Chapter 2) suggests that barrels and tins are in the same category as the items prohibited in the list, and so are included under 'any other item'. Whatever the result, it may be capricious. The drafter's over-particularity has posed problems of interpretation.

The clause could be made clearer by substituting a general word or words for each list, along these lines:

- 'bring keep store stack or lay out': *allow*
- 'materials equipment plant bins crates cartons boxes receptacles for waste or any other item': *thing*
- 'is or might become': *is*
- 'unsightly or in anyway detrimental': *unsightly or detrimental*
- 'the Premises or the area generally': *the premises or the neighbourhood.*

The clause could then be rewritten:

> On and after [*date*], not to allow on the land anything that is unsightly or detrimental to the premises or to the neighbourhood.

Pronouns

Legal documents drafted in the traditional style tend to avoid personal pronouns, such as *she, they, we*. More formal substitutes are used – 'the said', 'the aforesaid', and the like. This style, perhaps adopted in the mistaken notion that it promotes precision, makes legal documents

---

65 See *Lavery v Pursell* (1888) 39 Ch D 508 at 517 (Chitty J); *Hobbs v London & South Western Railway* (1875) LR 10 QB 111 at 121 (Blackburn J).

impersonal and stuffy. In contrast, the modern style of drafting has no qualms about using personal pronouns in legal documents. As David Mellinkoff puts it:

> The 'plain language movement' has rediscovered the pronouns 'you' and 'I'. Some now hail these born again pronouns as the key to legal simplification. The pronouns are short, easy to read, and give an appearance of intimacy lacking in a third person label. Any normal person would rather be an 'I', or even a 'you', rather than a 'Party of the First Part'.[66]

The 'I', 'we', and 'you' style is now becoming common in modern legal drafting. Properly used, it can greatly improve the accessibility of legal documents.

Although we embrace this trend towards pronouns, two cautionary notes should be added. First, the chatty style of 'you' and 'we' may be out of place in a document where one side wishes to impress the other with the formality of the obligations being undertaken and the potential seriousness of their breach. To quote Mellinkoff again:

> The 'You' and 'I' format also has an inherent frailty that dictates cautious use. The very virtue of conversational informality lends itself to conveying a sense of camaraderie that may be essentially inconsistent with the adversary relation of the parties. If pronouns get too friendly, they tend to induce an unwarranted relaxation of attention to detail.[67]

Second, used thoughtlessly the style can produce drivel. Consider the following example:

> You will not become bankrupt, commit an act of bankruptcy, call a meeting with your creditors or reach any arrangement with them, or allow anyone to present a bankruptcy petition against you.

Some of these events are quite beyond the promisor's control – for example, the promise not to allow anyone to present a bankruptcy petition. Essentially, what the drafter intended was a promise not to trigger the prohibited events by getting into financial difficulties. It would have been better to draft those events as triggers for remedies enforceable by the other party to the document. To speak of bankruptcy as a breach of obligation is to stretch the language unduly.[68]

---

66 *Legal Writing: Sense and Nonsense*, p. 96.
67 Ibid., p. 98.
68 *Cadogan Estates Ltd v McMahon* [2000] 3 WLR 1555 at 1561 (Lord Hoffmann) and 1567 (Lord Millett).

If pronouns are employed to create a personal and informal style, rarely should it be necessary to define formally for whom the pronouns stand. Yet provisions like this are sometimes seen:

> The words 'you' or 'your' mean Cardmember, that is, the person named on the enclosed Card. The words 'we', 'our' and 'us' refer to American Express Europe Limited or its successors.

Almost always, context makes these kinds of definitions tautologous.

Inclusive language

Allied to the topic of pronouns is the matter of gender-neutral, or inclusive, language. The traditional style of legal drafting prefers the male pronoun, sometimes adding the interpretative rider that 'male includes female'.[69] This is so even where the document is a standard form, such as a mortgage or lease, designed for use by males and females alike.

The modern style of drafting – as with writing generally – avoids the exclusive use of the male pronoun and deliberately adopts a gender-neutral approach. Some drafters achieve this result simply by replacing 'he' with 'he or she', with the occasional inversion 'she or he' as if to correct past infelicities by positive linguistic discrimination. This can produce strained language. It is much better to redraft in a way that remains idiomatic.

The New Zealand Law Commission, in its 1996 *Legislation Manual*, suggests a number of techniques for avoiding the male pronoun.[70] The commission takes as its example the clause 'A member of the Tribunal may resign his office', and suggests the following devices:

- Omit the pronoun: 'A member of the Tribunal may resign office.'
- Use both masculine and female pronouns: 'A member of the Tribunal may resign his or her office.'
- Repeat the noun: 'A member of the Tribunal may resign the office of member.'
- Use the plural: 'Members of the Tribunal may resign their offices.'

Other techniques may also be used:

- Convert a noun to a verb form (a practice to be encouraged in any case, as we mentioned in Chapter 5). So the clause 'The landlord shall give his consent to an application if he is satisfied...' can be recast 'The landlord must consent to an application if satisfied ...'.

---

69 Sandra Petersson, 'Gender Neutral Drafting: Historical Perspective' (1998) 19 *Statute Law Review*, p. 93.
70 Report No. 35, *Legislation Manual: Structure and Style* (Wellington, 1996), p. 47.

- Use a relative clause. Thus, 'Where a landlord re-enters under the lease, he may ...' becomes 'A landlord who re-enters under the lease may ...'.
- Use *they* and its variants as a singular pronoun. Hence 'The landlord may revoke his consent if ...' becomes 'The landlord may revoke their consent if...' This technique is increasing in popularity. It is found in both private legal documents and in statutes.[71] The *Oxford English Dictionary* traces its ancestry to the Rolls of Parliament of 1464. However, some drafters still find that it jars.

Whichever technique is used, of course, the drafter must be careful to ensure precision and consistency. It is also preferable, stylistically, to adopt a technique that does not draw attention to itself: for example, if a document is intended for single parties, to draft in the plural will seem incongruous. Those matters apart, no legal requirement demands retention of the traditional 'male-only' style. It can always be replaced by inclusive language without loss of legal precision or effectiveness.

Problems with 'and', 'or'

Legal drafters often overlook the potential for ambiguity inherent in the conjunctions *and* and *or*. The most celebrated example in England is the case which has come to be known as *Re Diplock*.[72] The judges who considered the case as it progressed through the various levels of courts expended an estimated 70,000 words on whether the phrase 'charitable *or* benevolent' created a valid charitable trust in a will.[73] In the end, the House of Lords ruled that it did not.[74] The issue arose because of the principle that a gift does not create a charitable trust unless every object or purpose of the gift is exclusively charitable; and not every benevolent object is 'charitable', as the law understands that word. Clearly, 'charitable *and* benevolent' is preferable to 'charitable *or* benevolent', since *and* cuts down the type of organisation that can benefit.[75]

The potential for difficulty in the use of these conjunctions is heightened by cases which have held that *and* is not always conjunctive,

---

71 J. Burnside, 'She – He – They' (1999) 110 *Victorian Bar News* (Spring), p. 53, discusses private documents. Statute examples are the Australian *Corporations Law* and the Ontario *Tobacco Tax Act* (which also uses 'themself' as a singular pronoun). For a more detailed examination, see Corporations Law Simplification Program, *Drafting Issues: A Singular Use of THEY* (Simplification Task Force, Commonwealth Attorney-General's Department, September 1995).

72 Ending in the House of Lords under the name *Ministry of Health v Simpson* [1951] AC 251.

73 The estimate is from F. L. Lucas, *Style*, 2nd edn (London: Cassell, 1974), p. 18.

74 In *Chichester Diocesan Fund and Board of Finance v Simpson* [1944] AC 341.

75 *Re Sutton* (1885) 28 Ch D 464 ('charitable and deserving'); *Re Best* [1904] 2 Ch 354.

and *or* is not always disjunctive. These cases show that context may require the words to be construed in ways contrary to their normal meaning.[76] To illustrate: *and* was found to be disjunctive – effectively meaning *or* – in *Attorney-General of the Bahamas v Royal Trust Co.* There, the Privy Council was asked to interpret the following clause:

> To use the income therefrom and any part of the capital thereof for any purposes for and/or connected with the education *and* welfare of Bahamian children and young people.

Their Lordships held that, since education would normally be for the welfare of a child, some wider meaning had to be given to 'and welfare'. Further, if welfare was ancillary to education, a purpose 'connected with' welfare would necessarily be connected with education, so the reference to welfare would again be otiose. With such abstruse reasoning, *and* was held to be disjunctive. In the result, the gift was void because it was not wholly charitable.[77]

And was also found to be disjunctive in the following phrase, which formed part of the objects clause of a theatrical association: 'To present classical, artistic, cultural *and* educational dramatic works'.[78] The court held that the plays authorised could be classical *or* artistic *or* cultural *or* educational, or any combination. To have found otherwise would have narrowed the repertoire to plays with *all* the named characteristics, which was clearly not intended.

The Privy Council, too, treated *and* as disjunctive in the following clause:

> [The property] shall be held by my trustees in trust for such charitable benevolent religious *and* educational institutions societies associations *and* objects as they in their uncontrolled discretion shall select.

Lord Buckmaster said of the word *and* in this clause:

> It is, in their Lordships' opinion, impossible to use the word 'and' as a link intended to join all the words together and make the gift available only for such institutions or objects as satisfied each one of the conditions represented by each of the separate words. Apart from the fact that such a restriction would all but render the gift inoperative, it is plain from the use of the word 'and' in the phrase 'institutions societies associations and objects' which occurs twice in immediate succession to the words in question, that 'and' must be regarded as 'or'.

---

76 See (1940) 56 LQR 451 (note by REM).
77 [1986] 1 WLR 1001, PC.
78 *Associated Artists Ltd v Inland Revenue Commissioners* [1956] 1 WLR 752.

The trust failed because the clause allowed the trustees to choose a body that was not charitable in the legal sense.[79]

In contrast, the House of Lords construed *or* conjunctively in the following statutory provision:

> If any oil to which this section applies is discharged from a British ship, the owner *or* master of the ship shall ... be guilty of an offence under this section.

The House of Lords held that both the owner *and* the master could be guilty of an offence. Lord Wilberforce said that in logic there was no rule that *or* must always carry an exclusive force; whether it does so depends on the context.[80]

'And/or'

The contrived conjunction *and/or* is becoming common in legal drafting. Scrutton LJ once described its use as so liberal in the document before him that it gave the appearance of being sprinkled 'as if from a pepper-pot'.[81] In recent times it has even appeared in statutes.[82] All this is despite judicial strictures against its use. In the United States, judges have condemned it as an 'abominable invention ... as devoid of meaning as it is incapable of classification by the rules of grammar and syntax'; as 'that Janus-faced verbal monstrosity, neither word nor phrase, the child of the brain of someone too lazy or too dull to express his precise meaning, or too dull to know what he did mean'; and as one of those 'inexcusable barbarisms which was sired by indolence and damned by indifference'.[83] In England, Viscount Simon LC, when discussing confused pleadings before the court, spoke of 'the repeated use of the bastard conjuction "and/or" which has, I fear, become the commercial court's contribution to basic English'.[84] In Australia, the phrase was described as 'an elliptical and embarrassing expression which endangers accuracy for the sake of brevity'.[85]

---

79 *Attorney-General for New Zealand v Brown* [1917] AC 393, PC, at 397.
80 *Federal Steam Navigation Co. v Department of Trade* [1974] 2 All ER 97, HL at 110. The Act referred to is the *Oil in Navigable Waters Act* 1963.
81 *Gurney v Grimmer* (1932) 44 Lloyds L Rep 189.
82 For example, the Australian *Trade Marks Act* 1995.
83 *American General Insurance Co. v Webster* 118 SW 2d 1084 (Texas, 1938); *Employers' Mutual Liability Insurance Co. v Tollefsen* 263 NW 376 at 377 (1935); *Cochrane v Florida East Coast Ry Co.* 145 So 217 at 218 (1932).
84 *Bonitto v Fuerst Bros & Co. Ltd* [1944] AC 75 at 82.
85 *Fadden v Deputy Commissioner of Taxation* (1943) 68 CLR 76 at 82 (Williams J). See also *Burwood Project Management Pty Ltd v Polar Technologies International Pty Ltd* (1999) 9 BPR 17,355 (exercise of option 'by A and/or B' invalid).

No doubt the popularity of *and/or* springs from its usefulness in compressing sentences. Thus, the drafter writes in a lease 'The landlord shall provide electricity and/or gas'. But while brevity is generally to be commended, over-compression of expression tends to mislead. Here, the use of *and/or* obscures the reality that the landlord has an option, satisfied by providing *either* gas or electricity, with no obligation to provide both. The word *and* is superfluous, which is why its presence tends to confuse: the drafter should have written 'The landlord must provide electricity or gas, and may provide both'.

Drafting in the present tense

The modern technique is to draft in the present tense. This contrasts with the traditional style, which often adopts more complex tense constructions as if required for precision. However, documents generally speak in the present, and so it makes more sense to draft in the present tense. This makes for clearer, crisper drafting, and should never cause ambiguity. For example, traditional phrasing includes:

- If the purchaser *shall fail* to pay, then ...
- If the purchaser *should fail* to pay, then ...
- If the purchaser *shall have failed* to pay, then ...

The modern drafter says:

> If the purchaser *fails* to pay, then ...

The technique of drafting in the present tense is especially useful in simplifying the structure of definitions. For example, instead of

> In this agreement, residence *shall include* a house.

The modern style prefers

> In this agreement, residence includes a house.

Deeds

Many legal documents take the form of deeds. In some cases this is because the law requires a deed (as distinct from a simple agreement) – for example, to create a legal interest rather than an equitable interest.[86]

---

86 For example, *Law of Property Act* 1925 (England and Wales), s 25; *Conveyancing Act*, 1919 (NSW), s 23B.

In other cases, drafters adopt the form of a deed because its formality helps to emphasise the solemnity of the transaction.[87] Whatever the reason for using a deed, some matters are relevant to drafting deeds in the modern style.

Formal parts of a deed

Some formal parts of a deed – such as the testatum ('Now this deed witnesses'), the habendum ('to hold unto'), and the testimonium ('In witness whereof the parties hereto') – are antique and can be discarded. In fact, the testatum and the habendum have all but disappeared already. The testimonium, though, has shown surprising resilience. Almost 400 years ago the eminent jurist Sir Edward Coke showed that the testimonium was unnecessary.[88] To jettison it now hardly seems radical.

Recitals

Recitals give the background to the document. They are easily identified, being traditionally heralded by the ubiquitous *Whereas*. Sometimes recitals are inserted out of habit, with no thought to whether they serve a purpose in the document. If they do not, they can be safely discarded.

In the hands of experienced drafters, however, recitals may serve a useful purpose. For example, a recital can create an estoppel, precluding the party who made the statement from later denying the truth of the matter recited.[89] By a related doctrine, a recital can operate to pass title to land. This is the doctrine of 'feeding the estoppel'. It occurs where a vendor (or mortgagor) who has no title to land which they have purportedly conveyed under a deed of conveyance recites in the deed that they have the title; by the doctrine, if the vendor (or mortgagor) later acquires title to the land, then the title passes to the purchaser (or mortgagee) by virtue of the recital without the need for any further conveyance.[90] Again, recitals can ensure the benefit (in later years) of the common statutory provision that recitals of facts in documents of a certain age are presumed to be correct.[91]

---

87 A deed being the most solemn form of document a person can make: *Manton v Parabolic* (1985) 2 NSWLR 361 at 367–9.

88 Edward Coke, *The First Part of the Institutes of the Laws of England; or a Commentary on Littleton* (first published 1628), p. 7.

89 *Bensley v Burdon* (1830) 8 LJ (OS) Ch 85; *Heath v Crealock* (1874) LR 10 Ch App 22; *Discount & Finance Ltd v Gehrig's Wines Ltd* (1940) 57 WN (NSW) 226; *Grant v John Grant & Sons Pty Ltd* (1954) 91 CLR 112.

90 *Re Bridgewater's Settlement* [1910] 2 Ch 342. Cf. *First National Bank Plc v Thompson* [1996] 2 WLR (CA): estoppel even without recital.

91 For example, *Law of Property Act* 1925 (England and Wales), ss 44, 45; *Conveyancing Act*, 1919 (NSW), s 53. Recitals of this kind can prove particularly useful in conveyancing documents, allowing later vendors and purchasers to rely on the matters recited.

Under long-settled principles of interpretation, recitals can also play a useful (though limited) role in construing documents. Stated shortly, these principles are:

- If the operative part of the deed is ambiguous and the recitals are clear, then the recitals govern the construction.
- If the recitals are ambiguous and the operative part is clear, the operative part prevails.
- If both the operative part and the recitals are clear but inconsistent with each other, the operative part prevails.[92]

Finally, on a more general level, sometimes background information is useful in a document to show where the parties have come from and what they propose to do. In this way, recitals can be used to set the scene for the heart of the deal, serving as a statement of purpose and helping interpretation.

Even where recitals are useful, however, there is no need to perpetuate a formalistic style. If recitals are thought necessary, they can be grouped under a heading such as 'Background', rather than the more formal 'Recitals'; and *whereas* can be dispensed with entirely.

Amending documents

Modern drafters would do well to consider the ways in which they amend standard-form documents. The usual style is to adopt the traditional parliamentary convention. For example, at the end of standard-form contract provisions the drafter will add amendments along these lines:

- In clause 27, delete 'agent' and insert 'stakeholder'.
- In clause 35, delete 'rescission' and insert 'termination'.
- In clause 47, after 'notified' insert 'in writing', and delete 'not' where thirdly appearing.

Unless the number of amendments is few, this amending technique is cumbersome. It forces the reader to go backwards and forwards in the document, trying to garner meaning from fragmented information. It is better to delete the clauses to be amended, and then include their full text as amended. Another option is to state the overall effect of the amendments, and then set out the detailed textual amendments in a schedule.

To illustrate the latter technique, imagine a large residential development where the freeholder has let the entire site on a long lease to a housing association. The lease identifies an area of the land for special-needs

---

92 *Leggott v Barrett* (1880) 15 Ch D 306 at 311; *Ex parte Dawes* (1886) 17 QBD 275 at 286; *O'Loughlin v Mount* (1998) 71 SASR 206 at 217–18.

housing, which is to be sublet to a mental health trust, which will manage
the units in that area. The scheme is now to change in the following ways:
the land allocated for special-needs housing is to be altered, and the
housing association itself is to manage the units with the help of specialist
staff. To achieve these changes will require numerous amendments to
various parts of a lengthy document. A deed of variation merely making
textual amendments to the original documentation is likely to be
incomprehensible. Far better to state the effect of the new arrangements
boldly in the body of the deed, and then to put the textual amendments
in a schedule.

Standard forms

We end this chapter with some comments on the use of standard forms
in legal drafting. More and more in modern legal practice, information is
conveyed by means of standard forms. Sometimes, the use of forms is
prescribed by statute, leaving the drafter with little scope for presenting
material more effectively. At other times, their use is optional.

Statutory forms

Model forms provided by statute have been widely available to the legal
profession for many years. In England and Wales, for example, the *Settled
Land Act* 1925 set out in its first schedule 'examples of instruments
framed in accordance with the provisions of this Act'. Another Act, the
Law of Property Act 1925, contained forms relating to mortgages and
other matters. The purpose was to provide forms that would be treated as
effective for the objective in mind: thus, the *Law of Property Act* provided
that instruments 'in the like form or using expressions to the like effect,
shall, in regard to form and expression be sufficient'. Most other jurisdictions have statutory provisions in the same vein. Generally speaking,
however, the legal profession has been reluctant to accept the statutory
invitation to use forms of this kind. For whatever reason, lawyers have
preferred to produce their own forms.

Forms used for land registration purposes are in a different category. Their use is generally mandatory, for the land registration system
hinges on their use.[93] These forms generally abandon the mumbo-jumbo
that bedevils traditional conveyancing documents, being drafted on the
premise that instruments (and entries in the register based on them)

---

93 In England and Wales, the forms spring from the *Land Registration Act* 1925. In Australia,
   they are promulgated under the various Torrens title statutes, such as the *Real Property Act*
   1900 (NSW).

should be clear, simple and definite. They contain no formal commencement; recitals are discouraged; lengthy clauses transferring quasi-easements and other appurtenant rights are absent;[94] and the testatum, habendum and testimonium (discussed above) are discarded. In short, they reflect an appreciation that both the form and language of traditional conveyancing documents are needlessly complex.

Even where the use of statutory forms is mandatory, some flexibility is generally allowed in their use. Statutes usually authorise the use of forms 'substantially to the same effect' as the prescribed forms. This permits forms to be modified to suit the particular transaction, but it can give rise to disputes over whether a form as varied is 'substantially' the same as the form as prescribed.[95]

Precedents

Of course, not all forms are generated in response to statutory prompting. Most legal firms have standard forms – generally called 'precedents' – from which they tailor documents for particular transactions. Sometimes these precedents are based on forms provided by publishers; sometimes they are drafted by the firm itself. Standard forms of this kind are a necessary part of the modern lawyer's practice, but they should be drafted in clear, modern English, in line with the principles advocated here.

Conclusion

This chapter has reviewed some of the matters to be considered when drafting in standard, modern English. The list of techniques it discusses is not exhaustive. Some drafters use other techniques in their documents. But by following the principles set out in the chapter, drafters will succeed in producing documents that are easy to understand and that exhibit that level of precision which the traditional style of legal drafting fervently praises but often fails to achieve.

---

94 See Theodore B. F. Ruoff and Christopher West, *Land Registration Forms*, 3rd edn (London: Sweet & Maxwell, 1983), p. 2.

95 For Australian examples, see *Perpetual Executors and Trustees Association of Australia Ltd v Hosken* (1912) 14 CLR 286; *Crowley v Templeton* (1914) 17 CLR 457; *Gibb v Registrar of Titles* (1940) 63 CLR 503.

7   Using the Modern Style

In earlier chapters we have discussed the many benefits of drafting legal documents in modern, standard English. In this final chapter we give step-by-step examples of drafting in the modern style. We illustrate with clauses drawn from four types of private legal documents, all commonly encountered in legal practice: leases, company constitutions, wills, and conveyances.

Lease: how to bring it to an end if the property is damaged

Original version

If the whole or a substantial part of the Premises shall at any time during the Term be destroyed or damaged then the Landlord shall have the right at any time before rebuilding or reinstatement shall have commenced to give notice in writing to the Tenant to determine this Lease and at the expiry of one month from the service of such notice the Term shall cease and determine but without prejudice to any claim for any antecedent breach of the Tenant's covenants herein contained (and if the tenancy is one to which Part II of the Landlord and Tenant Act 1954 applies[1] then a statutory notice in the form required by that Act shall also operate as notice under this sub-clause).

This clause exudes many characteristics of traditional legal writing:

- use of *shall*
- unusual tenses: 'shall have commenced'
- use of capital letters to indicate important terms: 'the Term', 'this Lease'
- unnecessary doublets: 'destroyed or damaged', 'rebuilding or reinstatement', 'cease and determine'
- lack of punctuation
- 'such' used as an adjective

---

1 This Act applies in England and Wales only.

- unusual word order: 'herein contained'
- avoidance of pronouns
- pomposity: 'commenced', 'determine', 'antecedent'
- special meaning for words in ordinary use: 'determine'
- antique words no longer in ordinary use: 'herein'
- tautology: 'a statutory notice in the form required by that Act'
- legal jargon: 'without prejudice to'.

Plain version

The original version can be rewritten:

(a) If a substantial part of the premises becomes damaged, the Landlord may give the Tenant written notice to bring this lease to an end.

(b) The Landlord must serve the notice on the Tenant before the Landlord begins to reinstate the premises.

(c) The lease ends a month after service of the notice, but the Landlord may still pursue any claim against the Tenant for breaches occurring before the lease ends.

This version does not attempt to deal with the bracketed words in the original, because their meaning is not clear. If the drafter meant by them that the notice is to dovetail with the 1954 Act, then a further paragraph could be added:

(d) If the tenancy is one to which Part II of the Landlord and Tenant Act 1954 applies, a notice under that Act may also constitute a notice under this sub-clause and the date of termination specified is the date on which the lease ends.

Two chief points arise from an exercise such as this. First, the revision forces a fundamental reappraisal of the original: as Robert Eagleson has said, 'To write plainly means to return to the heart of the matter'.[2] Second, difficulty in rewriting may expose a fundamental problem with the subject matter, as with the bracketed words in the original version. The review forces the conclusion that a notice under the 1954 Act serves one purpose, and a notice to bring the lease to an end following a disaster serves another. To elide the two types of notice, as though one notice can perform the two functions, confuses rather than helps. It is better to omit the bracketed words altogether.

---

2 Robert Eagleson, 'Plain English in the Statutes' (1985) 59 *Law Institute Journal*, p. 673.

Company memorandum of association: subsidiary objects clause

Original version

To improve, manage, construct, repair, develop, exchange, let on lease or otherwise, mortgage, charge, sell, dispose of, turn to account, grant licences, options, rights and privileges in respect of, or otherwise deal with all or any part of the property and rights of the Company.

This clause illustrates the lawyer's love for lists. Rather than choose one word that covers the field (but is no wider than necessary), the drafter compiles a list of near-synonyms in the hope of hitting the target. This technique Rudolf Flesch called the shotgun principle of legal drafting.[3] Much to be preferred is Dickerson's 'lowest common denominator' approach,[4] under which the drafter tries to select a word or words to cover the particular group or activity intended but no more.

Plain version

Using the Dickerson approach, the original can be recast in ordinary English, thus:

To deal with the company's property in any way.

The rewriting takes account of the following points:

- 'Deal with' adequately covers improve, manage, construct, repair, develop, exchange, let (on lease or otherwise), mortgage, charge, sell, dispose of, turn to account, grant licences, grant options, grant rights and grant privileges; nor is 'deal with' too wide for the purposes of the clause.
- 'In respect of' is unnecessary.
- 'The property', without further elaboration, implies all or any part of it.
- The company's rights are part of its property, so they need not be mentioned separately.

---

3 Rudolph Flesch, *How to Write Plain English* (New York: Barns & Noble Books, 1979), p. 41.
4 Reed Dickerson, *Fundamentals of Legal Drafting*, 2nd edn (Boston and Toronto: Little, Brown & Co., 1986), p. 18.

Will: attestation clause

Original version

Signed by the above-named Sarah Smith as her last will in the presence of us present at the same time who at her request in her presence and in the presence of each other have hereunto subscribed our names as witnesses.

Attestation clauses in wills are designed to show that the statutory requirements for signing ('executing') wills have been satisfied. Most jurisdictions impose statutory requirements on executing wills. In England and Wales, for example, the requirements are set out in s 9 of the *Wills Act* 1837 (replaced by s 17 of the *Administration of Justice Act* 1982, for wills taking effect after 1982). The section reads as follows:

No will shall be valid unless –
(a) it is in writing, and signed by the testator, or by some other person in his presence and by his direction; and
(b) it appears that the testator intended by his signature to give effect to the will; and
(c) the signature is made or acknowledged by the testator in the presence of two or more witnesses present at the same time; and
(d) each witness either -
    (i) attests and signs the will; or
    (ii) acknowledges his signature,
in the presence of the testator (but not necessarily in the presence of any other witness), but no form of attestation shall be necessary.

Notice that, while various permutations of acknowledgment or signature are possible, the statute specifically provides that no form of attestation is necessary. Nonetheless, every professionally drawn will contains an attestation clause, because without one the probate authorities usually require an affidavit stating that the will has been executed in accordance with the statutory formalities.

Plain version

Here is a redraft of the original version:

Signed by the testator in our presence and attested by us in the presence of her and of each other.

This was the form judicially approved in *Re Selby-Bigge* (Hodgson J expressing the view that to save labour and for the sake of neatness, skilful practitioners desire to reduce words to the minimum).[5] In practice, probate officials welcome an even shorter form, enabling them to see at a glance that the statutory provisions have been satisfied:

> Signed by the testator in our presence and then by us in hers.

Where the testator is female, the circumspect drafter may prefer *testatrix* to *testator*. But in modern English, *testator* has become gender-neutral, like *actor, juror, prosecutor, administrator* and *executor*. In any case, no judge would be perverse enough to rule a will invalid on the ground that a female deceased had executed her will as 'testator', especially in the face of the common statutory provision that in all documents the masculine includes the feminine and vice versa.[6]

Will: distribution in unequal shares

Original version

> In trust to divide the same into ten equal shares (and the words 'share' or 'shares' in this clause shall be always read as referring to such equal shares) and to hold one share in trust for my niece Doris Jeffries and to hold one share in trust for my nephew Kenneth Hyne and to hold one share in trust for my niece May Martin and to hold one share in trust for my niece Dora Wiles and to hold one share in trust for my niece Phyllis Stoneman and to hold one share in trust for my niece Ruth Ellis and to hold one share in trust for my nephew Raymond Hyne and to hold the remaining three shares in trust for my niece Carmin Hecker Provided that if any of the trusts declared by this clause shall fail then the share or shares as to which the said trusts shall so fail (including any share or shares accruing by virtue of this provision) shall accrue to and be added equally to the other shares hereby given and be held in trust accordingly.

The form of this clause – one long, unpunctuated sentence – makes it particularly difficult to read. Further, the proviso is obscure. One way of divining meaning is to attempt a redraft.

Plain version

To divide it as follows:
* one-tenth for my niece Doris Jeffries
* one-tenth for my nephew Kenneth Hyne

---

5 [1950] 1 All ER 1009 at 1010.
6 In England, see s 61 of the *Law of Property Act* 1925. In New South Wales, see s 181 of the *Conveyancing Act* 1919. See also Robin Towns, 'Plain English' (1998) 142 SJ 821. For gender-neutral drafting, see Chapter 6.

- one-tenth for my niece May Martin
- one-tenth for my niece Dora Wiles
- one-tenth for my niece Phyllis Stoneman
- one-tenth for my niece Ruth Ellis
- one-tenth for my nephew Raymond Hyne
- three-tenths for my niece Carmin Hecker.

If any of those beneficiaries dies before I do, his or her share is to be added equally to that of the survivors.

The clause still poses some difficulties. Where Carmin Hecker survives but one or more of the others does not, the relationship between the shares changes. If one of the lesser beneficiaries dies, Carmin Hecker's share becomes a little under three times what the others receive. If all but one of the other beneficiaries die, three-tenths accrue to the lesser beneficiary and three-tenths to Carmin Hecker; the lesser beneficiary then ends up with two-fifths and Carmin Hecker with three-fifths. To preserve the original relationship between the shares, an entirely different wording would be needed for the closing sentence:

> If any of those beneficiaries dies before I do, his or her share is to be added to those of the survivors in the same mathematical relationship that the specified shares of the survivors bear to each other.

To illustrate this redraft: if Carmin Hecker survives with only one of the lesser beneficiaries, six-tenths are available to split between them in the ratio of 1:3. Thus, three-twentieths go to the lesser beneficiary and nine-twentieths to Carmin. Add those fractions to their direct fractions, and the lesser beneficiary gets five-twentieths (one-quarter) and Carmin fifteen-twentieths (three-quarters). Assuming this is what the testator intended, a plainer wording might be:

> If any of those beneficiaries dies before I do, the fund is to be divided between the survivors in the same ratio that their shares specified in this clause bear to each other.

Or even shorter:

> If any of those beneficiaries dies before I do, the fund is to be divided between the survivors in the same ratio.

Or perhaps even better:

> If any of those beneficiaries dies before I do, the fund is to be divided between the survivors proportionately.

New land obligations: buyer's restrictive covenant

Original version

THE Purchaser to the intent and so as to bind the property hereby conveyed and each and every part thereof into whosesoever hands the same may come to protect such parts of the adjoining or neighbouring land and premises situate at Exon in the said County of Devon and forming part of the Vendor's Blueacre Estate as for the time being remains unsold or as shall be sold with the express benefit of this covenant as are capable of benefiting HEREBY JOINTLY AND SEVERALLY COVENANTS with the Vendor that the Purchaser and his successors in title will at all times hereafter observe and perform the following restrictions stipulations and conditions

Plain version

This example of legalese could be recast in ordinary English, as follows:

(a) To burden the property and to benefit the retained land, the buyers separately and together promise the seller that they will observe the stipulations which follow.

(b) 'The retained land' is every part of the seller's Blueacre Estate, Exon, Devon, which is near the property and is capable of benefiting from this promise, and which either remains unsold or has been sold expressly with the benefit of this promise.

Two commonly used phrases in the original version merit detailed analysis: 'each and every', and 'jointly and severally'. Like other doublets, their use should always be questioned (see Chapter 1).

'Each and every'

This doublet appears often in traditional legal drafting. The two words are closely related: 'each' derives from the Old English *aelc*, and 'every' from the Old English *aefre aelc*. There could be no objection to using either 'each' or 'every' by itself. But is the doublet necessary? The drafter's particular concern seems to have been the consequences of later subdivision of the land. Is the covenant to burden the purchased land as a whole only, or is it to burden also any parcels into which it might later be subdivided? And is the covenant to benefit the 'adjoining or neighbouring' land as a whole only, or is it to also benefit that land if it is later subdivided? Under present law, in the absence of some contrary indication, both the burden and the benefit of restrictive covenants probably pass with the later-subdivided parts of those lands.[7] But the law relating

---

7 Burden, *Law of Property Act* 1925, s 79; benefit, s 78. See *Federated Homes Ltd v Mill Lodge Properties Ltd* [1980] 1 WLR 594, CA; *Roake v Chadha* [1984] 1 WLR 40; *Shropshire County Council v Edwards* (1983) 46 P & CR 270; *Gyarfas v Bray* (1990) NSW ConvR 55–519; P. Baker, 'The Benefit of Restrictive Covenants' (1968) 84 *Law Quarterly Review*, p. 22; Hayton, 'Restrictive Covenants as Property Interests' (1971) 87 *Law Quarterly Review*, p. 539.

to the enforceability of covenants following subdivision is complex, and the drafter does well to clarify the position and to set out the scheme as the client would like it to be. Nevertheless, the drafter's purpose could be achieved just as well by referring to 'each' part or to 'every' part, without recourse to the uncritical 'each and every'.

A related drafting point concerns the interpretation of 'any part' – as in a prohibition against dealing with 'any part' of premises. Drafters frequently expand the prohibition into one against dealing with 'the whole or any part' of the premises. But since the sum of the parts is the whole, a prohibition against dealing with any part of a property necessarily prohibits a dealing with all of it.[8] A drafter who wants to prohibit a dealing with part only should say so directly, by using such words as 'not to deal with part only of the premises'.

'Jointly and severally'

'Jointly and severally' is a phrase found rarely in ordinary English. Yet it features prominently in legal documents. An example is the following boilerplate from a lease:

> Where two or more persons are included in the expression 'the Landlord' and 'the Tenant', covenants expressed to be made by the Landlord and the Tenant shall be deemed to be made by such persons jointly and severally.

'Jointly and severally' has no legal magic. It simply means 'together and separately'. Where more than one person is under an obligation 'jointly and severally', the obligation can be enforced against them all collectively or against any one of them individually. Likewise, where more than one person is given a duty or a power 'jointly and severally', the duty or the power can be exercised by them all collectively or by any one of them individually.[9]

Drafters who persist in using 'jointly and severally' should realise that the phrase bears little meaning for the lay reader. They should also appreciate an ambiguity it may create where an obligation is entered into 'jointly and severally' by more than two persons, say X, Y and Z. There can be no doubt that the obligation is by X, Y or Z separately, and X, Y and Z collectively. But what about X and Y together, or X and Z, or Y and Z? A court would probably hold that these combinations must submit to the obligation. Nevertheless, the matter is not free from doubt. The

---

8 *Field v Barkworth* [1986] 1 WLR 137.
9 Although context may require otherwise: see *Kendle v Melsom* (1998) 72 ALJR 560, where the Australian High Court held that receivers appointed 'jointly and severally' had to act together.

drafter could remove that doubt by substituting for 'jointly and severally' the phrase 'separately, together or in any combination'.

Conclusion

These and similar examples indicate the direction for legal drafters. They show that legal documents can be expressed in standard, modern English without loss of legal precision. The challenge to those who oppose modernising legal drafting is then apparent: why should the law use the language of yesterday? Why should legal language be subject to special rules, locked in a unique linguistic code accessible only to those with the key?

We have sought to explain why legal documents are drafted in a traditional style, and why moves to improve drafting techniques are so compelling. We have shown how the traditional style of drafting hinders understanding and creates dangers for lawyers and clients alike. In contrast, modern, standard English helps improve understanding and remove the dangers. And importantly, modern, standard English can be as legally effective and linguistically precise as traditional legal language. Nothing in logic or law stands in the way of using modern, standard English in the legal documents of the twenty-first century. Using the techniques we have outlined, the modern lawyer can produce documents which are clear, accessible and litigation-proof.

Further Reading

The following are some of the many books on legal drafting. We have listed only those that emphasise the benefits and techniques of drafting in standard, modern English – or 'plain English' as it is usually described. We list them alphabetically by author, allowing us to sidestep the invidious task of ranking them in order of merit.

Adler, M., *Clarity for Lawyers* (The Law Society of England and Wales, 1990). A practical guide to clear drafting, written for practising solicitors by a practising solicitor and former chair of Clarity.

Asprey, M., *Plain Language for Lawyers* (2nd edn, Federation Press, 1996). The standard Australian text, combining theory with practical insights.

Child, B., *Drafting Legal Documents* (2nd edn, West Publishing, 1992). A student text, with many illustrations from case law and legal documents.

Dick, R., *Legal Drafting in Plain Language* (3rd edn, Carswell, 1995). A practical guide for lawyers, written by one of Canada's best-known authors on the subject.

Dickerson, R., *Fundamentals of Legal Drafting* (West Publishing, 1965). A highly influential text, although encouraging a style which today might seem somewhat conservative.

Eagleson, R., *Writing in Plain English* (Australian Government Publishing Service, 1990). An excellent guide to plain writing, designed primarily for the Australian civil service but of universal application.

Garner, B., *The Winning Brief* (Oxford University Press, 1999). A practical discussion of 100 tips for persuasive briefs. Aimed chiefly at American advocates, but with many practical insights for lawyers generally.

—— *A Dictionary of Modern Legal Usage* (2nd edn, Oxford University Press, 1996). The classic American guide to legal usage, by an author with deep learning and a keen appreciation of the techniques of drafting in modern, standard English. A work of erudition and wit.

—— (ed.), *Scribes Journal of Legal Writing* (West Publishing). An occasional journal, with articles by leading lawyers with expertise in writing.

Good, C. E., *Mightier than the Sword* (Blue Jeans Press, 1989). A highly practical discussion of the principles of clear legal writing.

Law Reform Commission of Victoria, *Plain English and the Law* (Victorian Government Printer, 1987). An in-depth report on the use of plain language in law, which influenced the plain language movement in many parts of the world.

Mellinkoff, D., *Legal Writing: Sense and Nonsense* (West Publishing, 1982). More of a 'how to' than the same author's *Language of the Law*.

—— *The Language of the Law* (Little, Brown and Co., 1963). A scholarly and highly readable history of legal language, making a classic argument for plain language.

Piesse, E., *The Elements of Drafting* (9th edn, Law Book Co., 1995, ed. Aitken, J.). A short and practical introductory work, written for students but also useful for readers seeking an overview of legal drafting principles.

Ross, M., *Drafting and Negotiating Commercial Leases* (4th edn, Butterworths, 1994). A thorough, clause-by-clause review of the contents of a modern commercial lease, with plain language precedents developed by the author and Richard Castle.

Wydick, R., *Plain English for Lawyers* (3rd edn, Carolina Academic Press, 1994). A step-by-step lawyer's guide to plain writing. Began life as a highly influential law review article, later expanded into this (short) book.

Index